D0742090

About Island Press

Island Press is the only nonprofit organization in the United States whose principal purpose is the publication of books on environmental issues and natural resource management. We provide solutions-oriented information to professionals, public officials, business and community leaders, and concerned citizens who are shaping responses to environmental problems.

In 2005, Island Press celebrates its twenty-first anniversary as the leading provider of timely and practical books that take a multidisciplinary approach to critical environmental concerns. Our growing list of titles reflects our commitment to bringing the best of an expanding body of literature to the environmental community throughout North America and the world.

Support for Island Press is provided by the Agua Fund, The Geraldine R. Dodge Foundation, Doris Duke Charitable Foundation, Ford Foundation, The George Gund Foundation, The William and Flora Hewlett Foundation, Kendeda Sustainability Fund of the Tides Foundation, The Henry Luce Foundation, The John D. and Catherine T. MacArthur Foundation, The Andrew W. Mellon Foundation, The Curtis and Edith Munson Foundation, The New-Land Foundation, The New York Community Trust, Oak Foundation, The Overbrook Foundation, The David and Lucile Packard Foundation, The Winslow Foundation, and other generous donors.

The opinions expressed in this book are those of the author(s) and do not necessarily reflect the views of these foundations.

Environmental Economics for Tree Huggers and Other Skeptics

Environmental Economics for Tree Huggers and Other Skeptics

William K. Jaeger

Washington • Covelo • London

Library of Congress Cataloging-in-Publication Data

Jaeger, William K. (William Kenneth)
Environmental economics for tree huggers : and other skeptics / William K. Jaeger.
p. cm.
Includes bibliographical references and index.
ISBN 1-55963-664-5 (cloth : alk. paper) -- ISBN 1-55963-668-8 (pbk. : alk. paper)
1. Environmental economics. 2. Environmental policy--Economic aspects. I. Title.
HC79.E5J335 2005
338.9'27--dc22

2005013824

Printed on recycled, acid-free paper

Manufactured in the United States of America
10 9 8 7 6 5 4 3 2 1

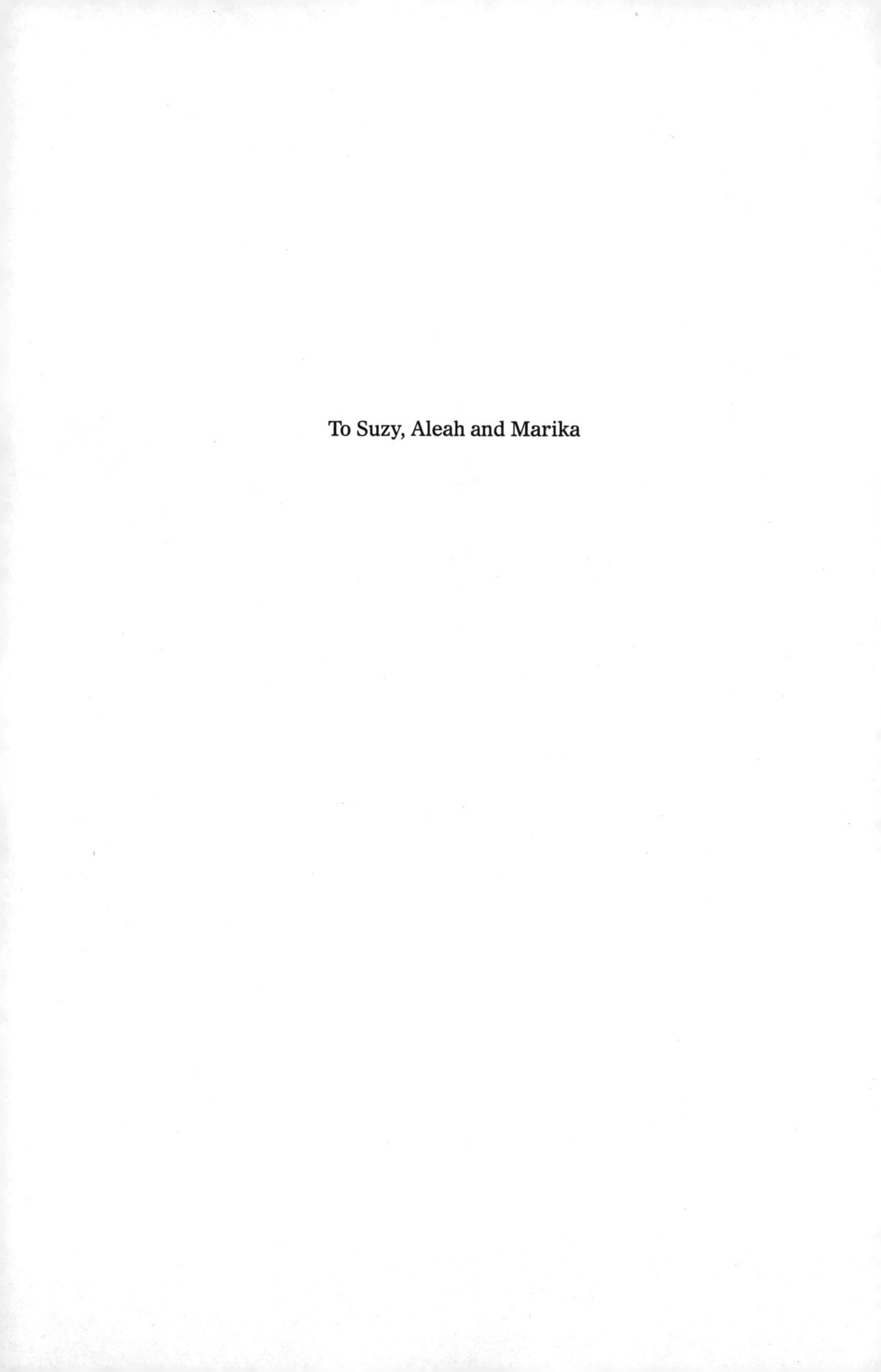

To Suzy, Aleah and Marika

Table of Contents

Preface

This book is a response to two concerns. First, the list of serious environmental and natural resource problems in need of attention grows longer by the day. Second, there is a widely held perception that economics is to environmentalism what Spam is to French cuisine: it's either completely irrelevant or it's in some sense antagonistic.

The first concern is hard to argue with. Not only have economic expansion and population growth taken a toll on our air, water, forests, oceans, and atmosphere, but broad systemic changes and harmful pollutants that are finding their way into the food chain may jeopardize the health and sustainability of individual species and whole ecosystems. In addition, growing demands on dwindling supplies of resources such as water, arable land, and forest products have raised tensions and sparked violent conflicts in many parts of the world.

The second concern is also unmistakable based on remarks I hear from students, activists, academics, policymakers, and the general public. Frequently, when introducing myself as an economist who works on environmental issues, I am greeted with a slight tilt of the head and a furrowing of the brow, as if to say: What *possibly* could economics have to do with environmental problems?! Aren't economists interested only in money? This kind of reaction is not limited to casual encounters with the general public, but also in discussions with university professors and in one case a member of Congress.

For those skeptics who see economics as irrelevant, or even antagonistic, to environmental progress, and whether they regard the label "tree hugger" as derogatory or complimentary, I have one message: economics is power! There is no getting around the fact that economic arguments can carry a lot of weight and be very influential in policymaking. So if you want to make a strong case for solving an environmental problem, and if there is an economic case supporting your views, then economics can be a powerful ally to your cause. The reverse is also true and equally important. If opponents of environmental protection use economic arguments, those arguments can also be very influential. But if those arguments are flawed, misinterpreted, or overstated, then being able to expose the shortcomings of those arguments is equally valuable. Yes, economics is power, but power can make mischief just as it can promote positive social change.

So why does economics have such a bad reputation? One problem, clearly, is the perception that "economics" is only about the stock market, consumer spending, interest rates, and the gross domestic product. Since environmental quality and species diversity are not "market commodities," many people believe that, at best, economics has nothing to say about them or, at worst, economics judges them to be worthless. Such criticisms of economics were at least partially true fifty years ago (when environmental concerns were not on many people's radar screens the way they are today). And those criticisms probably do reflect the views of some individual economists today (just as some geologists see beautiful landscapes only in terms of their potential for drilling and digging). But when we distinguish the *practice* (the social science of economics) from the *practitioner* (an individual economist), the former can be said to be largely neutral (some qualifications to this will come later).

True, many environmental topics involve nonmarket issues, like scenic vistas, but that does not make them noneconomic issues. Just because a beautiful view doesn't have a price doesn't mean it doesn't involve trade-offs and incentives for keeping or destroying it. Indeed, economics is actually a very broadly based social science that can be used, and has been used, to examine and understand things such as the conduct of families, the structure of organized religions, the ways we use time, the importance of cooperation, the role of "status seeking" in society, the decision to have a child, and many more topics not directly involving markets and money. In the realm of environmental resources, "environmental economics" and "natural resource economics" have become large, well-established, and important fields of economics, involving many active researchers and university professors, with professional associations, academic journals, and hundreds of peer-reviewed journal articles and dozens of books published every year.

Since economists began to pay attention to environmental issues in the 1950s and 1960s, the field of environmental economics has grown dramatically and has contributed to a better understanding of the causes of environmental problems, the strengths and drawbacks of alternative ways to address environmental problems, and the ways to measure and compare the value people place on specific environmental resources. Some of the important progress that has been made in recent years on many environmental issues has come about because of, not in spite of, the insights and powerful analytical tools developed by economists.

For example, many environmentalists are familiar with the idea of the "tragedy of the commons" popularized by Garrett Hardin in 1968, but few are aware that the central idea of that work was first pointed out by an economist, Scott Gordon, in 1956. Environmentalists are also familiar with the idea of sustainability, but few are aware that the essential idea was contained in the economist Sir John Hicks's definition of income in 1939. And more recently, John Nash, in work that won him the Nobel Prize in Economics in 1994, explained how cooperation can help solve problems of the tragedy of the commons.

Economists have also made important contributions to the design of creative policy tools for environmental problems, and for understanding why different policies can be expected to achieve different outcomes. Although economists are well known for favoring market-based instruments such as pollution charges and tradable pollution rights, they have also contributed to our understanding of the advantages of and opportunities for approaches such as deposit-refund systems, transferable development rights, habitat conservation plans, clean technology subsidies, and many more.

Still, some skeptics simply do not see a role for economics. They see a role for biology, ecology, and atmospheric chemistry because those fields study the physical systems where the symptoms of environmental problems appear. These fields do not, however, help us understand the ultimate cause of these problems: people. Indeed, just to define or identify what constitutes an environmental "problem" is to ask a social question, one requiring a judgment about the magnitude of harm, or loss, or the severity of consequence in human terms, based on people's values.

Environmental economics recognizes that the social system and the natural system are interconnected parts of the whole. Each part has its own forces and processes, actions and reactions, and linkages and feedbacks. The socioeconomic system involves incentives and disincentives, opportunities and constraints, laws and markets, political jurisdictions, wants and needs, ethics and morals. To understand the workings of the whole system, we need to understand enough about both subsystems to predict cause and effect, action and response. In some cases this may be as straightforward as recognizing that dumping waste in a river will kill fish; in other cases the interactions are more complex, as in a chess game, where a given move can set in motion a string of actions and reactions quite different from the sequence of events for a different path.

Wishful thinking won't solve these problems and, let's face it, the economy is not going to go away. People have wants and needs, and they respond to incentives, prices, and profit motives. People tend to want more for less, to avoid costs, and yes, to get away with things (like polluting or not paying their fair share). If there is a case to be made for trying to actually change people's values and preferences, this book makes no attempt to do so. In general, economists take people's preferences as is: Some people like SUVs, others tofu. Some want to backpack in a wilderness, others want to shop or watch NASCAR. But don't shoot the messenger! Economics should not be blamed for the preferences people have; human nature seems to be the culprit—perhaps with the help of history, advertising, corporate greed, and political influences.

Given all that, the goal of this book is not only to show just how valuable and important economic analysis can be for understanding the causes of environmental problems, but also to provide the reader with the tools necessary to see ways, perhaps really creative ways, to go about solving these problems. Another goal of this book—since many people are just plain scared of economics—is to be accessible and nonthreatening to readers. The theory, graphs, and equations used are kept as simple as possible, but at the same time they provide all the basic tools for understanding the ideas and insights that economics has to offer.

This book is also more of a "primer" than an exhaustive six-hundred-page textbook trying to cover all of economics and all environmental issues. It can be used most successfully when combined with case studies or supplemental readings in economics or from other fields. And it is also meant to serve as a handy reference for professionals in government, nongovernmental organizations, and the private sector. Finally, although no prior economics training is needed, the coverage of microeconomics principles is fairly brief, and the text does not include extra exercises and problem sets. Readers who have had prior exposure to introductory microeconomics should have no trouble with the theory covered and may find it to be a welcome refresher. For readers with no prior exposure to economics, who would like some additional reinforcement of these concepts, suggestions on further readings are found at the end of each chapter.

One last point: economists sometimes distinguish between "environmental economics" and "natural resource economics." The former topic focuses on nonmarket goods such as clean air and biodiversity; the latter topic focuses on marketable commodities such as fossil fuels, timber, water, and fish. But there is so much overlap between environmental issues and natural resource issues that keeping them separate is often difficult and awkward. For example, examining the economics of timber production without simultaneously looking at forest habitats, watersheds, wildlife, and recreation would be silly. With few exceptions natural resources are also environmental resources, and this book addresses both.

1

Economic Analysis in Brief

Much of what constitutes "economic analysis" is not really very controversial. It is simply a way of thinking about choices and about the costs, benefits, and trade-offs that underlie those choices. A basic notion in economics is that we make trade-offs "at the margin." We do this on a daily basis, for example, when we allocate our time between work and play, or when we allocate money between spending and saving. Groups of individuals—such as households, organizations, towns, or countries—face similar kinds of collective choices, and economics has a systematic way of thinking about these trade-offs as well and of applying these ideas to a wide range of situations. Economics also tries to understand how individuals behave and how they respond to incentives of various kinds. This makes it possible to evaluate how a given change in incentives—such as a change in government policy—is likely to alter individuals' actions.

Economic analysis is essential for the environment because environmental issues are fundamentally economic ones: people cause environmental problems because of their choices, and people distinguish small environmental problems from large ones based on their values. It follows that finding solutions to environmental problems requires understanding those values and those choices. That is what economics tries to do. It tries to understand people's individual incentives and choices, as well as the collective opportunities and constraints faced by society as a whole.

To help us get started, let's take a look at some key economic concepts and ideas and then apply them to the example of water. Water provides a good example because it is both a resource and a commodity, and it's also an essential ingredient in ecosystems and habitats. The availability of water depends on many things, including the choices made by individuals and households, towns and cities, and countries. So, as we introduce these key economic ideas, we'll consider how they relate to the allocation of water and how a small community might apply these economic ideas and tools to water allocation issues.

One note of caution: What follows is a compact overview of some big issues and ideas, which may make the delivery in this first chapter seem more like a fire hose than a drinking fountain to some readers. Don't despair. The intention here is to introduce some key ideas and to entice. A more detailed, step-by-step approach follows in the remaining chapters. Also, a number of key concepts used throughout the book are shown here in bold, followed by brief definitions or explanations. More detailed discussions of each can be found in later chapters.

Marginal versus Total Value

One of the most fundamental concepts in economics is the idea of **marginal value**, such as the value of one additional gallon of water, one more hour spent studying, or the value of one more dollar spent on junk food. When we make choices that involve the allocation of a resource to a particular use, or when we give something up that is valuable to us, almost always we are doing this "at the margin." This means we are making only an incremental change in the amount of the resource being allocated to a particular use as compared with other uses, for example, when a household allocates water for drinking, bathing, or gardening.

When we do this, it makes sense to consider the incremental or **marginal benefit** of this particular change. Even though the value of the first unit of a particular good or service may be very high to us, it is likely that with additional quantities the marginal value will decline. Economists call this **diminishing marginal utility.** It is extremely important to recognize the difference between marginal value and total value because while a particular good may have an extremely high total value (for the whole amount used), this does not necessarily mean that the marginal value of one additional unit of that good is also extremely high. For example, because we cannot live without water, the total value of water can be thought of as being infinite. But the value of an additional gallon of water may be close to zero if we are at the point where all our current needs for water have been satisfied.

Economists illustrate this graphically as in figure 1.1, where the marginal or incremental value of one additional unit of a good (like water) or a service (like a haircut) may be very high when the quantity used (in a given period of time) is low, but will generally decline at higher levels of consumption or use. At a very high level of use, the marginal value of water will eventually fall to zero (somewhere off the right end of the horizontal axis in figure 1.1). But at a very low level, water will have an exceedingly high marginal value—for example, when thirst becomes a life or death situation.

Since the total value is just the adding up of all the incremental or marginal values from the first gallon to the last gallon, even

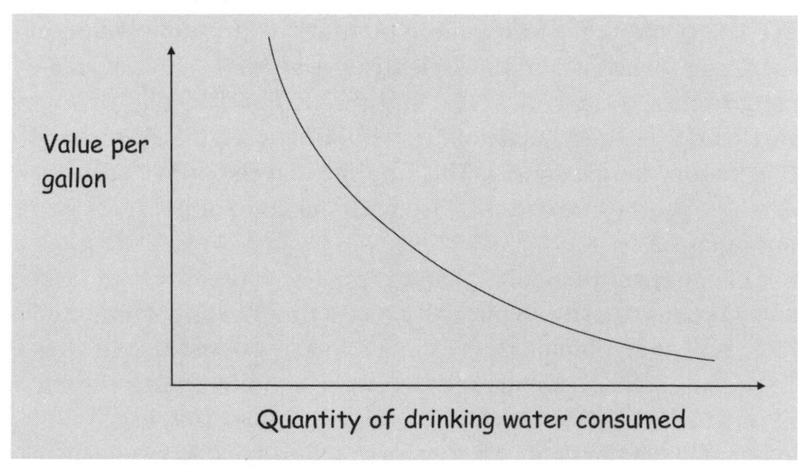

FIGURE 1.1 The declining marginal value of drinking water

in a situation where the marginal value is very low, the total value may be very high for an example like water. The marginal value at low levels isn't even shown in figure 1.1 because it goes off the top of the graph. If the marginal value is infinite at very low quantities, then the total value will be infinite as well, even though the value of the last gallon consumed is very low. Individually and collectively, we face many choices, but these usually involve incremental changes in resource allocation. That is why we should often focus on the incremental changes in value for a given use rather than the total value.

Opportunity Cost

A second key concept in economics is **opportunity cost**. Nearly all choices involve trade-offs. That means that a choice to allocate a resource to one use necessarily implies not putting it to some other use. By not putting a resource to that other use, you give up the benefits from that other use, and this is the opportunity cost. Using water to water the garden means giving up its value for drinking or bathing. Cutting down a tree to build a house means giving up its value as part of a forest. Spending time exercising implies giving up the value of that time for working.

In general, the more of a thing we take away from one use and put to another, the higher the opportunity cost. The relationship can be appreciated by looking again at drinking water in figure 1.1. If we begin with a large quantity of drinking water, but then take away water for irrigating a garden, we move from right to left in figure 1.1. The marginal value of a unit of water that could be used for drinking will rise as we take away additional units for gardening. This implies that the opportunity cost of water used to garden will rise with the amount used, as shown in figure 1.2.

Economists recognize that as units of a resource are taken away from one use and put to a second use, the opportunity cost rises and the value of the resource in the second use declines. Because of this, we expect there to be a point where the marginal values of the resource for the two competing uses will be equal. This is the point where shifting units of the resource one way or the other will not increase the combined total value for

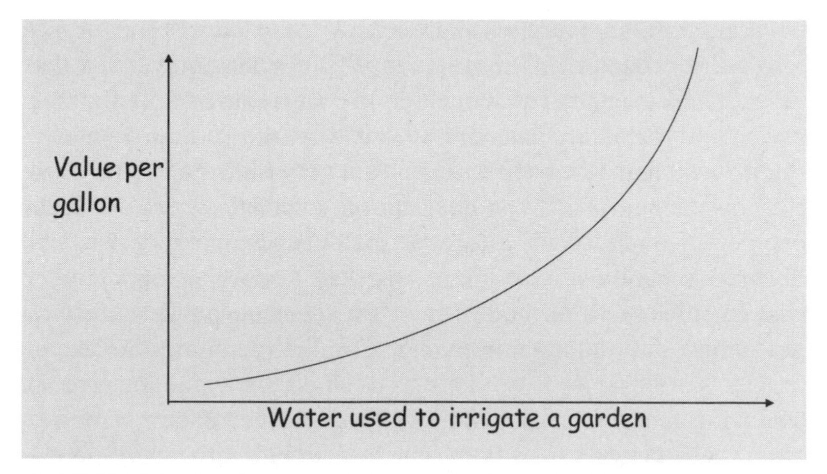

■ **FIGURE 1.2 The rising marginal cost of using water for gardening**

the two uses. In the case of water, if a household uses water for gardening up to the point where the marginal value from that use is just equal to the marginal value from using water for drinking or bathing, then the sum of the total value from each use will be maximized, and the household will have gotten the most total value, or benefit, out of its water use. We call this efficiency.

For a water-using community, these same ideas about opportunity cost and making trade-offs at the margin will apply. The competing demands of different individuals for water will require compromise and trade-offs among different individuals' priorities. If the community's water delivery system is inadequate for a growing population, a system of larger pipes could be installed—at a cost. This means the funds used for replacing pipes would not be available for other uses. The reliability of the community's water supply might be greatly improved by damming a nearby river, but with a cost, the adverse effects on recreation and fishing.

The stark reality that we must make trade-offs—that more of one thing implies less of something else—seems often to be missed by individuals whose own interests are narrowly focused, especially when the opportunity costs are at the community or societal level. Some individuals in the community may oppose any damming of rivers, no matter how many other rivers there may be. To look at a different example, librarians may insist that all books have enormous value and are worth saving, or that our nation's libraries are inadequate and that we should do everything possible to bring them all up to a very high standard. While this may be a priority for a librarian, in a society where different people have different interests, preferences, and goals, the librarian's view neglects these two key notions of opportunity cost (money spent on books can't be spent on public safety or museums) and diminishing marginal value (doubling the size or numbers of libraries is unlikely to double their value to society). The point is not that librarians or river advocates are wrong to have these views, but rather that in a world with many people with diverse interests and priorities, compromises and trade-offs are unavoidable.

A related concept to opportunity cost in economics is **substitution.** Whether a particular good or service has a high or low value at the margin will depend on how important it is to individuals. If there are no substitutes for a particular good, and the good is essential, then it will likely have a very high value. But if the good is not essential or if there are **close substitutes**—goods that can serve the same or similar purpose—then the marginal value of the good will be low. Water is essential for survival, and since there are no substitutes for it, it will have a very high value over some range of quantities. The community may value a river very highly as a source of water for drinking, but a particular river may not have a high value if there are several other streams nearby that could be used instead.

By contrast, if the substitute good is costly or inconvenient, or if it is an imperfect substitute, then there will be lost benefits when the substitution is made. Water that is located one hundred miles away may be a poor substitute for water that is immediately available.

Public Goods

In general, economists are quick to sing the praises of competitive markets—the "invisible hand" that has the potential to allocate resources efficiently. But economists also recognize that there are many situations in which markets cannot be relied upon to achieve an efficient, or desirable, allocation of resources. The example most relevant to environmental concerns is the notion of a **public good.** A public good cannot be divided up and sold individually to consumers according to their preferences. The benefits or services from a public good are **nonrival,** which means that the good can be consumed or used by one person without reducing the amount available to others. Drinking water is a rival good: if I drink it, it is no longer available for others to drink. A radio broadcast, by contrast, is nonrival: I can listen to it without reducing the amount available for others. I can also enjoy clean air or a scenic, free-flowing river without reducing the amount available for others to enjoy.

Public goods may sound like a great thing, but they also create a problem. Everyone has incentives to use them; no one has a strong incentive to provide or protect them. Clean air, migratory seabirds, wilderness areas, and national security are just a few of the public goods that will not be produced or maintained at the desired levels simply by "letting the market work." Individuals have an incentive to be **free riders,** meaning they can let others produce or protect these public goods and then enjoy them without contributing toward their cost. This free rider problem is a fundamental source of conflict between social goals and individual incentives, providing a clear rationale for collective (e.g., government) intervention to make decisions about the level or quantity of these goods to provide, how to provide them, and who should pay.

In our hypothetical community, the infrastructure for delivering water to households from an upstream source is a type of public good. The risk of flooding may be a collective risk for the community, one that might be reduced with a flood control dam, another kind of public good. But individual households are unlikely to build flood control dams on their own. If some members of the community joined forces to build a dam for this purpose, free riders, who didn't share in the cost of the dam, would still be protected from flood risk. Should all community members be required to pay for the dam? Should everybody pay the same amount? What about the poor, or those who live in locations with little risk of flooding?

Value-Added

The potential value of a resource to society must be measured in terms of the incremental or **net benefits** associated with an increase in the availability of that resource. To measure net benefits, we need to subtract the **incremental costs** involved in making the additional goods or resource available. For example, if our community taps a source of irrigation water that produces $1 million worth of crops, this does not mean that the value of the water to society is $1 million. If equipment was used to build the infrastructure for dams and canals, then these are one-time or **fixed costs** that must be subtracted from the value of the end result. Moreover, if the crops grown in the irrigation project are grown using seeds, fertilizers, tractors, and labor, then the costs of these inputs must also be subtracted from the value of the output, if we are interested in measuring the net benefit to the community. This difference between gross value and net value, or **value-added,** is often overlooked in discussions of projects or policies.

As another example, assume we know that there is $1 billion worth of oil somewhere in the ground in country X, but we do not know exactly where it is. Does that mean that the value to society of exploiting it is $1 billion? No, certainly not. If it would cost $0.5 billion just to figure out where it is, and another $0.1 billion to drill and pump it out, and another $50 million to ship it to where people would consume it, then the value to society of the oil is much less than the total value at the selling point.

Benefit-Cost Analysis

Individuals make personal choices based on their own preferences, market information, and what they perceive to be the opportunity costs and net benefits. For society as a whole, there is no equivalent internal mental process to rely on. Since society's "preferences" are not as easily known as an individual's, these kinds of collective choices are even more difficult. For example, if our hypothetical, water-using community is considering replacing the pipes that deliver water, or switching to a system of wells and pumps, or building a dam to control flooding or improve water supply, there are many costs and benefits to consider and take account of, and the values and preferences of individuals in the community will differ.

One approach to this kind of complex problem is benefit-cost analysis, an important tool used by economists to evaluate policy options or projects that involve collective trade-offs. It identifies the impacts of a policy or project and estimates the value of those impacts as benefits and costs. The value that people place on the goods and services affected is the basis for estimating the project's benefits and costs. For goods and services that are sold in markets, the market price provides a measure of the marginal value of the good. For goods and services that are not sold in markets, we cannot observe what people actually pay, so we try to estimate what people would be "willing to pay," which is a difficult practical matter.

Economists generally use a monetary unit such as dollars as a convenient common unit of measure for comparing the value of different kinds of goods and services. In principle, we could compare all goods in terms of the number of tomatoes people would be willing to give up to acquire them, but dollars are clearly a more convenient and familiar unit of exchange. The idea behind this is that the perceived benefits of a policy or project can be measured in terms of the goods and services that people are prepared to give up in exchange for those benefits.

These economic notions about how and why individuals make choices give rise to a way of aggregating the "values" placed on goods and services. Using these measures gives us a way to systematically summarize information about the different preferences, priorities, and values within a diverse society. For water system investments, these approaches can illuminate the trade-offs between improved water supply or flood control and the value the community places on protecting a free-flowing river.

In many situations, however, benefit-cost analysis alone will not be adequate to make complex and difficult social policy decisions. Society has many objectives, not all of which are easily summarized using benefit-cost analysis. We often want to know how benefits and costs will be distributed among particular groups or individuals, how future generations will be affected, or how people's rights will be affected, and if the action will be fair.

For these reasons, it's important to use benefit-cost analysis with caution and to recognize its limitations.

Time Preference and Valuing the Future

A critical feature in economic analysis is the treatment of benefits and costs that occur in the future. This is particularly important when we're concerned about the world we're leaving for our children. Unlike benefits and costs that occur now or at the start of a project or when a policy is initially introduced, the benefits and costs that occur in later time periods are **discounted,** meaning that they are given less weight. Building a flood control dam involves costs now; the benefits may not occur for many years, so they are discounted.

Why? Because the opportunity cost of using funds for a project today is the interest those funds could earn if deposited in a bank. In the same way that the relative price of two commodities is a measure of people's willingness to give up one good in exchange for another, the interest rate is a measure of people's willingness to give up a dollar in one period in exchange for a dollar in another period. Some individuals may be willing to delay consumption (for a price); others may be willing to pay that price in order to have resources now rather than in the future. The market that emerges between borrowers and lenders finds its equilibrium at the market-clearing price, the market interest rate.

Interest rates also reflect the "time value of money." This is because individuals can borrow funds for a productive investment such as starting a business, planting fruit trees, or doing research. The investment generates a return to pay back the loan and still leave a payoff for the investor. To judge whether a particular investment justifies borrowing funds, the future benefits of the investment are compared with the interest that could have been earned lending to others.

From society's perspective, however, there are reasons why the market interest rate doesn't provide the best guide for "social discounting." The reasons for these differences generally have to do with public goods, market distortions, and externalities. There is a large theoretical literature on the topic, which is complex and difficult to summarize in a few paragraphs. But the main point is that society should often use a discount rate lower than the market interest rate. Just how much lower is a perennial topic of debate.

Difficult Choices Are Difficult Choices

Some skeptics of economics claim that economic analysis is inappropriate or counterproductive when applied to situations involving moral principles, such as trying to put a value on human health or human life. There is no doubt that situations involving trade-offs where lives are at risk, such as how much to spend on a flood control dam or airline safety, or how high to set the speed limit on our highways, are difficult and make us uncomfortable. But such situations are inherently difficult, and these difficulties are not created by economics. While saving lives is unquestionably beneficial to society, it also involves costs, for example, by not using resources to save lives in other ways or for improving others' quality of life.

Contaminants in a community's drinking water, such as arsenic, can cause illness and death. These risks can be reduced or eliminated at a cost, but how much should a community be willing to pay to save lives in this way? If accessing a distant, but arsenic-free, water source would cost millions of dollars, would it be better to spend that money on improved fire protection or research on childhood diseases?

The spirit of the economics approach is that we not shy away from difficult choices, that we should be explicit about them. One way to be explicit about these kinds of choices and their implications is to compare the benefits and costs of alternative courses of action using a common measure. Economists use an approach that translates into a dollar metric the marginal costs of saving a "statistical life." Some critics charge that economics is being taken too far and that putting a price on life is an absurd exercise. But abandoning economics, or condemning benefit-cost analysis, will not eliminate these difficult social choices. Leaving the trade-offs implicit rather than explicit will, perhaps, allow some to avoid the discomfort of facing up to them directly. But being explicit about these choices and debating them openly is in society's best interest. We can and should debate how much value we put on saving human lives, as compared with protecting biodiversity, or ensuring that we have good libraries, or any of the other collective and individual goals in society. We cannot save all lives from all threats, and we cannot cure all diseases and eliminate all suffering. We cannot reduce the risks of driving or flying to zero. At some point we decide that it is too costly—at the margin—to give up more of other goods and services in order to reduce these risks further. Individuals make trade-offs of this kind all the time, and so must society.

Institutions

Even if we can imagine the optimal allocation of water in our hypothetical community, how do we get there? What are the mechanisms by which water is allocated among individuals within households, among households within a community, and among the different uses of water for consumption, recreation, wetlands, and flood control reservoirs? Clearly, if we leave it to individual choices, conflict, waste, and free riding are likely to be the result. So we need to have a process or a mechanism to avoid conflicts, waste, and free riding. Economists call these mechanisms institutions. Institutions are the humanly devised mechanisms that guide and constrain individuals' choices. They resolve conflicts, reduce uncertainty, and make the world more predictable; they also align individual choices with the interests of society as a whole. Sometimes the mechanisms that coordinate things in society are quite simple: "first come, first served"; "stay to the right"; "line forms to the rear." Often, however, such simple rules don't work well, and more complex institutions are needed.

Markets are one important mechanism for the allocation of resources, and many economists focus their attention here. But many other economists, including environmental economists, pay attention to the many other kinds of institutions. These include private property and markets, but also regulations, fees and taxes, social norms, codes of conduct, as well as those simple rules like first come, first served. In fact, water law in the western United States is largely based on first come, first served (also known as the prior appropriations doctrine). Private property works well for some land uses, less well for wetlands, wilderness, and whale populations. Informal rules can keep order in some communities and within households. Regulations and enforcement are often needed to curb the harms individuals may impose on each other. How society tries to implement or affect those choices can mean the difference between success and failure, between high cost and low cost, and between small achievements and large achievements.

Our fictional community will want to find the most effective way to control and allocate the use of water and to pay for water-related public goods. As we will see later on, it is likely that a combination of institutional approaches will evolve that includes private ownership, government regulation, incentive-based approaches, and informal agreements.

What's Ahead

The ideas and concepts introduced here play important roles in the economic way of thinking about how people behave and make choices, and how and why natural resources are allocated or misallocated. Situations where resources are misallocated represent opportunities where changes could be made that would improve benefits or reduce costs, making society, and the environment, better off. The example of water allocation in a community illustrates just how complex these situations can be, given the multiple, interacting ways that water provides both private and public goods and services.

Some of the chapters ahead revisit these essential concepts in much more detail, while others build on these ideas and apply them to specific kinds of environmental issues and problems. These chapters utilize a graphical approach for representing benefits, costs, and trade-offs. For readers who are unfamiliar with microeconomics and the graphical approaches that economists use or for those who need a refresher, the next two chapters provide a crash course.

PART 1
Tools of the Trade

2

Trade-Offs, Efficiency, and Demand

We can live without diamonds, yet they have a very high price. We cannot live without water, yet it typically has a very low price. Does this suggest something is terribly wrong? Economic reasoning says no. Understanding this diamond-water paradox is just one of the goals of this chapter and the next one, where the essential building blocks for economic analysis are developed step by step. Central to this economic reasoning is marginal analysis: the evaluation of trade-offs between marginal benefit and marginal cost in order to identify the efficient allocation, the one that maximizes net benefits. Producing the highest net benefit is, in many ways, the bottom line for much of economic analysis. The concept of efficiency has to do with getting the highest net benefits possible, getting the most value out of the resources at our disposal.

Most of these ideas can be represented with graphs that, along with a few simple algebraic equations, are the main analytical tools used throughout the rest of this book. Most of the graphs in this book are actually quite simple, yet they make it possible to understand a surprising array of important and sophisticated ideas. Some readers may want to jump ahead to see what economics has to say about reducing pollution, improving fishery management, or slowing tropical deforestation. If that's the case, then give part 2 a try. But if you don't fully understand the analysis and graphs you find there, come back to chapters 2 and 3 for the basics and chapters 4 through 8, where the basics are expanded and applied to a number of environmental issues.

Now, a few general points about the most common kind of graph you will be seeing. These graphs typically represent the quantities of an individual item (tons of steel, acres of land, gallons of water, tons of pollution) that is used (bought, sold, produced, consumed, emitted, or destroyed) during a given period of time (e.g., tons per month, gallons per year). The quantity of the item is shown on the horizontal, or *x*, axis. On the vertical, or *y*, axis, we indicate a marginal value per unit (either a benefit or a cost). The idea is to represent the incremental or marginal benefits or costs associated with changes in quantity. If the marginal cost or marginal benefit doesn't change with quantity, then the relationship is flat (horizontal).

These marginal benefits and marginal costs are generally measured in monetary units, for example, in dollars per unit where the unit may be a ton, gallon, or parts per million (ppm). Of course, many of the benefits and costs we are interested in here are not bought or sold in markets (e.g., the cost of air pollution or the benefit of preventing extinction for a species), so putting a value on them is difficult. There are a number of techniques economists use to value these kinds of nonmarket benefits, and these are discussed in chapter 14. But for now let's proceed under the assumption that these benefits and costs can be measured.

Trading Off Benefits and Costs

Let's begin with a simple example where cookies are allocated in a small school classroom. The teacher makes the cookies every day, and the students can buy them. We'll assume that it costs the teacher $0.50 to make each cookie for all the ingredients, including labor and energy. Thus, we can represent marginal cost (MC) as a horizontal line in figure 2.1, reflecting the fact that the marginal cost of $0.50 is the same at all quantities.

Given the preferences of the students (some students like cookies more than others, some have larger appetites or more money to spend), what they are willing to pay (their "maximum willingness to pay") for a cookie will differ, as will their willingness to pay for their first cookie compared with their second or third cookie. We've assumed some hypothetical preferences for the students in this particular classroom, and we've represented what they would be willing to pay (in dollars per cookie) with a set of bars in figure 2.1. Each bar represents one student's willingness to pay for a cookie, and we've arranged these from highest to lowest in the graph.

The way to interpret this is that the first bar shows the person with the highest willingness to pay for a cookie ($1.50). The second highest marginal benefit (MB) is $1.25 (indicating two students would be willing to pay $1.25 for a cookie). Other students are only willing to pay lower amounts. Taken in this order, the marginal benefit for cookies declines as the number of cookies increases along this "staircase" of marginal benefits. The marginal benefit for the twelfth cookie is only $0.15; no student is willing to pay a positive price for a thirteenth cookie.

The marginal cost of these cookies is also represented in figure 2.1 as a horizontal line since we assumed the cost per cookie

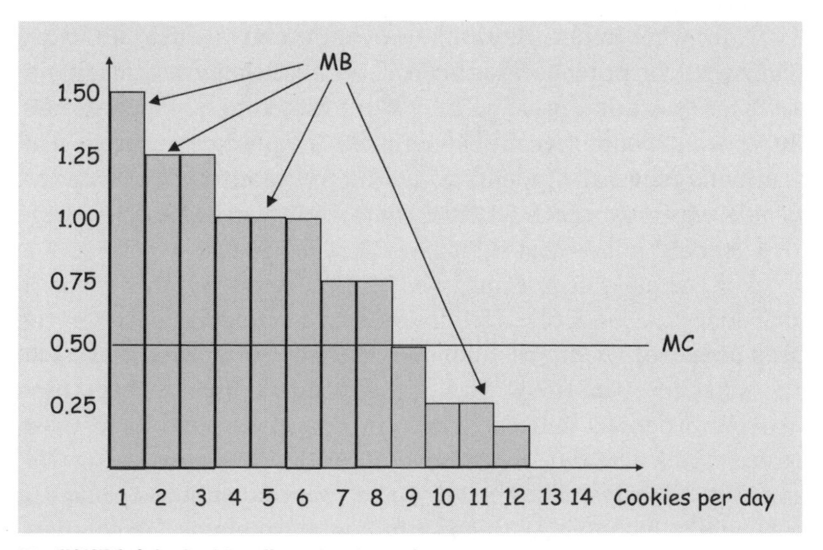

■ **FIGURE 2.1 Cookie allocation in a classroom**

is constant at $0.50 (MC could be represented with bars like MB, but all the bars would have the same height).

This simple example allows us to make some very important points about trade-offs, marginal benefits, marginal costs, net benefits, and efficiency. First, let's look at net benefit, which is equal to benefit minus cost. For the first student (the one willing to pay $1.50), we want to ask the question, what is the net benefit to her if she can buy a cookie at a price equal to its marginal cost ($0.50)? We have to subtract the value of what the student gives up from the value of what the student gets. The student gives up $0.50 and gets something with MB = $1.50, so the net benefit is $1.00. We say, then, that the net benefit of this transaction for that first student is $1.00. For the second and third students, the net benefit will be $0.75.

But what about the ninth student? If he has to pay a price equal to marginal cost, what is his net benefit from that transaction? The answer is zero! No net benefit. That student is neither better off nor worse off after buying a cookie. He gained something worth $0.50 to him, and he gave up exactly that amount (he could have used the $0.50 for something else later, and that is why he was only willing to give up $0.50 for a cookie). The ninth student is neither worse off nor better off; economists say that this particular student would be "indifferent" to buying a cookie or not buying a cookie.

Now what about the tenth, eleventh, and twelfth students? They would not buy cookies at $0.50 because their marginal benefit is less than that price. If they were forced to buy a cookie for $0.50, what would their net benefit be? It would be negative. The tenth and eleventh students would be worse off by $0.25 since a cookie was only worth $0.25 to them and they had to pay twice that. Benefit minus cost is $0.25 − $0.50 = −$0.25.

For the class as a whole, what we can see from this graph is that marginal benefit exceeds or equals marginal cost for the first nine cookies, but that beyond that the marginal cost exceeds the marginal benefit. It makes "economic sense" to have nine cookies produced and consumed in this classroom since these transactions generate net benefits. Of course, here we are assuming that all costs and all benefits are being taken into account in this simple example. With environmental problems, by contrast, there are often additional costs or side effects that alter the net benefits (in our example, this might occur if the students make a mess that the teacher must clean up or if eating cookies distracts from learning).

In the example we can say that nine cookies is the efficient amount. But what is the net benefit overall, for the whole class? Well, all we have to do is add up the net benefit for each student—the portion of each marginal benefit "bar" that is above the MC line. The total net benefit for these is $4.50, and this is the maximum net benefit possible in this "market."

We can end up short of the maximum net benefit in two ways: too few cookies or too many cookies. What if we made only six cookies and sold them to the first six students at marginal cost? The total net benefit would then be $4.00, or less than $4.50. In this case we would conclude that this is not the efficient level of cookies, because it does not maximize net benefits.

This may be a good place to point out that we don't need to assume there is a market operating to compare benefits and costs. In many environmental examples there is no market, or the market does not take all of the costs or benefits into account. Even for our cookies-in-the-classroom example, we don't need to have cookies bought and sold to compare costs and benefits. For example, let's assume that cookies are given away to all twelve students with positive marginal benefits. We can still ask, what would be the net benefit? This time, let's get at the net benefits differently, by first summing total benefits across all students and then subtracting the total cost. The total benefit would be the sum of the areas of all the bars ($9.65 is the total). And now let's add up the total cost of the twelve cookies (12 × $0.50 = $6). The cost is not the cost to the students in this case, but it is still the cost to the teacher of making these cookies. The difference between total benefits $9.65 and total cost $6 is $3.65. And this is less than the maximum of $4.50.

Why is this net benefit lower than $4.50, even though more students got to enjoy eating cookies? Does the fact that the students didn't pay for the cookies cause the net benefit to be less than $4.50? No. The reason is that for the tenth, eleventh, and twelfth students, their marginal benefit (willingness to pay) is less than the cost of producing the cookies, as illustrated in figure 2.2. As a result, the total net benefit is actually reduced by making these three cookies and selling them to these last three students: total net benefit is \$−0.25 for two of them and \$−0.35 for the third.

We can see from this that in order to allocate a resource to gain the highest net benefit, the quantity allocated to any particular use (like making cookies for students) should increase so long as the marginal benefit exceeds the marginal cost but should stop at the point where marginal benefit is just equal to marginal cost. If we continue to increase the quantity to a point where MC is higher than MB, then the total net benefit will be less than the maximum possible.

Economic theory assumes that people know what they want and thus can identify the point where the MB for good X is equal to the MB for the amount of good Z they could have instead. Another way of saying this is that the MC of X is the opportunity cost of using resources (money) to buy X, since that money could have been spent on Z. Money is just the medium of exchange between X and Z, or between X and other goods and services.

The staircase of marginal benefits for cookies in our classroom could be referred to as a demand curve, representing the quantity that would be demanded in a market for each price. In other parts of this book we'll stick to the label MB, but in some

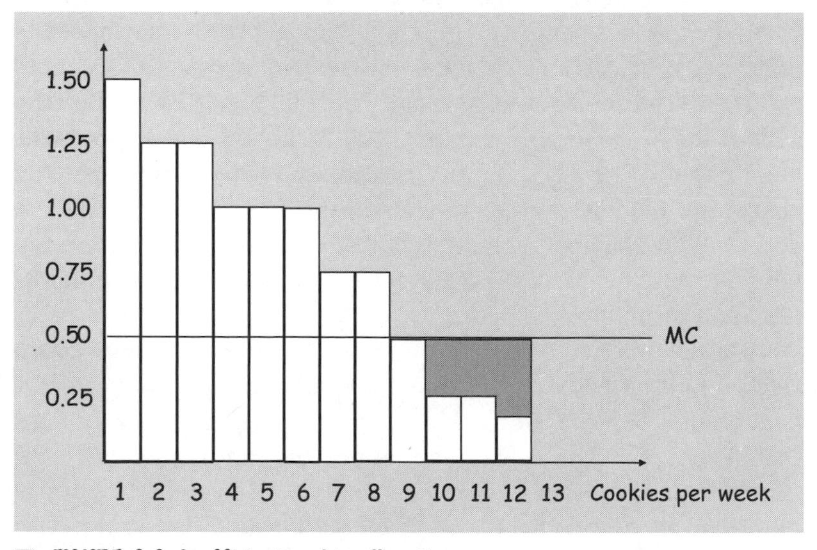

FIGURE 2.2 Inefficient cookie allocation

cases where we clearly are talking about markets, we'll refer to demand and designate the curve with a big D.

Shortly, we will also be representing MB and D as a continuous curve rather than a staircase of discrete steps for individuals (think of a staircase with thousands of steps viewed from a distance). This MB or demand curve may be steep or flat, and many kinds of changes in an economy can cause the whole curve to shift to the left or the right. As you will soon see, these factors can be enormously important. In a market, whether the demand curve is steep or flat, or whether it shifts a lot or a little in response to some other kind of change in the economy, can have enormous implications for environmental problems and the policies aimed at correcting them.

But let's not get ahead of the game. Let's start by recognizing that individuals' preferences include the ability and willingness to make substitutions among different goods and services, depending on their relative prices. If gasoline is expensive, consumers may take the bus more frequently. If coffee is cheap, they may consume less tea. In some cases goods are "complements" rather than "substitutes." For example, if air travel becomes more expensive, the demand for hotel accommodations at tourist destinations is likely to fall. A decline in the cost of bread could lead to a rise in the demand for jam. Economists are very interested in these relationships, and they often measure them by estimating the proportional change in the quantity demanded of one good in response to a percentage change in the price of another good. These measures are called elasticities; more on that later.

We will want to talk in much more detail about supply (firms, profits, and choices in production), but for now I'll ask you just to accept a few ideas about the marginal cost or supply side of a market, in order to be able to make some preliminary observations about how competitive markets find their equilibrium and why economists think there is something special about that equilibrium.

Market Equilibrium

We can take these insights from our simple cookie example and shift to a more general case where the marginal benefit curve is continuous rather than a staircase of discrete levels. Let's also make the marginal cost curve slope upward, meaning that the marginal cost increases with the quantity produced rather than stays constant (as was the case for a horizontal cost curve). We do this to reflect the idea that at a low price only low-cost supplies would be offered in a market, but that as the price rises the quantity supplied would likely increase as well. This is the same—well, opposite—reasoning for having a marginal benefit curve that slopes down, because the number of willing buyers and the quantity demanded declines as the price increases. We'll get into the reasons behind the slope of the MC or supply curve in more detail in the next chapter.

Putting these two curves together in figure 2.3, we see MB (demand) sloping downward and MC (supply) sloping up. How does a market find that point where marginal benefit is just equal to marginal cost? It works like this: Starting at any arbitrary price, there will be a quantity demanded and a quantity supplied (the point on the demand curve at that price, and the point on the supply curve at that price). If demand (D) exceeds supply (S), this scarcity will lead consumers to offer to pay more to get what they want, and this will push up the price, which will increase the amount supplied and reduce the amount demanded. This upward pressure will continue as long as there is a shortage, or until the point where the two curves intersect: the market equilibrium where MB = MC and S = D. If, by contrast, we begin at a price where supply exceeds demand initially, suppliers will lower prices to unload their surpluses. This will create downward pressure on prices, which will increase the amount demanded and reduce the amount supplied. This downward pressure will continue as long as there is a surplus, or until market equilibrium is reached where, once again, MB = MC and S = D.

What's so great about this market equilibrium (aside from having no shortage and no surplus)? In a "competitive" market, this market equilibrium is the place where the net benefit is maximized—and there is a simple way to see this from the graph. When a market allocation is in equilibrium as with Q* in figure 2.3, total benefit (TB) can be measured as the area under the demand (or marginal benefit) curve between zero and Q*. (Look back at figure 2.1 to see why the area under the curve is equal to

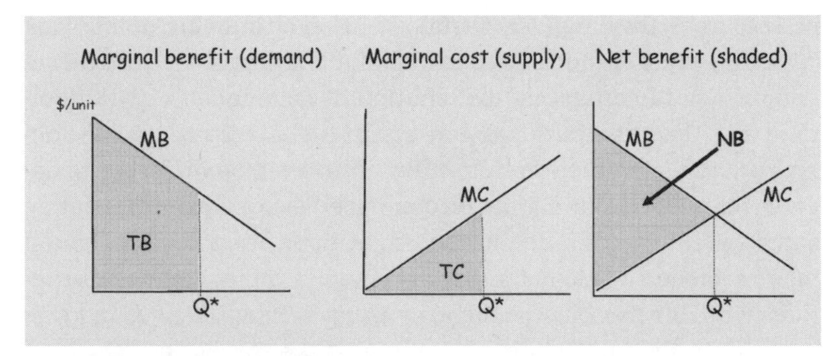

■ **FIGURE 2.3 Marginal benefit, marginal cost, and efficient allocation**

the total benefit.) Similarly, total cost (TC) can be measured as the area under the supply (or marginal cost) curve between zero and Q*.

Since the net benefit (NB) is just the difference between total benefit and total cost, it will be equal to the area between the demand and supply curves from zero and Q* (the shaded area in the third panel in figure 2.3). As with the cookie example, this area (net benefit) will be maximized at Q* since all exchanges for which MB > MC have taken place. Since we are at the point where MB = MC (and since the demand curve is downward sloping and the supply curve is either upward sloping or horizontal), any additional exchange would be for units where MB < MC, and thus the net benefit will be reduced. This is the crux of market efficiency.

Key Definition: *Pareto efficiency, social efficiency* 

Efficiency is a central concept in economics, so let's take a few minutes here to define it carefully and explain its importance. Economists use the terms **Pareto efficiency** or **Pareto optimality** in recognition of the Italian economist Vilfredo Pareto who, in 1906, said **an allocation of resources is efficient if no other allocation is possible that will make at least one person better off without making another person worse off.** Pareto efficiency is a very precise and useful way to think about different allocations of resources from a given initial situation or starting point. This "starting point" qualification is important and refers to the initial endowment of resources (distribution of land, income, commodities) and the existing legal and institutional setting (ownership rights, laws, jurisdictions, etc.). By contrast, two different property rights situations cannot be compared using Pareto efficiency since switching from one to the other, in either direction, would make someone worse off. Later on we will want to compare situations with different institutional settings such as changes in laws, property rights, or liability rules, and there we will use the concept of **social efficiency,** which compares the allocations that occur with different policies, or institutional arrangements, and evaluates them from the perspective of maximizing net social benefits.

So what's so important about efficiency? If you avoid waste or minimize costs for one activity, more resources will be available for other activities. Students who study efficiently have more time for their other interests. A community with efficiently run schools can have lower taxes or can spend more on public health, libraries, or police protection. It's pretty clear that people care enormously about efficiency even though they might not use the word. The public is regularly outraged when it hears about government inefficiency such as idle workers, defective construction, or expensive projects that end up being useless. Nobody likes to spend time or money on something only to be disappointed or to find out that there was an easier or cheaper way.

Goals and efficiency are interdependent. For environmental issues, society's willingness to set specific environmental goals depends on their costs and benefits. The costs will depend on the efficiency of the approach taken, and the benefits will depend on choosing the right goals. By emphasizing efficiency, society can achieve greater environmental benefits, at lower cost, and over a wider set of issues than if efficiency were not given appropriate attention. The differences between efficiency and inefficiency can be very large: in later chapters we will see examples where either costs or benefits vary by factors of 10 or 20. What policymaker would use all her available resources to achieve one goal when she could achieve twenty similar goals at the same total cost?

The third graph of figure 2.3 is deceptively simple. Before we go into more detail, perhaps this is a good place to step back for a minute and think about the interplay of MB and MC. If there is no market, as with many environmental examples such as clean air, the ozone layer, or species diversity, then identifying where MB = MC is located is important, as is assessing how large or small NB is likely to be if we can achieve efficiency. In most cases what goes on in these "nonmarkets" is heavily influenced by the things that go on in markets, such as environmental damage from industrial production, farming, and resource extraction. The interplay can be large or small depending on the slopes of these curves and whether they shift one way or the other in response to a particular change in the economy or government policy. The size of the net benefit can also be small or large, and it may change by a little or a lot owing to other changes taking place elsewhere in the economy such as a change in population or income. In short, many important kinds of economic analysis involve evaluating the position and shape of these curves, and how sensitive ("shifty") they are to changes in government policy or other forces.

Demand Response

The response of demand to price is what gives the demand curve its slope: steep if demand is relatively unresponsive, flat if it is relatively responsive. A steep curve also means that the marginal benefit changes a lot when the quantity changes; a flat demand curve indicates that the marginal benefit doesn't change much with a change in quantity. This steepness or flatness of demand can be very important for understanding how the market will respond to policy, or for understanding how costly a change in policy may be. The cost of reducing carbon emissions, or the effectiveness of a $20/ton carbon tax, depends on whether the demand for carbon-intensive products is steep or flat.

Key Definition: *Price elasticity of demand* 

The most common way that economists describe how demand for a resource changes in response to a change in price is with the

price elasticity of demand (PED). PED measures the percent change in quantity demanded as a result of a given percent change in price. Mathematically, we can write this as PED = $\%\Delta Q / \%\Delta P$, where Q is the quantity of the resource demanded, P is the price, and $\Delta\%$ is the percentage by which each changes. For demand elasticities, the sign of PED is always going to be negative since we expect the change in demand to move in the opposite direction as the change in price. If the proportional change in quantity demanded is less than the proportional change in price, PED > -1 and we call this inelastic demand. If the proportional change in quantity demanded is greater than the proportional change in price, then PED < -1 and we call this elastic demand. For PED $= -1$, we refer to unit elasticity, meaning that a 5% rise in price will result in a 5% decline in quantity demanded. The price elasticity of demand provides an indication of how easily consumers can find substitutes for a given commodity. If Coke drinkers can easily switch to Pepsi, then the price elasticity of demand for Coke will be highly elastic. By contrast, if motorists have no close substitutes for gasoline, then demand will be inelastic especially for commuters who have no alternative for getting to work.

In addition to demand from consumers, we are often interested in the demand for inputs by firms, and this kind of demand can be characterized in the same way. We refer to this as derived demand, meaning that the demand for an input by producers is "derived from" (depends on) the final demand for the products being produced (more on this in chapter 3).

For example, the demand for high-sulfur coal will have direct implications on air quality (assuming for the moment that technologies to "scrub" pollutants from their emissions are not being used). We may wish to know what the costs would be for reducing air pollution by limiting the use of high-sulfur coal. In figure 2.4 we consider a limit on the use of high-sulfur coal for a case with inelastic demand (case A) and one with elastic demand (case B). The cost (reduction in net benefit from the use of coal) for a reduction from Q to Q′ would be much larger for the case with inelastic demand versus elastic demand, as indicated by the reductions in net benefit (shaded areas). Case B might represent a situation where other fuels were readily available at reasonable cost (i.e., low-sulfur coal, natural gas).

Key Definition: *Cross-price elasticity of demand* 

There are two additional types of elasticity that are important for many policy questions: the cross-price elasticity of demand and the income elasticity of demand. **The cross-price elasticity of demand (CPED) measures how the demand for one good responds to a change in the price of a different good.** It provides an indication of whether two goods are substitutes or complements. If the two goods are substitutes like coal and heating oil, an increase in the price of one will result in an increase in the quantity demanded for the other, so that CPED > 0. If the two goods are complements like cars and gasoline, an increase in the price of one will result in a decrease in the quantity demanded for the other, so that CPED < 0. These elasticities indicate how the demand curve would shift when the price of another good changes and in which direction.

Key Definition: *Income elasticity of demand* 

Finally, the **income elasticity of demand (IED) measures how demand for a good responds to a change in income** (Y) and, like the other elasticities, is the ratio of the percent change in quantity demanded to the percentage change in income, or

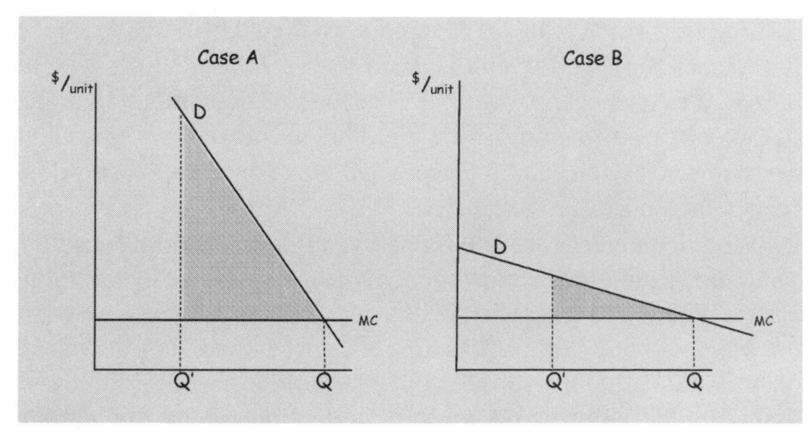

FIGURE 2.4 Inelastic and elastic demand for high-sulfur coal

IED = %ΔQ/%ΔY. If coal and oil have high-income elasticities of demand, then IED > 1, and an economy with rising per capita incomes will see consumption of these fuels rising faster than the increases in income. Again, this will be reflected in a shift in the demand curve when income changes.

How important are these elasticities? In addition to telling us whether pollution can be reduced at a low or high cost, they can tell us whether it will be easy or costly for farmers to reduce their use of chemical fertilizers. Elasticities can tell us whether subsidized public transportation can be expected to reduce highway congestion, or whether subsidies for energy efficiency improvements in the home can be expected to lower electricity demand. Indeed, many aspects of public policy questions about environmental and natural resources can be framed as questions about the magnitude of these elasticities. Let's look at a couple of illuminating examples.

First, consider how local governments frequently face questions about changes in zoning or the creation of open space such as suburban greenbelts. Because local governments are often funded from property tax revenues, objections will be raised because reducing the amount of developable land in the jurisdiction will decrease property tax revenues. But is this necessarily the case? For this analysis we can characterize the supply of land as a vertical line since the supply is fixed at the amount available (and we can't add more the way we make cookies). If we set aside lands for open space, we will reduce the amount of usable land, shifting that vertical line (the supply) to the right. This decrease in the supply of land is indicated in figure 2.5 by the shift from $S_1$to S_2. The market for land will respond to this shift in supply. Prices will rise to find a new equilibrium between supply and demand, and the change in price will depend on the slope, or elasticity, of demand.

What happens to the total value of all such land in the jurisdiction? Initially, the total property value (P × Q) was equal to the area ABCD. With an inelastic demand (relatively steep demand curve), the price rises proportionally more than the decline in quantity, and the new total property value is equal to the area AEFG, which is greater than the initial value. In addition, open

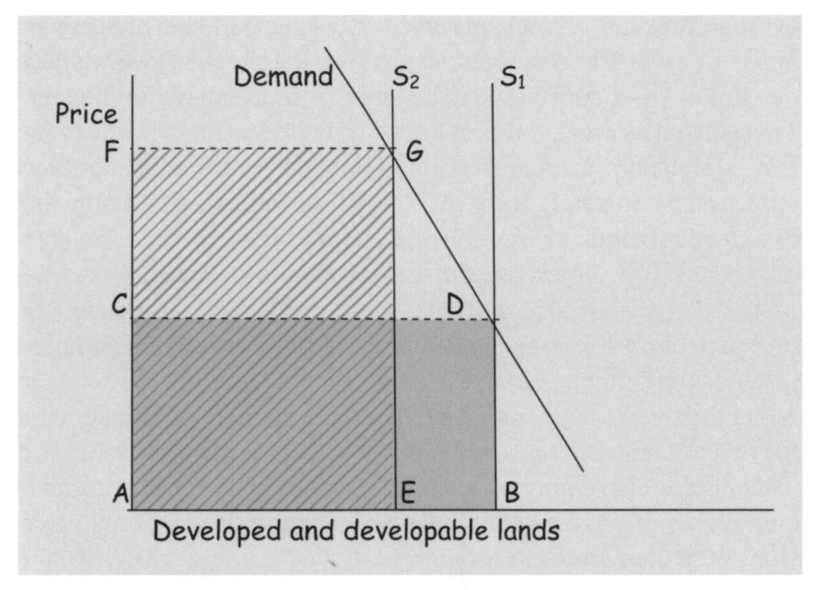

■ **FIGURE 2.5 Price response when supply of land is reduced**

space tends to increase the value of properties that border or are near the open space, and this could increase revenues even more by shifting the demand curve (for properties near the greenbelt) to the right and raising land prices even more. In these circumstances, reducing the land available for development would actually increase tax revenues, not decrease them.

Let's look at a second example involving the regulations in the U.S. auto industry known as the CAFE (corporate average fuel economy) standards, which are aimed at improving auto fuel efficiency in large part to reduce air pollution. Americans are well known for how much they drive. In order to drive you need a car, but once you have a car the cost of driving will be mostly a function of the fuel cost when driving. We expect the marginal benefit from driving (the demand curve) to slope downward as in figure 2.6. The marginal cost of driving is represented as a horizontal line, indicating that we are assuming that the cost of gasoline and the fuel economy of your car do not change when you drive more miles during a month. So what happens when government regulators require increased fuel economy? Increasing average fuel economy means more miles per gallon, which means more miles per dollar (spent on gas), which means fewer dollars per mile. The CAFE standards actually make driving cheaper! This shifts the marginal cost curve down because it reduces the marginal cost of driving (assuming gas prices are unchanged) as indicated by the shift from MC to MC′ in figure 2.6. This means that people will drive more. If the demand for driving were elastic, then a 10% improvement in fuel economy would lower the cost of driving by 10%, and this would increase the miles driven by *more* than 10%, so that gasoline consumption and air pollution would actually increase!

Is that what happens? Fortunately, estimates of the demand for driving with changes in average fuel economy suggest that it is inelastic. There may be a small increase in driving, but this is unlikely to offset more than a small portion of the gains made from improved miles per gallon with CAFE standards. Still, the main point here is that the difference between elastic and inelastic responses can be very important, and ignoring them can cause well-intentioned policymakers to seriously miss the mark when trying to achieve a policy goal.

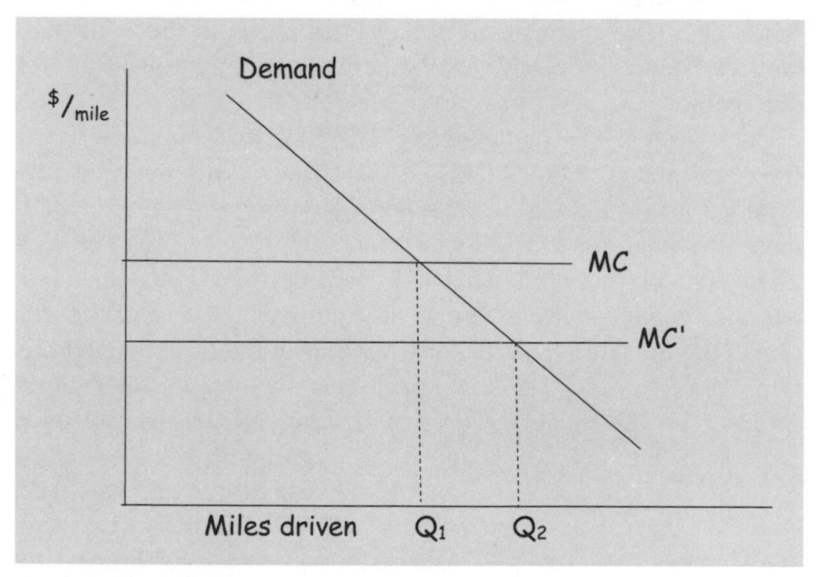

FIGURE 2.6 Fuel economy and the demand for driving

Demand Shifters

There are many factors that could alter, or shift, a demand curve. These factors include changes in population, income, the price of other goods, or simply a change in people's preferences. The one factor that does not cause a shift in the demand curve is a change in price, and that is because the effect of price on quantity demanded is reflected in a *movement along* the demand curve, not by a shift in the curve.

The difference between a large shift and a small shift can be very important when evaluating the costs, benefits, or effectiveness of policies. For example, one way to discourage environmentally harmful actions is to lower the costs of an alternative, for example, with a government subsidy. Whether the policy is effective will depend on the shift in demand. Some African countries have considered subsidizing kerosene in order to discourage demand by households for fuelwood collected from forests and woodlands (which have been severely degraded by excessive fuelwood collection). Figure 2.7 shows two possible effects of a kerosene subsidy, one that shifts the demand for fuelwood by a small amount (case A) and one that shifts the demand for fuelwood by a large amount (case B). For case A, the policy will do little to solve the problem. It will reduce fuelwood collections from Q to Q′ only. For case B, the shift from Q to Q′ will be large and the policy will be much more effective.

In this example, as in many other situations, the responsiveness of demand to other changes in the economy is important and can tell us much about the actions, reactions, positive feedback, negative feedback, and potential for low-cost solutions to environmental problems. These relationships provide a basis for addressing many environmental problems because we can evaluate how demand is related to negative environmental impacts, and also what the likely effect would be from a policy change or other government action.

But before we can move to looking at environmental policy, we first need to have a more complete picture of the market economy. We need to understand production and the supply side of market allocation. The next chapter takes up these issues. Once we have done that, we can integrate the two sides of the market

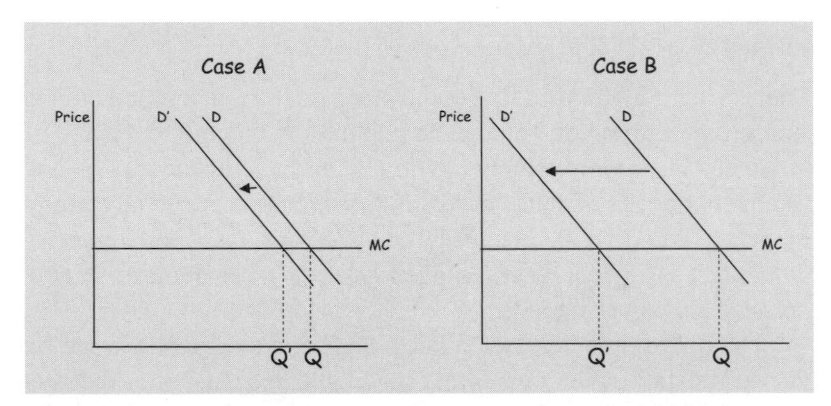

■ **FIGURE 2.7 Shift in demand for fuelwood in Malawi with a kerosene subsidy**

and return to some of the key ideas about resource allocation for the whole economy.

Recommended Readings and References

For a comprehensive introduction to microeconomics, there are many excellent textbooks such as the unique and highly recommended approach in Paul Heyne, Peter J. Boettke, and David L. Prychitko, *The Economic Way of Thinking*, 10th ed. (Upper Saddle River, NJ: Prentice Hall, 2002). An excellent alternative is William J. Baumol and Alan S. Blinder, *Microeconomics: Principles and Policy*, 9th ed. (Mason, OH: South-Western College Publishing, 2004). For more depth, see an intermediate microeconomics text such as Robert H. Frank, *Microeconomics and Behavior* (New York: McGraw-Hill/Irwin, 2002); Walter Nicholson, *Intermediate Microeconomics and Its Applications* (Mason, OH: South-Western College Publishing, 2000); and Hal Varian, *Intermediate Microeconomics: A Modern Approach* (New York: W. W. Norton, 2002).

3

Production, Profit, and Supply

The supply side of a market is just the reverse of the demand side. While demand is based on marginal benefit, which determines consumers' willingness to pay, supply is based on marginal cost, which determines producers' willingness to sell. In a market, supply comes from firms or producers that combine inputs to make the goods and services that consumers will buy. Economists sometimes refer to these inputs as factors of production, meaning labor, capital, and land, as well as other more specific inputs such as energy, chemicals, water, steel, wood, and seeds.

Key Concept: *Opportunity cost* 

In the last chapter we indicated that the supply curve tends to be upward sloping: marginal cost increases with quantity. At a very general level an upward-sloping supply curve is quite intuitively based on **opportunity cost.** In order to produce more goods in market X, we must draw inputs away from other uses such as producing other goods in other markets. As inputs are drawn away from other uses, the marginal value of using those inputs in those other markets is likely to rise. The cost of inputs for producing X will depend on their opportunity cost, or the value of using them elsewhere, and this cost tends to rise as the production of X rises.

Just as consumers substitute among goods and services, firms make similar kinds of substitutions. Capital can be substituted for labor (tractors, automated machinery, or computers). Labor can be substituted for land (using more labor to tend crops as a way to get more output per acre). There may be limits to the degree of substitution: if you are producing bottled water, you are going to need water. Over long periods of time, research and development (R&D) can raise the productivity of labor or land, which makes R&D a form of capital that is substituted for labor or land. Firms also may enter or exit an industry, or expand or reduce the size of their operation, which affects supply. And since the supply of goods in each industry is just the sum of the actions of all the individual firms, we need to understand a few things about how those firms operate, how they make decisions.

Firms, Profits, and Production

Each firm in an industry will make its own decisions about combining and substituting inputs to produce output. Standard economic theory assumes that firms try to maximize profits, and in a competitive market where many firms are producing the same commodity, only the firms that can keep their costs low will survive. Low-cost firms can keep prices low to attract customers. High-cost firms will be unable to cover their costs at competitive prices. The airline industry is a visible example of this kind of competition, where extinct firms like Pan Am and TWA were unable to compete. Farms and restaurants are also industries where financial failure is common.

When economists talk about a competitive industry, they have in mind a situation where each firm is small relative to the size of the market. This means that the firm does not have any influence over the prices of products or inputs, and so it behaves as though these prices are fixed. The firm can sell all it wants at the market price for its product and buy all the inputs it wants at the going rate.

A few key concepts related to profits, entry, and exit in an industry will come in handy later on. Figure 3.1 illustrates several key ideas about the economics of a firm in a competitive industry. First, firms have two kinds of costs, fixed costs and variable costs. Fixed costs are things such as buildings, land, large equipment, or contracts with managers or other employees. These costs are independent of the level of production. Variable costs vary with the output level and include the materials and other inputs that go into the product being produced. The distinction is important for understanding why the average cost curve in figure 3.1 is different from the marginal cost curve.

Typically, we recognize that before you can produce even one unit of a commodity, you need some capital equipment, and that because of these expenses, it would be very costly to operate at a very low level of output. As output increases, average cost declines—over some range of output levels. But we also understand that at some point a firm can get too big and unwieldy, making it difficult to produce as efficiently as it did at some intermediate level. For this reason, we generally assume that average costs start to rise when a firm gets too big. The idea of the U-shaped average cost curve in figure 3.1 is that there is an optimal-size firm and that firms will do best if they can operate at the lowest average cost. Of course, that level will vary by industry and technology. The optimal-size pizza restaurant is different from the optimal-size airplane manufacturer.

Marginal cost will generally rise over the range of output levels we are interested in. The MC curve will always cross the AC curve at the minimum average cost. (If you think about it long enough, you can probably figure out why this has to be the case.)

If a firm producing TVs has costs like those in figure 3.1, and it wants to maximize profit, what will it do? The profit for a firm is just equal to the difference between revenues and costs. If the firm produces one additional TV, its marginal revenue is just P, the price of the TV. Its marginal cost is indicated by the MC curve. So as long as $P > MC$, the firm should increase output. If $P = MC$, the firm should stop. In figure 3.1, if the price were P_2, the firm would produce at Q_2.

If we want to be able to identify or measure the profit of the firm based on something like figure 3.1, it is useful to recognize

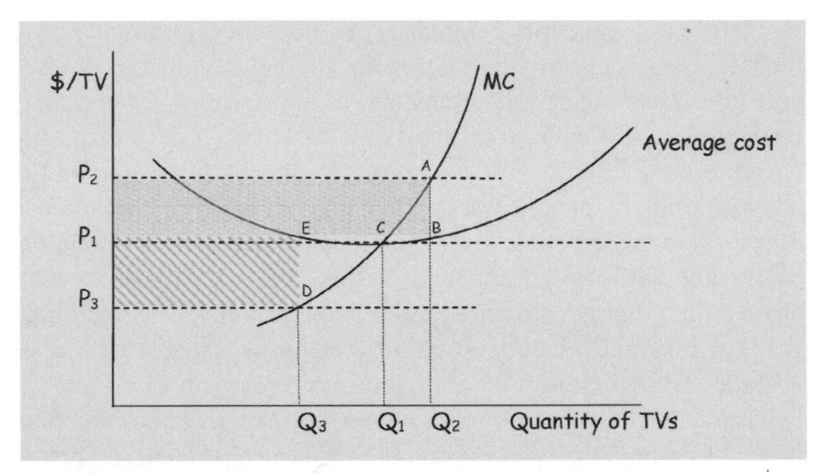

FIGURE 3.1 Profits, costs, and output for a firm producing TVs

that profits are equal to total revenue (TR) minus total cost (TC) for any output Q. Another way to measure profit is to take *average* revenue (P), subtract *average* cost (AC), and multiply this by Q. To see that these two different ways of measuring profit are the same algebraically, we need only to recognize that TR = P × Q (since price in a competitive market is both the marginal revenue and the average revenue), and also that TC/Q = AC, so AC × Q = TC. The second way to measure profit, (P – AC) × Q, can be identified by the shaded area in figure 3.1 as the profit-maximizing output Q_2, when the price is P_2. This is the case because A – B is equal to P – AC, and output is Q_2, so that the area of the rectangle is equal to (P – AC) × Q.

What happens if the firms in the TV industry find themselves at P_2? Well, the firms are making positive profits equal to (A – B) × Q_2, or the shaded area. This attracts new firms; output rises, which puts downward pressure on price. As price falls, incentives for new firms to enter diminishes until, at P_1, no new firms are interested in entering, and profits equal zero (MR = P = AC, so (P – AC) × Q = 0).

What happens if the firms in the TV industry find themselves at P_3? Well, in that case the firms are making negative profits since (D – E) × Q_3 is less than zero and equal to the striped area. This situation will discourage firms, and some are likely to leave the industry (in search of positive, or at least zero, profits); output declines, which puts upward pressure on price. As price rises, the incentives for firms to exit the industry will diminish until, at P_1, no additional firms will be interested in leaving, and profits will once again be zero.

Taken together, all these ways that firms respond to price changes give us an industry supply curve. It may be flat or steep, and that will depend on how existing firms respond by moving along their marginal cost curves, as well as the entry or exit of firms. The industry supply curve is just the horizontal sum of all the firm supply curves, as illustrated in figure 3.2.

The central point here is that profits end up being zero because positive or negative profits will trigger the self-correcting mechanisms of entry into or exit from the industry until profits settle back to zero. But "zero profit" in this sense does not mean the company is broke. In fact, it means that the firm owner is earning just enough to be satisfied. Well, perhaps grumbling a bit, but not really willing to go elsewhere for better opportunities. Why? Well, because elsewhere, in any other competitive industry, the situation is going to be exactly the same.

Supply Response

Key Definition: *Price elasticity of supply* 

We can measure the responsiveness of supply in a market the same way we measured the responsiveness of demand, with elasticities. **The price elasticity of supply (PES) measures the percentage change in quantity supplied as a result of a given**

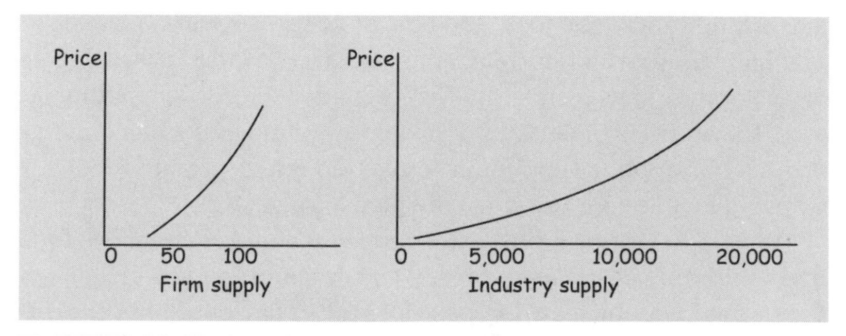

FIGURE 3.2 Firm supply and industry supply

percentage change in price. Mathematically, we can write this as PES = %ΔQ/%ΔP, where Q is the quantity supplied, P is the price, and %Δ is the percentage by which each changes. Unlike PED, we expect PES to be positive since the change in supply is generally in the same direction as the change in price. If the proportional change in quantity supplied is less than the proportional change in price, then PES < 1 and we call this inelastic supply. If the proportional change in quantity supplied is greater than the proportional change in price, then PES > 1 and we call this elastic supply. For PES = 1, we call that unit elastic, meaning that a 10% increase in price will lead to a 10% increase in quantity supplied.

Although supply curves shift in response to changes elsewhere in the economy, we don't frequently talk about the "cross-price elasticities of supply." We are, however, interested often in how changes in the market price of a commodity will alter the firm's demand for inputs. This is the notion of derived demand, taken up next. Another way that supply curves, which are also marginal cost curves, can shift is in response to government policies that may raise (tax) or lower (subsidize) a firm's costs. Examples of how these kinds of policies will shift the supply curve can be found in the section on market distortions.

Derived Demand

The demand for inputs by firms is very similar to the demand for goods and services by consumers. One key difference is that this demand for inputs is dependent on the demand by consumers for the goods and services being produced. Economists call this derived demand. As an illustration, let's look at the demand for labor in U.S. agriculture. Given market prices that consumers are willing to pay for food, the cost of processing and transporting, and the production technologies that farmers are using in order to minimize their costs (using land, chemicals, machinery, etc.), there will be a derived demand for farm labor like D_1 in figure 3.3. For a labor supply curve like the one depicted, the labor employed will be Q_1 and it will be paid a wage W_1.

What if foreign suppliers are suddenly able to send more food to the U.S. market at lower cost? The demand for U.S.-produced food would decline, causing prices to fall. This would make profits negative, and some farmers would reduce or stop production, which in turn would affect the derived demand for labor in agriculture. This change in demand for the product would cause a shift in labor demand from D_1 to D_2 in figure 3.3. The market for farm labor will need to find a new equilibrium, and it will do that with a decline in wages and a decline in employment to D_2 and W_2. A similar shift in derived demand could have occurred if farm employers were required to pay more for workers insurance. A shift of the derived demand in the opposite direction (up and to the right) might occur if labor-saving farm machinery became more expensive (so that farmers would choose to rely somewhat more on manual labor).

While we're on this topic, what might this representation of a labor market tell us about the impact of environmental regulations on the job market? First, the introduction of environmental regulations could shift the demand for labor to the left or the right. The reason for this is that labor could be a complement or a substitute to the regulations; the regulation could be labor using or labor reducing. Indeed, some evidence indicates that environmental spending by industry is labor intensive so that it actually creates additional jobs in some industries, while other evidence finds that air pollution regulations in the United States have led to modest

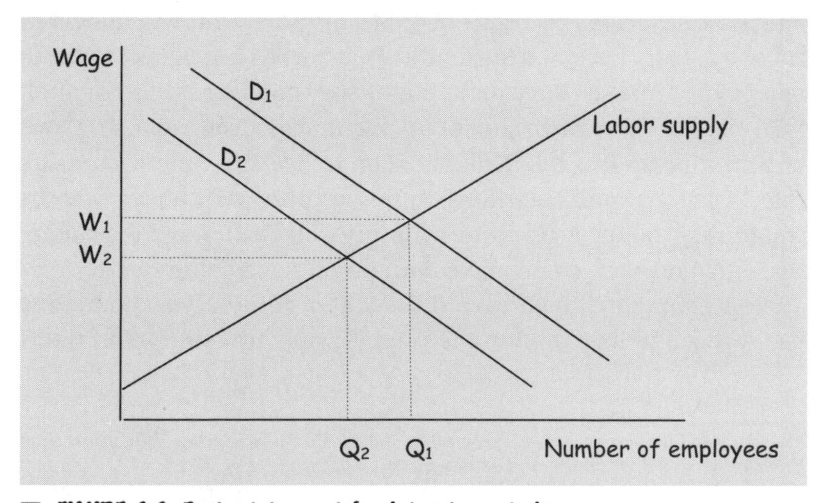

■ **FIGURE 3.3 Derived demand for labor in agriculture**

manufacturing job losses in some regions.[1] Second, the graph indicates that if environmental regulations do cause the demand for workers to shift to the left, there will be market forces at work to reestablish a new equilibrium rather than leave a gap between supply and demand. True, unemployment is a persistent feature of the economy, but this unemployment exists for reasons mostly having to do with shifts in labor demand among different industries and locations, and the time it takes for workers who lose their jobs to find new ones. Overall, the evidence suggests that environmental regulations do not slow job growth, deepen recessions, or prevent an economy from achieving full employment.

Deficient Markets

In order for market allocation to be efficient, it has to allocate goods and services efficiently, but it also has to allocate inputs efficiently. The markets where derived demand for inputs meets input supply must also find that equilibrium where MB = MC. If they don't, then the allocation of inputs will be inefficient, and the net benefits from allocating inputs will not be maximized. Let's look at an example.

For a variety of reasons, markets for water do not always exist or work very well, in some cases because of legal restrictions on the transfer of water between uses or locations. Take the situation described in figure 3.4. Much more water is allocated for use A (e.g., irrigated agriculture), whereas much less water is allocated for use B (which might be municipal, residential, hydropower, or industrial use). At the margin, the value of a unit of water in use B is much higher than in use A, and this suggests that B users would be willing to pay a price well above what it would take to get A users to willingly sell. Voluntary exchange, through a market, could make both buyers and sellers better off.

For example, if a portion of the water currently available for use A (e.g., ΔS indicated in the figure) were transferred to the B

[1]See Richard D. Morgenstern, William A. Pizer, and Jhih-Shyang Shih, *Journal of Environmental Economics and Management* 43, no. 3 (May 2002): 412–436; and Michael Greenstone *Journal of Political Economy* 110, no. 6 (December 2002): 1175–1219.

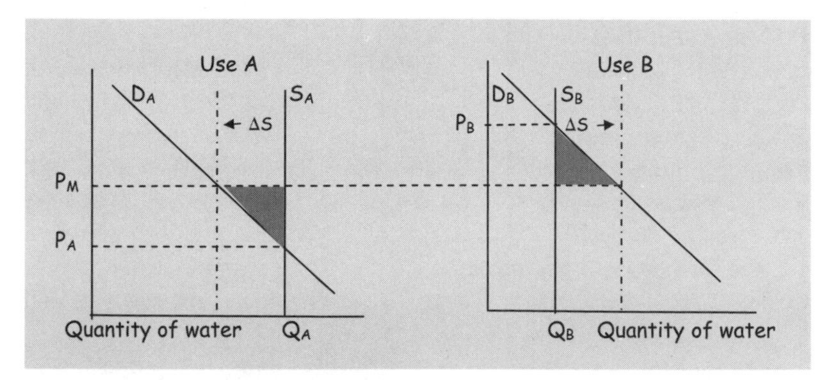

■ **FIGURE 3.4 Potential gains from a water market**

user group, we can represent this as shifting supply S_A to the left by ΔS and shifting supply S_B to the right by the same amount. Let's assume this transfer of ΔS occurs as the result of a voluntary market exchange at price P_M. The net benefit for A users is the shaded triangle in the right-hand panel indicating the difference between their benefits (payments from group B) and the costs (the lost marginal benefits from ΔS). For the B group, the net benefit is the shaded area in the left-hand panel indicating the difference between the benefit (the gain in marginal benefit from ΔS) and the cost (the payments to group B). Both groups see a net benefit equal to these shaded areas.

In this hypothetical example, the ratio of the marginal values before the trade occurs (P_B/P_A) is about 3 to 1. In reality these differences can be 20 to 1, for example, in some parts of the western United States (see box 1) where, among other things, legal restrictions or jurisdictional barriers prevent water markets from functioning efficiently. Some of the reasons for these obstacles have to do with what are called third-party effects, where small rural communities would see their economies shrink if irrigation water were sold to distant uses.

Profits and Economic Rent

When a competitive market is in equilibrium, the last consumer to enter the market is one for whom the marginal benefit is *just* equal to the price (the last consumer's marginal cost): MB = P. On

BOX 1

The Klamath Water Crisis and the Lack of a Water Market

In the spring of 2001, the U.S. Bureau of Reclamation (BOR) announced that farmers who irrigate the 190,000-acre Klamath Reclamation Project (KRP) in southern Oregon and northern California would get no water that year from the Klamath River because of a combination of drought conditions and Endangered Species Act directives to maintain adequate instream flow and lake levels to protect coho salmon and two other species of endangered fish. That decision by the BOR prompted protests, marches, civil disobedience, and political fallout that received national attention throughout that year. Estimates of the economic damage suffered by the farmers ranged from $30 million to $40 million. Federal and state public funds spent drilling groundwater wells and compensating farmers for their losses topped $50 million.

More than half of the irrigated land in the Upper Klamath Basin, however, is outside the jurisdiction of the BOR. There are nearly 300,000 acres of privately irrigated lands upstream and outside the federal KRP, and those farmers irrigated their lands in 2001 under state law without restriction. One other key difference between the KPR acres and the non-KPR acres is that most of the very high productivity lands are in the KRP, and most of the least productive irrigable lands are outside the KRP. As a result, the marginal value of irrigation water across the different areas varies by a factor of 20!

Unresolved legal issues and history made it impossible to have a water market in 2001, although some progress has been made since. If farmers in the KRP had been able to lease water rights from non-KRP farmers (leaving more water instream in the upper portions of the watershed so that KRP farmers could divert it later on), the efficiency of the water that *was* available for irrigation could have been increased significantly. Would this have made much of a difference in terms of the costs of the 2001 crisis? One analysis based on some economic simulation models suggests that the costs could have been reduced from $33 million to less than $9 million.

Source: William K. Jaeger, "Conflicts over Water in the Upper Klamath Basin and the Potential Role for Market-based Allocations," *Journal of Agricultural and Resource Economics* 29, no. 2 (August 2004): 167–184.

the supply side, the last firm to produce the last unit of the commodity is also one for which the marginal benefit (the price received) is *just* equal to marginal cost: P = MC. It's easy to see that the firm receives no extra benefit, or profit, on this last unit produced and sold (MC = P). But it's not so obvious why profits are zero for all units produced by all the firms. This is partly because of the way that economists define profits, and this in turn is related to that fundamental idea of opportunity cost.

Here's how it works. If there are competitive markets for all the inputs that a firm uses to produce a commodity (labor, land, energy, materials, supervisors), and if the firm can make substitutions among different inputs to some extent, then we can expect the firm to be using each input up to the point where the marginal value is just equal to its price (just as consumers will consume a commodity up to the point where MB = P). If, after paying for all its inputs, the firm gets a price from the market that is above the firm's marginal cost, what do you think will happen? Other firms will see this as an opportunity for excess benefit or "profits" and will enter the market. This will increase supply and drive down the price to where, you guessed it, the price is just enough to cover the firm's costs. At that point, profits are zero. And if all firms are identical, then profits will be zero for all firms. Economists use **economic profit** to refer to excess benefit, something above the normal returns expected in a competitive market.

But what if all firms are not identical? What if some firms have a cost advantage that other firms don't have, for example, farmers who have the best land or restaurants that have the best location or view? After all, the situation with identical firms having identical costs and zero profits will look like a horizontal supply curve, and we generally draw supply curves to be upward sloping.

In that case those advantages will result in economic or scarcity "rents," not economic profit. Here's how economists make the distinction. If a farmer has land that is 10% more productive than that of all other farmers, he can produce 10% more wheat than everybody else with the same inputs and make more profit. But are his costs lower per ton of wheat? Economists say no, because his very special land is worth more than other farmers' land. So if we recognize this opportunity cost (he could sell or lease his productive land for more than the land used by other farmers), then his costs (for cultivating the land himself) are really higher when you include this opportunity cost. So producing 10% more leaves him right where everybody else is: zero profits. Alternatively, he could lease his land to somebody else and just sit back and enjoy the rents from his land.

This situation is depicted in figure 3.5, indicating a fixed supply of highly productive farmland. The demand for this land will raise its price/opportunity cost to P*, a level reflecting its value in farm use. In general, the value of an input will be determined by the market just like commodities, and even if the owner inherited this productive farmland, or land with a great location for a downtown restaurant, its (opportunity) cost is the economic cost to consider. When the concept of profit is viewed this way, we expect profits for all firms in competitive markets to be zero because all costs, including opportunity costs, are taken into account.

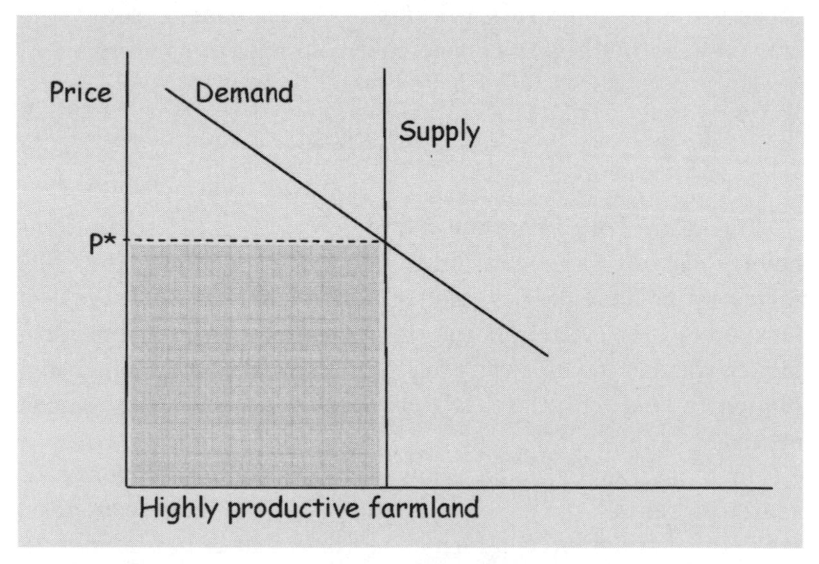

■ **FIGURE 3.5 Economic rent from a scarce resource**

What happens to economic rents if the supply of productive farmland is hugely abundant? (Hint: shift the vertical supply curve in the figure way out to the right.) The price falls to zero, meaning no economic rents. Anybody can just go farm some land, and as a result nobody would buy or lease it from somebody else. Michael Jordan had a highly productive resource, his basketball skills, and he earned huge economic rents (a multimillion-dollar salary). What if players with his basketball skills were hugely abundant? The price for that particular skill level could fall to zero, and they would receive no economic rents.

Short-Run versus Long-Run Substitutions

For many policy issues, there is an important distinction between the short-run and the long-run responses by firms and individuals. For economists, the short run is a period when firms and individuals are "locked in" to some past decisions, so that they have "fixed costs" that they cannot avoid. If gas becomes more expensive on a Monday, you don't trade in your gas-guzzling car on Tuesday. But over a period of months or years, individuals might respond to price changes by buying more fuel-efficient cars or by making other gradual adjustments in their behaviors and choices. If capital equipment becomes more expensive, firms may rely more on labor-intensive technologies after their existing equipment wears out. Households may, over time, convert to natural gas if the price of heating oil stays high for a period of time. These are substitutions that can be made, but they are generally made only over a period of time.

This distinction is important because it can have important implications for policy. Consumers and producers are more responsive in the long run than in the short run because they have more time and more opportunities to respond to a lower, or a higher, price in the long run than in the short run. Demand is generally more elastic in the long run, and so is supply. And because necessity is the mother of invention, research and development (think of this as investment in "knowledge capital") can lead to additional substitutions from high-cost to low-cost inputs or goods.

Let's take the example of a gas tax, introduced as a way to reduce pollution. If we look only at the short-run elasticity of demand (which is much easier to estimate based on market data), we might conclude that a gas tax will have little effect on driving since demand is quite inelastic (a steep demand curve, like the short-run demand depicted in figure 3.6). However, if we had an estimate of the long-run elasticity of demand, we might see that the demand curve is flatter, like the long-run demand depicted in figure 3.6. Starting at Q_1, demand might decline to Q_2 in the short run, but over a longer period of time demand would decline to Q_3. Since the effectiveness of many market-based environmental policies depend on the responsiveness of firms and individuals to a change in incentives, economists and policymakers should bear in mind the difference between short-run responses and long-run responses.

Debates about energy conservation and achieving energy independence often raise the question of how effective incentives might be. Pessimists may refer to elasticities reflecting the short-run responses to suggest that incentives will have little effect. However, more responsive changes can be expected over longer periods of time and at various levels. Consumers can alter their use of energy, the kinds of cars and home heating equipment they rely on, even where they live in relation to where they work. Firms can make substitutions between labor and capital (e.g., more expensive but energy-efficient motors) or between different sources of energy and change their use of transportation or location of production. Over very long periods of time, research and development induced by higher energy prices may give rise to newer and more energy-efficient technologies. When all these long-run possibilities for substitutions at multiple levels are taken into account, the prospects for reducing dependence on fossil fuel energy may be much more encouraging than short-run analysis would suggest.

Some projections estimate that worldwide consumption of fossil fuels will continue to rise for another one hundred to two hundred years before starting to decline, with troubling implications for carbon emissions and climate change. However, one economic study of this question looked very closely at the range of substitutions among different kinds and grades of energy resources (oil, coal, natural gas, and solar energy), the range of energy uses, and the recent trend of technological change with respect to solar

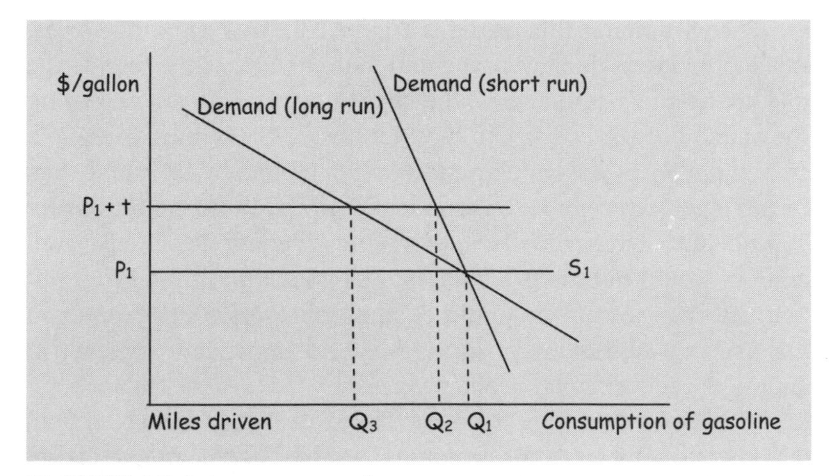

■ **FIGURE 3.6 Long-run versus short-run responses to a gas tax**

energy. Based on a simulation model of the world's economy with different assumptions about future cost reductions for solar energy and the substitutions that could be expected to occur with such changes in relative prices, the analysis finds that carbon emissions are likely to begin to decline within fifty years and that 90% of the world's coal will never be used.[2]

Recognizing the difference between short-run and long-run elasticity can mean the difference between a sensible policy change and a futile or counterproductive one. Let's look at an example. In March 2000, gas prices in the United States were unusually high. Presidential candidate George W. Bush proposed reducing the gasoline tax to offset the rise in prices. On the face of it, the action sounded reasonable, but the economics tell a different story. First, this was a short-run problem and Bush was proposing a temporary, short-run solution. Gasoline supplies are extremely unresponsive in the short run, given the time it takes to produce, ship, and refine petroleum, and then to distribute gasoline. So the short-run supply curve is nearly vertical (completely inelastic). Demand may not be highly elastic, but compared with supply it is much more flexible and responsive.

[2]Ujjayant Chakravorty, James Roumasset, and Kinping Tse, "Endogenous Substitution among Energy Resources and Global Warming," *Journal of Political Economy* 105, no. 6 (1997): 1201–1234.

The situation is illustrated in figure 3.7, where S_1 is the existing supply curve including the national gas tax. If we reduce the gas tax (paid by producers), the supply curve will shift down by the amount of the reduction: suppliers would be willing to sell the same amount of gasoline at a lower price since they would then be paying a lower gas tax. The market, however, would find a new equilibrium. Given the lack of responsiveness in supply, consumers would bid the price up and, as you can see from the figure, the change in price would be negligible. No relief from high gas prices would likely result because no significant increase in supply is occurring in the short run.[3]

If prices would stay the same following a gas tax reduction, what would happen to the revenues that had been collected from the gas tax? They would end up in the pockets of oil refineries and OPEC producers. So the policy change would have no effect on supplies in the short run and no real benefits to consumers, and it would cost the U.S. government revenues. In all respects, a really, really bad idea.

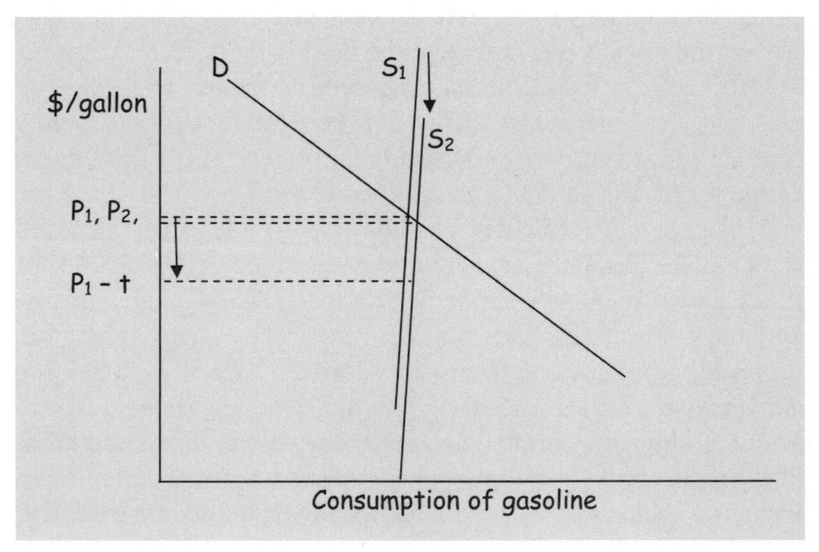

FIGURE 3.7 Short-run responses to a gas tax

[3]This example draws on Paul Krugman, "Gasoline Tax Follies," *New York Times*, March 15, 2000.

Production Possibilities

Up to now we've looked at consumers choosing among goods and producers choosing among inputs. The third and final category of choice we need to consider is how much of each good to produce. These choices aren't generally made by one individual, as is the case for a consumer's choices or a firm's choices. Instead, the interactions of consumer choices, producer choices, and market prices determine a set of outputs for all goods and services. Overall efficiency would involve efficient allocation of inputs such as labor, land, water, energy, and materials in each use, and having the right combinations of labor, land, water, capital, and materials in each industry. The marginal productivities of each input would vary only to the extent that their prices (opportunity costs) varied.

Key Concept: *Production possibilities frontier* 

A simple graph can only represent this kind of trade-off for two goods such as food and clothing or for two classes of goods such as durable goods and nondurable goods, or between market goods and environmental goods. But the same principle would apply to every pair of goods in the marketplace. Here, we are interested in the "production possibilities" in an economy. For example, if we are producing only food and clothing, then the shaded area in figure 3.8 shows all the possible combinations of food and clothing that could be produced. In figure 3.8 we want to be on the outer edge, or frontier, of these production possibilities. **Economists call this edge the production possibilities frontier (PPF). For any production possibility, if more of one good could be produced without reducing the output of the other goods, then that production possibility is not efficient and not on the PPF.** So, only points on the boundary, the PPF, are considered efficient allocations. To see why, let's look at point B. Point B is clearly not efficient because point A is also possible, and point A has more food *and* more clothing than at point B. So we can say that point B represents inefficiencies or wasted resources in production.

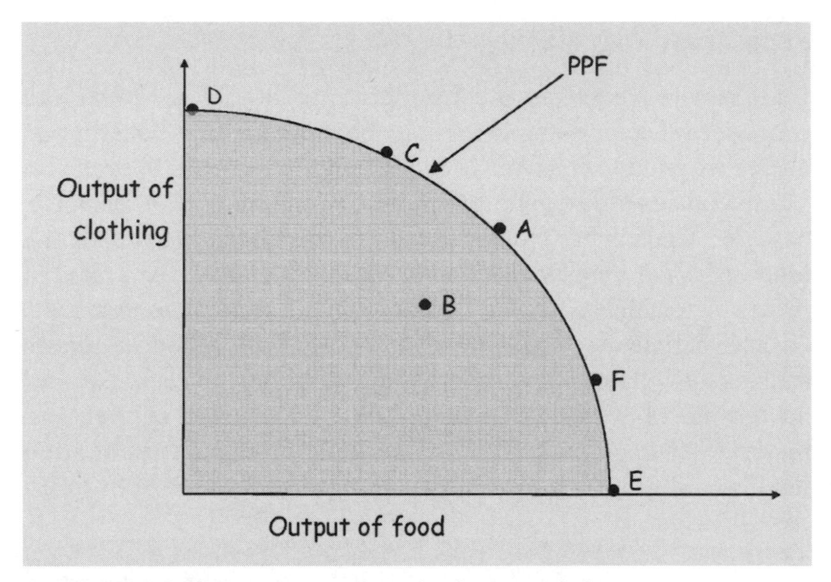

FIGURE 3.8 Production possibilities for food and clothing

Overall efficiency, however, requires more than just being on the PPF. It also requires finding the right point on the PPF, the point where the trade-off between food and clothing for producers is also best for consumers. For example, beginning at point A, we could reallocate resources and move along the PPF toward either D or E. Why would we do that? It depends on the relative value of the two goods when valued by consumers.

From point A, we can increase food production by a small amount if we are willing to give up a small amount of clothing. Let's assume the rate of substitution is one for one at point A. If consumers are willing to give up two units of clothing for one more unit of food, then it makes sense to move from A in the direction of E because the cost of producing more food (in terms of clothing) is less than what consumers would be willing to pay (give up). Given the way the PPF is curved, as we move from A toward E along the PPF, the marginal cost of food (in terms of forgone clothing) will rise, and the marginal cost of clothing (in terms of forgone food) will decline.

This is the same kind of trade-off we have seen elsewhere. Indeed, finding the right point on the PPF is similar to representing how a market finds its equilibrium.[4] Given the quantities of food and clothing at different points on the PPF, and thus the marginal cost of food in terms of clothing, we can represent the efficiency of this allocation along the PPF in one more diagram, figure 3.9, which reflects this final trade-off at the margin. For the preferences reflected in figure 3.9, efficiency occurs at point A rather than at C or F.

Key Concept: *Diminishing marginal returns* 

Why is the PPF curved rather than a straight line at a 45° angle? The PPF could be a straight line, indicating a constant rate of substitution between food and clothing in production. But it is more likely that the PPF will be curved as shown in the figure for two reasons. First, because there are usually unique or specialized factors of production used for each industry that are less productive when used in a different industry. And second, because of **diminishing returns,** the notion that as more and more of one factor is combined with a fixed amount of other factors, the marginal productivity of the factor being added will decline.

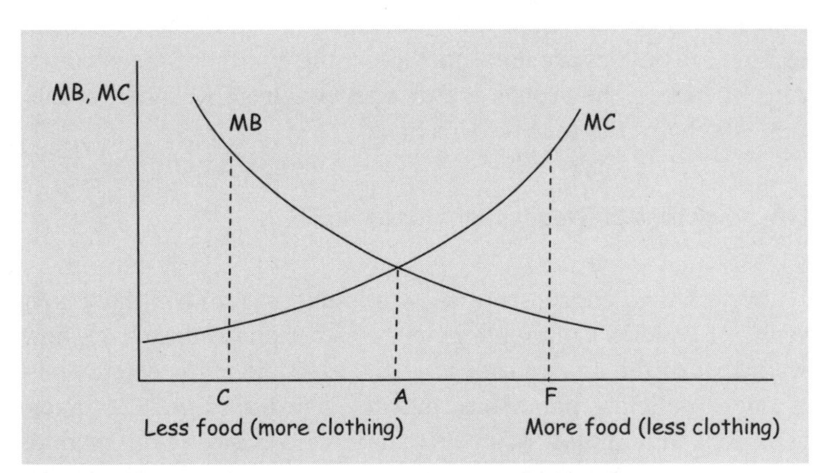

■ **FIGURE 3.9 Marginal value of food (in terms of clothing)**

[4]There is a more direct way to represent and evaluate the point on the PPF that would be optimal, but this would require introducing "indifference curves" and covering additional theory to derive and understand them.

From Efficiency to Market Distortions

Key Concept: *Perfect competition*

The main attraction of markets in economics is that they can achieve significant, even dramatic, net benefits through voluntary exchange between buyers and sellers, producers and consumers. If these markets exhibit what economists call **perfect competition,** they will maximize net benefits and be Pareto optimal. **For perfect competition, however, there must be (a) many small suppliers (so that they cannot influence price), (b) many consumers (also so that they cannot influence price), (c) producers able to freely enter and exit the industry, (d) a homogeneous commodity (so that all firms' products are perfect substitutes), (e) perfect information among all participants, and (f) no externalities.**

This, of course, is a tall order. Some standard exceptions include a monopoly (one supplier) or oligopoly (a few suppliers) where the supplier's decisions can influence the market price, giving them an incentive to reduce supply in order to raise the price and increase their profits. The absence of full information can also reduce efficiency, for example, in the market for used cars where buyers are uncertain about the quality of the product. And, of course, the problems caused by environmental externalities, which are the focus of this book.

Key Concept: *Deadweight loss*

We want to concentrate on two issues here. First, how government policies can create market distortions and, second, how we measure the size or extent of the inefficiency created. Government policies that create market distortions include taxes, subsidies, and quotas. Markets can be a little inefficient or a lot inefficient. We measure the level of inefficiency using the notion of **deadweight loss. Deadweight loss is the difference between the net benefits actually achieved and the maximum net benefits possible with an efficient allocation (at Q*).**

Let's take a simple example where government limits, say, the amount of steel that can be produced to Q_{max}. In figure 3.10 we see that this amount falls short of the amount that would be supplied at the competitive market equilibrium. At the Pareto optimum the total net benefit would equal the areas A + B, but with the supply restriction the net benefit is only equal to the area A. The deadweight loss, therefore, is equal to B, the shaded area.

Let's take another example, say, where government subsidizes milk production by paying farmers a direct subsidy, S, for every gallon produced. The supply curve shifts down by the amount of the subsidy because the marginal private cost (MPC), which includes the subsidy, is lower than the marginal social cost (MSC), which is the "true" cost to society, including the cost to taxpayers who ultimately pay the subsidy. This is described in figure 3.11.

Notice that the change in market price from P_1 to P_2 is less than the amount of the subsidy ($P_1 - S$ is below P_2). If demand were fixed at Q_1, the price might decline by the full amount of the subsidy and consumers would reap their entire benefit. This would occur only if the demand curve were vertical. Because the

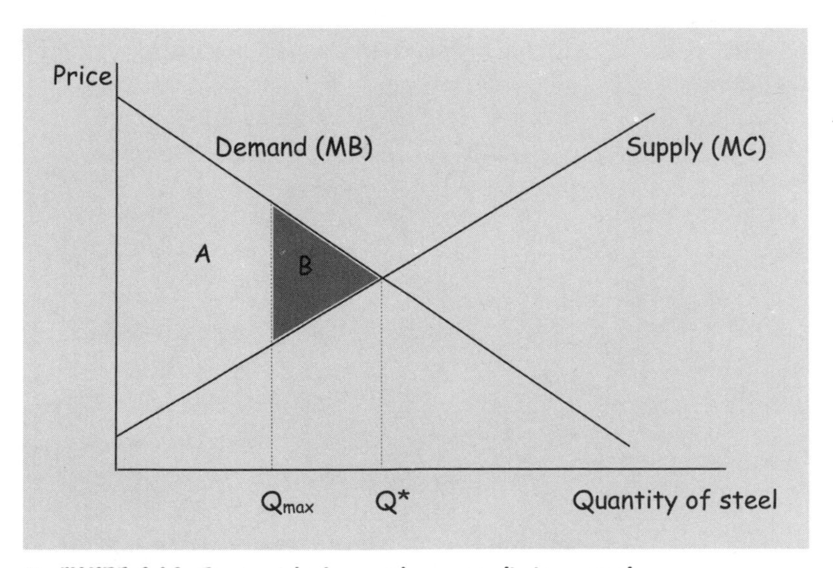

■ **FIGURE 3.10 Deadweight loss with a quota limit on steel**

lower price encourages higher demand, and this increased demand puts upward pressure on prices, the new market equilibrium occurs at Q_2 where supply increased to meet that demand. As a result, some of the benefits of the subsidy end up being transferred to producers because of the market adjustments that lead to a new equilibrium price at P_2. So who gets the subsidy? Both producers and consumers get a part of it, and the shares depend on the relative slopes of the demand and supply curves. Economists will refer to the "incidence" of a subsidy when they talk about who actually ends up benefiting from it. The same concept and term is used for taxes to recognize that even though a tax may be levied on producers (or consumers), markets will adjust in response to the shift in supply (or demand) caused by the tax, and these market adjustments will determine the "incidence of the tax," meaning who *really* ends up paying for it.

A third example involves a distortion of the demand curve, such as when there is an excise tax, T, paid by consumers at the time of purchase. Knowing they will have to pay a tax, consumers will recognize that the cost is going to be higher or, alternatively, that the marginal benefit, when the value of the tax is subtracted, will be less than it would be if there were no tax. Whether the consumer thinks of this as a higher cost or a lower benefit, demand will be lowered for a given (pretax) sticker

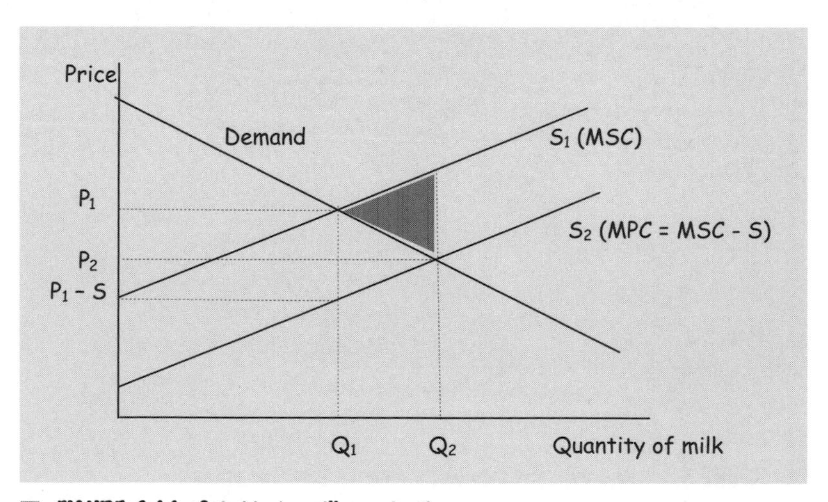

FIGURE 3.11 Subsidy in milk production

price. We can represent this as a downward shift in the demand curve as in figure 3.12 by the amount of the tax, T, so that the demand curve with the tax is below the untaxed demand curve. Consumers who would have been willing to pay $1 without a tax will now be willing to pay only $0.80 if they know they will be obligated to pay an additional 20¢ tax, so that the market equilibrium occurs at Q_T.

The revenues from the tax are generally assumed to be used for some government purpose (such as funding education or providing other public goods).[5] In that case then there is a reduction in consumer surplus owing to the shift down in the demand curve, but also a transfer of revenues to the government equal to the difference between D and D − T from 0 to Q_T (the striped area). The shaded area represents the deadweight loss, the portion of the net benefit that would have existed without the tax, but that isn't now a part of consumer surplus, producer surplus, or government revenues.

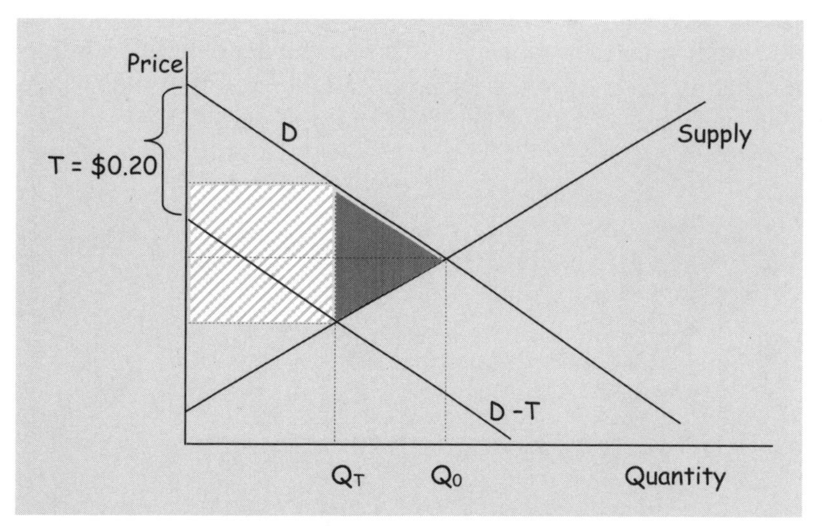

■ **FIGURE 3.12 Excise tax, deadweight loss, and revenue transfer**

[5]We could also represent this whole situation by a shift up in the supply curve by the amount of the tax, indicating that the price to consumers is the "after-tax" price including the tax. Either of these can depict the same situation: shifting the supply curve up by the tax is equivalent to shifting the demand curve down by the same amount.

Key Concept: *Marginal excess burden*

The deadweight loss may be large or small depending on how producers and consumers respond (if the shaded triangle is big or small compared with the amount of revenue). **The marginal excess burden is the additional deadweight loss created for every dollar of additional revenue generated by a tax.** Inefficiencies or deadweight losses also occur when there are other causes of a divergence between social and private benefits or costs. Graphs similar to figures 3.11 and 3.12 will be used later on to evaluate environmental situations involving public goods or externalities.

We can evaluate the size of the social gains and losses quantitatively if we have estimates of the marginal (social) benefits and marginal (social) cost curves. For example, if demand for video games can be represented (in dollars) as MB = 30 − (2/3) × Q (where Q is in thousands) and supply can be represented as a constant marginal cost of MC = $10, then we can represent this in the figure 3.13. If these estimates of supply and demand were based on actual data, then we could estimate the net benefit from this market as the area of the triangle **ABC,** or $\frac{1}{2} \times (\$20 \times 30{,}000) = \$300{,}000$ (area = $\frac{1}{2}$ base × height of the triangle).

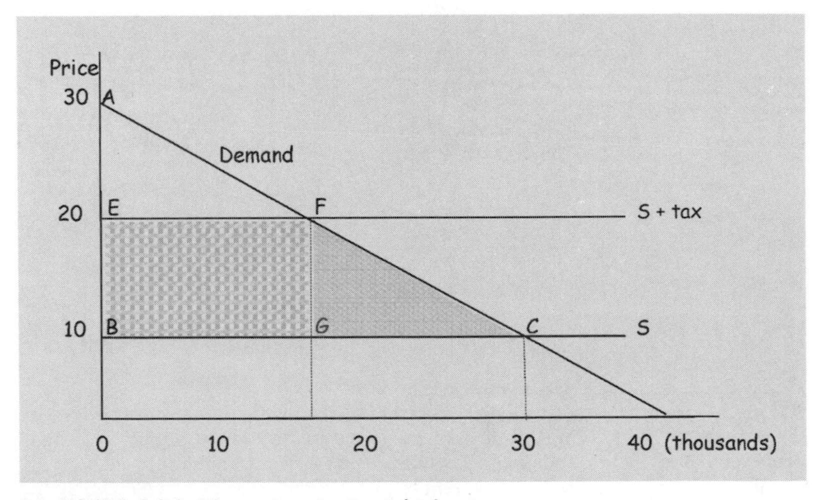

■ **FIGURE 3.13 Measuring deadweight loss**

Now suppose that video games were banned entirely. What would be the loss to society of eliminating all production and consumption of video games? The loss would be the elimination of the $300,000 in net benefits. The net benefits would go to zero, instead of the maximum of $300,000 at $Q^* = 30$. This example is the same as the earlier examples except that the distortion created by government results in the elimination of the market entirely, rather than just a distortion that keeps it from finding the optimal point (in this case, $Q = 30$).

Key Concept: *Transfer* 

There is one more important distinction that we need to be clear about in the case of a government policy: the difference between a deadweight loss and a **transfer**. **A transfer takes payments from one group of people and makes them available to a different group. Since one group gains what the other group lost, the transferred amount does not represent a deadweight loss.** Let's look at one more example. What would happen if, instead of a ban, a $10 tax on video games was introduced? In that case, the price would go up to $20, and quantity demanded would decline to 17,000 units. The consumer surplus would be reduced from the area of the triangle ABC to the area of the triangle AEF. So is the deadweight loss equal to ABC − AEF? No. The reason is that only the shaded triangle FGC is considered to be the distortion or deadweight loss caused by the tax. The other portion, the plaid-patterned rectangle EFBG, is a "transfer" from consumers to government: it represents the amount of revenue generated by the tax, $10 × 17,000 = $170,000. From society's perspective, only the deadweight loss is a "social cost"; the other change is a transfer that represents a private cost (of tax payments) for producers and an equal benefit (tax revenues) that government has available for other purposes (e.g., they could just be returned to all citizens in a tax rebate).

Taking Stock

Well, you did it. In the past two chapters you've covered much of the basics of microeconomics—although in abbreviated form.

Congratulations. The notions of making trade-offs at the margin and opportunity cost combine to help us think about how to achieve the highest total value, or net benefit, for many kinds of allocation questions. If we use resources efficiently at each level of resource allocation, input use, production, and consumption, then the economy will maximize net benefits and be Pareto efficient or Pareto optimal. Achieving efficiency, therefore, is just a matter of always finding that point where marginal benefit equals marginal cost. If all markets were perfectly competitive, that would be easy. Since markets are not perfectly competitive, and since many goods and services valued by society are not even produced or sold in markets, other ways of trying to allocate them will be needed.

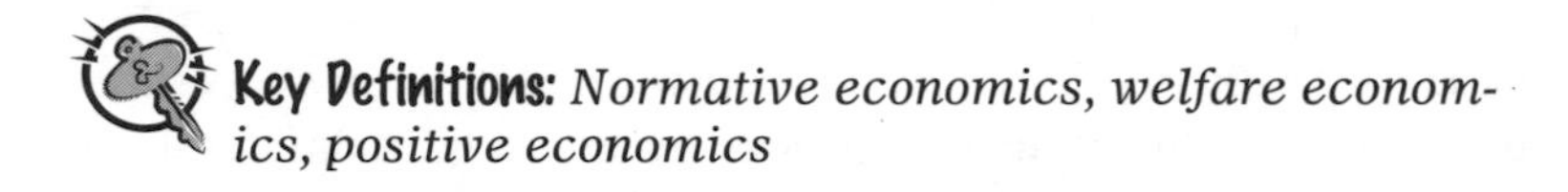
Key Definitions: *Normative economics, welfare economics, positive economics*

These first few chapters have used economic theory about demand, supply, production, and consumption to be able to talk about efficiency and inefficiency and about the costs and benefits and deadweight losses for a given resource allocation. This part of economics is referred to as **welfare economics, or normative economics, meaning the part of economics where value judgments are made, for example, when suggesting that efficiency is a good thing, or that policies with the high net benefits ought to be preferred over ones with low net benefits.** More on the basis of these value judgments is found in chapter 16, along with discussion of other considerations that should be taken into account when evaluating policy such as equity, fairness, and rights.

Not all economic analysis is considered welfare economics or normative, however. The alternative type is referred to as **positive economics, meaning the use of economics only to describe an economy and to evaluate and predict how the economy might respond and change in response to some action or change in other economic variables.** For example, how would a 10% increase in wheat prices affect wheat production? How would a decline in the interest rate affect housing starts? How would a drop in gasoline prices affect consumption of gasoline in the United States? A key characteristic of this kind of analysis is that it does not make direct value judgments about whether some change in the economy would be good or bad; it just describes cause-and-effect relationships and answers "what if" questions.

You can now use these basic tools of economic analysis to look more closely at environmental policy issues. There are, however, a few more general topics to cover: allocation across time periods, economic growth, international trade, and the notion of sustainability. Covering these topics in the next five chapters will give you an important perspective for appreciating some of parts 2 and 3, and this will also give you a firmer grasp of the graphs and other analytical concepts used throughout.

Recommended Readings and References

For more depth on the topics in this chapter, consult one of the microeconomics textbooks listed at the end of chapter 2.

4

Today versus Tomorrow

I would gladly pay you Tuesday for a hamburger today.
—Wimpy, from *Popeye the Sailor Man*

In the same way that we allocate resources between alternative uses, we also allocate resources between different time periods: making trade-offs at the margin in response to incentives. The marginal value of using additional resources this year diminishes at higher levels, and if using more resources this year means having less available next year, the opportunity cost will rise, and there will be a point where the marginal value today is outweighed by the marginal value of saving for the future. Think of the market for funds traded across two time periods in the same way you might think of the market for funds traded between two countries. In the latter case, supply and demand determine the market price, which is the exchange rate. In the former case, supply and demand determine the market price, which is the interest rate.

In the market for funds, lenders (supply) are motivated by their willingness to defer consumption in order to earn interest from a loan. This is related to people's preference for consuming now or in the future—their time preference. People seem to prefer things "sooner rather than later," and this is part of the reason for a positive interest rate: the price of current resources or income is higher than the price of future resources or income. Borrowers (demand) may also be motivated by the desire to consume now, but underlying much borrowing is the fact that borrowed funds can be invested in productive activities that will create additional value over time. Unlike a cake, which you can eat either today or tomorrow, productive capital grows over time. Planting trees creates future wood products, a fish population will grow over time (if protected), investing in your education can increase your productivity and income in the future, and research and development can create new, improved technologies, contributing to economic growth. We'll talk more about economic growth in chapter 7, but for now we want to focus on this "market across time," the interest rate, and how to evaluate alternatives involving costs and benefits in different time periods.

The Market for Funds

These "transactions across time" involve the market for funds, like at a bank. To simplify just a bit, let's assume that the supply curve in figure 4.1 reflects people's willingness to postpone consumption of their income until a later period. The demand curve in figure 4.1 represents people wanting to borrow to make productive investments. Investors' willingness to pay a premium to borrow money for their investments depends primarily on the expected return on their investments. As in earlier chapters, we are interested in the slopes of these curves and the factors that would make them shift one way or the other, since these changes would affect the equilibrium interest rate and the amount of investing on both private and public activities.

Consider what would happen if, suddenly, more people thought they had a great investment idea with a high future payoff. The demand curve would shift to the right, causing the interest rate to go up. This would push up the market equilibrium price—the interest rate. More investing would occur, but less than if the interest rate had stayed the same. Similarly, if many

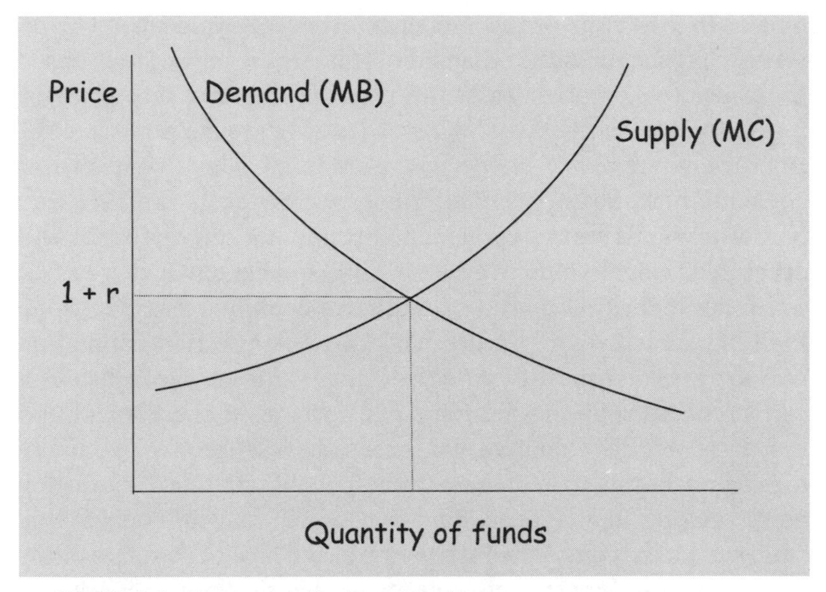

■ **FIGURE 4.1 The market for loanable funds**

more people felt a need to save for their future or for their children's future, the supply curve would shift to the right, causing the interest rate to decline, and more funds would be borrowed and invested at the new, lower interest rate.

This market functions like any other market really. The price is determined as the equilibrium price that equates supply and demand. When individual consumers, or investors, are making decisions about whether to consume, defer consumption, or invest in a particular activity or project, they are likely to use the market interest rate as a reference point, because it represents the opportunity cost for their decision. Why undertake an investment project with a 4% return if your funds could earn 6% in a savings account? Why continue in your current occupation if borrowing to pay for more schooling would get you a higher-paying job that would more than cover the loan repayment?

Discounting

When we make these kinds of decisions about borrowing, lending, saving, or investing, at some level we are doing what we call

discounting, weighing benefits or costs today against benefits or costs in the future. Even if a person's time preference (degree of impatience) is "neutral" (if they were indifferent to having $100 today or $100 next year), there is still a good reason for discounting. One hundred dollars today is worth more than $100 next year because it can be deposited in a bank to earn interest so that by next year the $100 will have grown to be worth more than $100. Discounting is different from adjusting for inflation, as explained in box 2.

We want to be able to compare benefits, or costs, that occur in different time periods. It's a bit like comparing the price of hotels in different countries; you need an exchange rate to make the comparisons. In the case of different time periods, you need an interest rate. To compare the future value (FV) of a payment at some year t with the present value (PV) of a payment now (t = 0), we use a simple formula:

BOX 2
Inflation and Discounting

Discounting is *not* about adjusting for inflation! Inflation is a rise in the general price level, usually caused by government policies such as increasing the money supply by printing more currency. A rise in inflation doesn't mean that people are better off.

If inflation were expected to be zero, we would still want to discount. That is because discounting has to do with the "time value of money," the opportunity cost of funds that can be invested or lent.

Since inflation tends to be positive (prices rise over time), what we need to do to focus on discounting is to adjust the "nominal interest rate" for inflation in order to get the "real" or inflation-adjusted interest rate. The real interest rate is more stable than the nominal interest rate. This is because people's willingness to borrow or lend is tied to the real interest rate; people are interested in the real purchasing power of what they may lose or gain today or tomorrow. So if inflation rises (or falls) by 3%, the market interest rate is also likely to rise (or fall) by 3%.

In the rest of the book, we will assume that either inflation is zero or that we're talking about the real interest rate.

$$FV_t = PV_0(1 + r)^t$$

This is the formula for compounding interest at interest rate r over t years. For example, the future value of $100 at an interest rate of 10% will be $110 in one year, or $121 in two years. Over longer periods of time, the compounding effect of earning "interest on interest" causes the future value to grow much larger. For example, the $100 earning 10% would become $1,745 after thirty years, or $1.38 million after one hundred years.

If we want to know the present value of some future payment (the amount today that would be equivalent to a given amount at some time in the future), all we have to do is rearrange this formula so that PV is on the left side, or:

$$PV_0 = FV_t /(1 + r)^t$$

This formula "discounts" the future. It computes the present value of a promise to pay $100 a year from now, as being worth only $90.91. The present value of a similar promise to pay two years from now is only $82.64. As with the compounding growth of the future value, the discounting of the present value has a much larger impact over a long time period. The present value of a promise to pay $100 in thirty years is worth only $5.73 when using a 10% discount rate; if the promise to pay is one hundred years in the future, its present value is less than a penny. People may use different discount rates depending on the opportunity cost they face: if people do not have access to a bank, or if there is risk involved in their investments, they may wish to discount future benefits and costs using a rate different from the market interest rate.

Let's try an example. An individual owns a tree plantation and can harvest the trees today and earn net revenues (revenues minus costs) of $50,000. If she waits one more year, the net revenue will be $53,000 (assume, for simplicity, that maintenance costs are zero). What should she do? Let's compare the present value of the two alternatives. Assume that she can borrow or save funds at a bank earning 8%. The present values of these alternatives are:

Sell now:	PV = $50,000
Sell next year:	PV = $53,000/(1.08)^1 = $49,074

In this case the value of harvesting now is higher than the present value of harvesting in a year. If the future value were higher, or if the discount rate were lower, then selling next year might have the highest present value. We'll revisit this particular kind of choice in chapter 11, which covers land and forestry policy.

The same kind of calculation is involved for livestock, fish farming, wine inventories, mineral resources, or any other investment: comparing costs and benefits currently with those that would occur in the future. If we think about an activity that would involve costs today and next year, maintenance costs every year, and benefits starting in year eight and continuing for twenty years, the computations can get complicated. All these different benefits and costs in different time periods can be distilled in one number, the net present value. **Net present value (NPV) is the sum of all the discounted benefits and costs of a project or policy.** For a project with benefits and costs in different time periods involves evaluating the net benefits in each period t (benefits, B_t, minus costs, C_t), discounting them, and then summing to get the net present value, or:

$$NPV = (B_0 - C_0) + \frac{(B_1 - C_1)}{(1 + r)^1} + \frac{(B_2 - C_2)}{(1 + r)^2} + \frac{(B_3 - C_3)}{(1 + r)^3} \ldots\ldots + \frac{(B_t - C_t)}{(1 + r)^t}$$

Key Definitions: *Net present value* 

There are a couple of ways that this formula can be simplified in specific cases. For example, consider a lake fishery that can produce $2,000 worth of fish (net of costs) each year indefinitely. What would be the present value of the losses, for example, if the fishery were destroyed, if the lake were drained and filled in, or if pollution killed the fish? This loss would amount to a negative "perpetuity" (which is an annuity or annual payment of a given value that continues forever). The present value of a perpetuity has a simpler formula—it is just the annual payment divided by the discount rate, or:

$$NPV_{(Perp)} = NB/r$$

For a discount rate of 6%, the loss of this fishery would represent a present value cost of $-2,000/0.06 = $-33,333.

In chapter 2 we described how efficiency is the result of having all resources put to their highest value use, when just the right balance is struck when allocating inputs, production, and consumption. The same is true for the allocation across time periods. Too much consumption and too little investment will be inefficient if it does not reflect the willingness of consumers and investors to lend or borrow across different time periods. In parts of the world where capital markets do not function well (e.g., rural parts of developing countries), it is believed that many valuable investments are not made simply because the option of borrowing is not available.

One way to think about the idea of efficiency in consumption versus savings and investment is with a consumption possibilities frontier much like the production possibilities frontier introduced in chapter 3. Instead of allocating resources between production of food and production of clothing, we are allocating resources between period 1 and period 2. Figure 4.2 illustrates a consumption possibilities frontier (CPF) between two periods. If we consume all our resources in period 1 (at C_1'), then we will have nothing available for consumption in period 2 (at C_2'). If we save and invest some of our period 1 consumption possibilities, our current consumption will be reduced to C_1'', but this increases our future consumption possibilities in period 2 to C_2''. If we save and invest even more so that we consume only at C_1''', the consumption possibilities awaiting us in period 2 will be C_2'''.

Which point would be efficient? This depends on the time preferences of individuals and the productivity of capital. A perfectly competitive market for funds would be expected to achieve a market interest rate and an optimal allocation. The interest rate in figure 4.2 is reflected in the slope of the CPF. For example, if the optimum occurs at point A, then the slope of the line tangent to the CPF at A will equal $-(1 + r)$.

The Social Discount Rate

When discounting is done for personal choices, or when firms make investments, the market interest rate can be used as the discount rate once it has been adjusted for inflation so that the

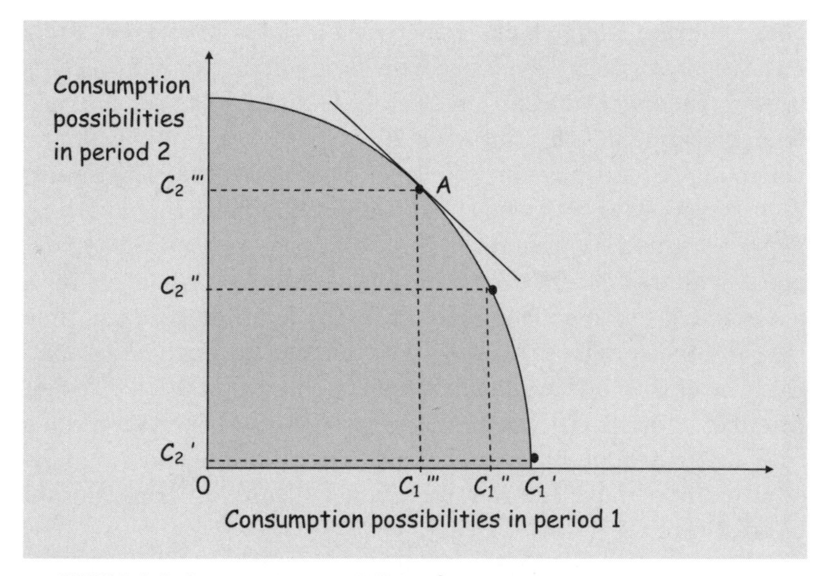

■ **FIGURE 4.2 Consumption possibilities frontier across time periods**

discount rate reflects the real interest rate. Societal choices or policy decisions have effects in different time periods that will also require adjustments for inflation, but there may be additional adjustments that society will want to make for "social discounting." Society may want to approach discounting differently than individuals do.

The first adjustment has to do with taxes on capital gains and investment income. Taxes create a wedge between the pretax and after-tax return on investment, and people's willingness to invest (their time preference) will be influenced by what they themselves get out of it, which is the after-tax rate of return. For example, if someone is willing to invest for a 6% rate of return, but they know that they must pay a 33% tax on their investment income, then they will require a 9% return on investment so that their "take home" or after-tax return will be 6%. Since social investments don't face these same tax obligations, social discounting should abstract from them as well.

A second adjustment that many economists believe is needed for social discounting has to do with risk. Most private investments carry some risk that the return will be lower than expected if, for example, a loan is not repaid or when a company or bank goes bankrupt. Given a choice between a risky investment and a risk-free investment, most people will be willing to make a risky investment only if the expected return is higher than for the risk-free investment. This differential is called a risk premium, reflecting a tendency for people to be risk averse. Since most investments have risks, most market interest rates include some degree of this risk premium. These risks, however, average out across individuals and over time. For society as a whole, or for a government making many kinds of investments at different time periods, these risks are also likely to cancel each other out. Because of this, it is argued that society should not use a discount rate that reflects risk premiums. Society should therefore use a rate that, in addition to adjusting for inflation and taxes, is adjusted to remove the risk premium reflected in most market interest rates.

What might a risk-free real interest rate be? Thirty-year U.S. treasury bonds are commonly cited as the best example of a risk-free investment because they are guaranteed by the U.S. government. Between 1995 and 2005, the return or yield on these bonds has been about 5.5%, during a time when inflation averaged about 2.5%. This suggests that the risk-free real interest rate is about 3%. If we also take account of the way that taxes affect the after-tax interest rate in private markets, then the after-tax risk-free, inflation-adjusted discount rate would be somewhere between 2% and 3%.

The literature on social discounting is large and dense, and it reflects many ongoing debates, including how to treat benefits and costs that will occur far into the future, for example, possible damages from climate change a hundred years or more in the future. Using standard discounting practices, these large numbers are reduced to miniscule amounts in present value terms. Many observers, including many economists, are very uncomfortable with this result, but no consensus has emerged about how to resolve this dilemma (some economists have recently advocated "hyperbolic discounting" where different discount rates are used for the near versus the distant future).

Overall, however, there is wide agreement that social discounting should involve a discount rate lower than the market interest rate, but how much lower is debatable. Some notable observers have suggested, on philosophical grounds, that a zero discount rate is the only morally defensible approach; otherwise, we are implicitly favoring current people over future people. But this view, too, is problematic. It could lead to advocating a policy that impoverished the present generation in order to offer small, but permanent, increases in income for future generations, even when these future generations are expected to have much higher incomes than the present population.

To sum up, discounting in the allocation of resources across different time periods is something that we all do, and it is also something that society must take account of when investing in public goods or when protecting environmental resources for future generations. The interest rate is the market price for borrowing and lending across time periods, just like an exchange rate is the rate at which we can transfer funds across national borders.

Recommended Readings and References

More detailed discussions of discounting can be found in Jonathan A. Lesser, Daniel E. Dobbs, and Richard O. Zerbe, Jr., *Environmental Economics and Policy* (Reading, MA: Addison-Wesley, 1997), chapter 13. A useful chapter on the topic of discounting is also found in William Cline, *The Economics of Global Warming* (Washington, DC: Institute for International Economics, 1992). Much of the economics literature on discounting is technical. A standard reference is Robert Lind, ed., *Discounting for Time and Risk in Energy Policy* (Baltimore: Johns Hopkins University Press, 1982).

Additional references include Maureen Cropper and Fran Sussman, "Valuing Future Risks to Life," *Journal of Environmental Economics and Management* 19 (1990): 160–174; Avinash Dixit and Robert Pindyck, *Investment Under Uncertainty* (Princeton, NJ: Princeton University Press, 1994); Martin L. Weitzman, "On the 'Environmental' Discount Rate," *Journal of Environmental Economics and Management* 26, no. 2 (1994): 200–209; and Martin L. Weitzman, "Gamma Discounting," *American Economic Review* 91, no. 1 (2001): 260–271.

5

Market Failures

Economists say that markets "fail" when they don't achieve an efficient (or desired) allocation of resources. This can occur for several reasons. In one example, monopolies are likely to restrict supply to push prices up and maximize their profits, but this comes at the expense of consumers and efficiency. In another example, markets do not achieve equity goals. For evaluating environmental problems, economists focus on two common sources of market failure, public goods and externalities.

Public Goods

Key Concepts: *Nonrival, nonexcludable, pure public good, congestible good*

Lighthouses are public goods; so is the ozone layer. The term "public good" is used to refer to a good that is **nonrival,** meaning that the consumption or use of the good by one individual does not subtract from the amount of the good or service available for others to enjoy. A second attribute of some public goods is that they may be **nonexcludable,** meaning that it is impossible, or prohibitively costly, to exclude or keep individuals from consuming the public good. A **pure public good** is one that has both these characteristics of nonrivalry and nonexcludability, without qualification. National security is a frequently cited example; radio and TV signals are very close to being pure public goods. Not all public goods are excludable, however, and most public goods are not perfectly nonrival. They are **congestible public goods,** meaning they are nonrival up to a certain level of use, but then beyond that point rivalry sets in, as with public highways, wilderness areas, or city parks. At high levels of use, the enjoyment or "consumption" of the public good by one individual *is* affected by the number of other users.

Our analysis of public goods focuses on two aspects: (a) the inefficiency or undersupply of nonrival or public goods by the market and (b) the dilemma of financing the provision of public goods at their optimal level. Nonexcludability makes it difficult or impossible to charge a price for a good like a radio broadcast since anybody with a radio can pick up the transmission. Famous works of art or other objects can be put in a museum and an entry fee can be charged, so they are excludable. But this does not completely eliminate the problem of efficiency for public goods. Indeed, both excludable and nonexcludable public goods involve market failures and inefficiencies, as we will see.

Key Concept: *Willingness to pay (WTP) for public goods is summed vertically*

The reason for this market failure can be illustrated by the following example, where the individual demands for, say, hours of radio broadcasting by three people are represented by the three demand curves D_A, D_B, and D_C. Because radio broadcasts are nonrival, all users can benefit from the same unit of the public good. **This implies that the marginal social benefit (MSB), or collective willingness to pay, for a public good will be the vertical sum of the demands, or individual's willingness to pay, at each quantity or level**—since all can listen to the same hour of broadcasting. The total demand is constructed by summing the individual demands vertically (rather than horizontally as in the case of a normal "rival" good) as indicated by the dotted line in figure 5.1. If this were a rival good, like pizzas or houses or cookies, the quantity demanded at each price would be summed horizontally.

Individuals will be willing to pay for radio broadcasts only when the benefits exceed the costs. According to figure 5.1, if the marginal cost is $15, only individual C will pay for some radio broadcasting (about ten hours). Individuals A and B will be able to enjoy the radio broadcasting paid for by individual C, but they would not be willing to pay for it themselves. Because of this free riding by A and B, there would be only ten hours of radio broadcasting even though the efficient level (where MSB = MC) would be about seventeen hours.

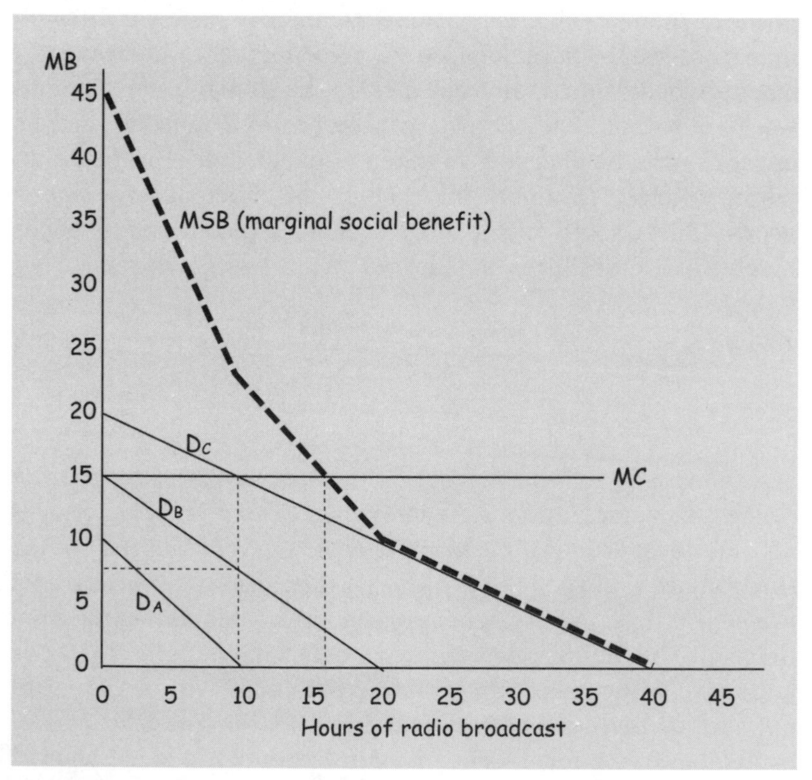

■ **FIGURE 5.1 The social value of a public good: radio broadcasting**

What if there were thousands of individuals with MB curves similar to the ones in figure 5.1, but with the marginal cost above $20? The market could easily "fail" to provide *any* units of this public good even though its collective value to society is very high. Most individuals are willing to pay for national security, but few would be willing or able to pay for an aircraft carrier or an army! This is a fundamental source of market failure—the failure to supply public goods at the efficient level.

Even if government intervened to produce the efficient level of seventeen hours of radio broadcast, how should it be paid for? Asking people to contribute based on how much they value the public good is unlikely to work owing to free riding (although many public radio stations try). For most public goods such as national security, public education, health, safety, and so on, general taxation is the way most societies pay for public goods. But funding public goods entirely from general tax revenues has the drawback that the total cost of providing the desired level of the public good (a fixed cost plus the marginal cost per hour of broadcast) will likely mean asking some individuals to pay more for the public good than they would want, and they would surely vote against doing so. So we face a dilemma: let the public good be undersupplied, or pay for it with taxation in a way that will force some individuals to pay more than what they would want to. Often some combination of low user charges and partial public funding is the resulting compromise.

At first glance, it would seem that excludability for a public good (the ability to control access) would solve the problem, but this is not the case. If it were possible to charge for listening to the radio, for example, if $8 were charged for each hour up to the ten hours being supplied, individual A would pay for only two hours and would not listen to the other eight hours of broadcasting, even though the marginal cost of allowing A to listen in would be zero. By forcing A to turn off the radio after two hours, there is a deadweight loss to society. Anytime the price is not equal to marginal cost this will happen, and the marginal cost (for one listener) is zero! The deadweight loss in this case is the area under A's demand curve between the actual level of two hours and the ten hours of total broadcasting

($(\frac{1}{2}) \times 8 \times 8$), or $32 of deadweight loss from pricing the public good at $8.

With public goods we can either accept undersupply or try to pay for the efficient level of the public good in distortionary and potentially unfair ways. Both have drawbacks. Herein lies the fundamental debate about government and the perennial political struggles over funding the military and the Environmental Protection Agency, subsidizing the arts, raising fares for subways, whether Amtrak should pay for itself, whether taxes should be used to build baseball stadiums, and so on.

Externalities

An externality is a cost or benefit affecting somebody other than those involved in an action or transaction. Competitive markets can be efficient only if all the costs and benefits accrue to the individuals directly involved (e.g., the buyer and seller). Somebody who heats his home with a woodstove may take account of the cost of firewood and the benefit he receives from being warm, but he is unlikely to take into account the external effects of his smoke imposed on people downwind.

Externalities can be positive or negative. Somebody who plants a beautiful cherry tree in her yard may do it because her enjoyment of the tree exceeds the cost of buying, planting, and maintaining it, but she is unlikely to also consider the enjoyment that her neighbors might derive from the tree. Smokestack emissions, solid waste sites, and effluent dumped in rivers are common commercial forms of negative externalities. Music, art, gardens, and pastoral views across farmlands are common examples of positive externalities. When a beekeeper operates in proximity to an apple orchard, each one benefits from the other.

The inefficiency that may arise from an externality is easy to represent with the graphs we developed earlier. Let's consider a paper mill that produces a useful product, paper, for market, but whose smokestack emissions are costly to the surrounding community. The factory's marginal cost curve is represented in figure 5.2, as is the demand or marginal benefit curve—assumed here to be for a large market so that demand is horizontal. In figure 5.2 marginal private cost (MPC) reflects the direct costs of production only. At the market price, P_M, the graph suggests the producer would produce at Q_M. For quantities above Q_M, the marginal benefit (P) is less than marginal private cost; for quantities below Q_M, additional net benefits can be had by increasing production up to Q_M.

Key Concepts: *Marginal external cost, marginal private cost, marginal social cost*

For products without externalities, this would be the end of the story. But in the situation described here, there is an additional cost that is "external" to the producer, the cost imposed on the community from smokestack emissions. If we add this **marginal external cost** (MEC) to the **marginal private cost** (MPC), we get the **marginal social cost** (MSC) indicated in figure 5.2. At each level of production the vertical distance between the MPC and MSC is equal to MEC. If MEC were constant at all levels of production, then the two lines, MPC and MSC, would be parallel. As drawn, MEC increases with the amount of paper (and pollution) produced per month.

Since the factory owner will choose to produce at Q_M where P = MPC, and the efficient level of production is at Q* where

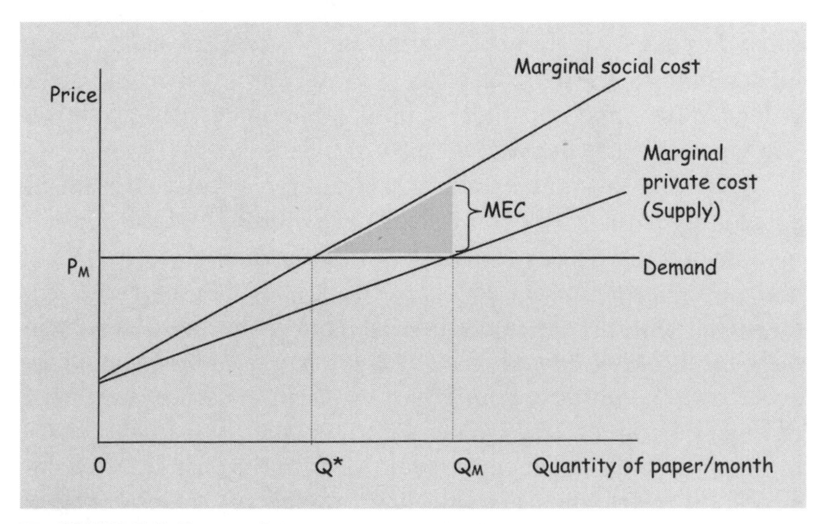

■ **FIGURE 5.2 Externalities in paper production**

P = MSC, this allocation is inefficient, and there is a deadweight loss represented by the shaded triangle.

Because of the way figure 5.2 is presented, one has the impression that to reduce pollution the firm must reduce the output of paper. In reality there are many ways that producers can reduce pollution or the damage from pollution, and these will often be preferable to just reducing output. For example, a firm can use a cleaner fuel or a cleaner furnace; it might install "scrubbers" that remove pollutants before they exit the smokestack. In some cases the waste products from production could be disposed of in different ways such as converting them into liquid or solid waste rather than airborne waste.

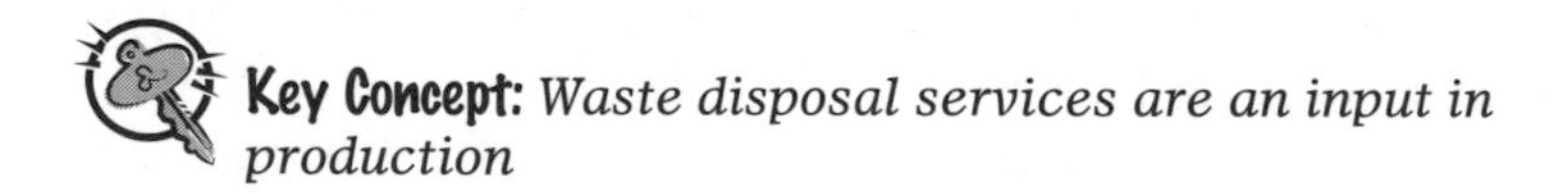
Key Concept: *Waste disposal services are an input in production*

In fact, economists tend to represent pollution as just another input into the production process like labor or capital. Think of this input as **waste disposal services.** Nearly all production activities generate some kinds of waste by-products, and these need to be disposed of. We can try to reduce the amount or toxicity of these by-products, and we can consider different ways of disposing of them (air, water, landfills, recycling, etc.). And there is likely to be some degree of substitutability between waste disposal and other inputs. In the same way that firms may substitute labor for capital or land, a firm may substitute capital, labor, materials, or alternative types of waste disposal for airborne emissions.

Given all these alternatives, a better way to represent an externality is just to plot emissions or "pollution" on the horizontal axis and the marginal benefits and marginal (external) costs of those emissions on the vertical axis, as shown in figure 5.3. The marginal benefit here is the benefit from being able to pollute, the benefit of not having to incur the costs of abatement. These are private benefits, meaning that the firm is better off when it can just dump its waste products into the air without concern for the costs, in the way that minimizes MPC. If the firm were unable to pollute at Q_M, then it would have to "abate": take actions to reduce emissions, which would be costly because the firm would be giving up marginal benefits (moving from right to left on the MB curve beginning at Q_M).

Key Concept: *MB for an increase becomes MC for a decrease*

This is an important point about interpreting the graphs that we will be using elsewhere in the book, so let's go over it one more time. **If we move from left to right (increasing emissions), there is a marginal benefit to the firm because it is producing paper in a low-cost way that earns the firm profits. If it is required to reduce pollution, then that benefit turns into a cost (moving from right to left). Similarly, if we move from left to right, there is a marginal external cost caused by the smokestack emissions that occur when paper is produced in that low-cost way. If the firm is required to reduce pollution, then that cost turns into a benefit (moving from right to left).**

So when we talk about abatement, or reducing pollution (as we will frequently in later chapters), we need to understand that we are moving from right to left, and as a result of that, benefits become costs and costs become benefits. This is an important kind of mental ambidexterity that we need to have for the analysis that will follow.

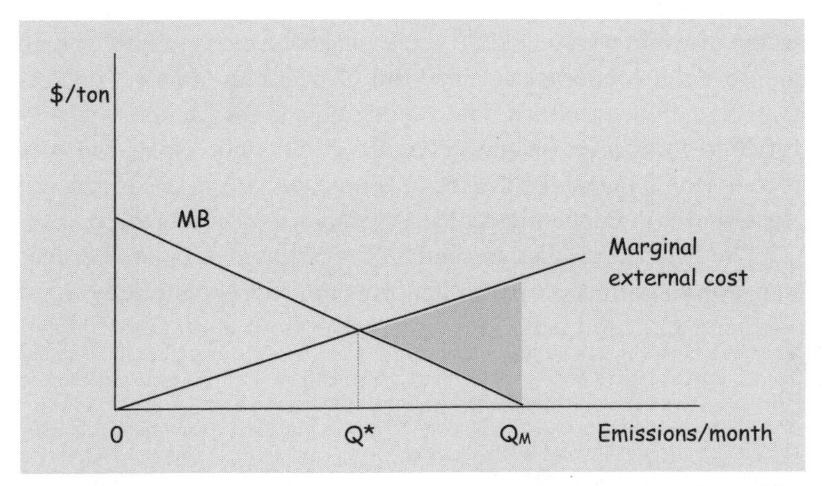

■ **FIGURE 5.3 Externalities in paper production when abatement is possible**

What to do about externalities? Economists often say that externalities need to be "internalized," meaning that some action needs to be taken to correct this kind of market failure. Precisely how government policies can control or internalize externalities of various kinds is the subject of chapter 10.

Tragedy of the Commons: Reciprocal Externalities

One type of market failure is sometimes referred to as a tragedy of the commons, a term ecologist Garrett Hardin popularized in a famous article of the same name in 1968. Many economists and other social scientists no longer like the term "tragedy of the commons" because it implies that all commons problems necessarily end in tragedy (overexploited and degraded resources).[1] They don't always end in tragedy—as we will see later when discussing common property institutions in chapter 9. Common pool resources can often be managed efficiently, as we will see. When tragedy strikes, they are sometimes referred to as open access resources.

The central idea here can also be described as a reciprocal externality, a kind of coordination problem found with pastures and fisheries, military arms races, cartels like OPEC, world population, and even international trade. Coordination problems occur when the self-interested actions of individuals, firms, or nations impose costs on others in a way that makes everyone worse off than what could be achieved with restraints, for example, through cooperation. This kind of problem is now a central feature in the economics field called game theory, and it is widely referred to as a Prisoners' Dilemma game. John Nash, the subject of the biographical film *A Beautiful Mind,* received the Nobel Prize in Economics in 1994 for his work on this topic.

The Prisoners' Dilemma can be represented with two herders who use a common pasture. The pasture will support two small

---

[1]Economists might also be just a bit miffed that Garrett Hardin became famous for his cleverly titled article, even though his main insight had been established fourteen years earlier by the economist Scott Gordon in an article about the overexploitation of fisheries. Garrett Hardin, "The Tragedy of the Commons," *Science* 162 (1968): 1243–1248; and Scott Gordon, "The Economic Theory of a Common Property Resource: The Fishery," *Journal of Political Economy* 62, no. 2 (1954): 124–142.

herds, but if one herder or both herders increase the number of animals to a large herd, the pasture will be degraded so that only meager nourishment is provided for the animals, and hence fewer benefits for the herders. Using arbitrary numbers to represent the payoffs for the herders, we can describe the dilemma as:

Payoffs for joint use of a pasture in a "cooperation game"

		Herder B	
		Small herd	Large herd
Herder A	Small herd:	100\100	40\130
	Large herd:	130\40	60\60

Each combination of choices is represented with the payoff for herder A shown before the slash (\) and herder B's payoff after the slash. If both choose a small herd, then A earns 100 and so does B.

The idea is that each herder makes his decision independently, not knowing what the other will do. They can choose to graze a small or a large herd. When choosing a large herd over a small herd, they gain benefits but at the expense of the other herder. When considering only their own benefits, we can see that A is better off with a large herd no matter what B chooses to do. A payoff of 130 is better than 100 if B chooses a small herd, and 60 is better than 40 if B chooses a large herd. The same analysis is true for B. The two choices are often referred to as cooperation (small herd) and defection (large herd). The problem or dilemma is that both herders would be collectively better off if they both cooperated (chose small herds where 100 + 100 = 200), which is higher than the sum of payoffs for any of the other situations.

Given these payoffs, the "dominant strategy" based on independent, self-interested consideration is to defect—to depart from the mutually beneficial, low level of grazing. Nash showed that if the herders both defect and end up at 60\60, there are strong disincentives for either herder to change, and they are highly likely to stay there and endure their "tragedy of the pasture." This outcome is referred to as a Nash equilibrium. The same kind of outcome occurs for arms races when two countries devote excessive resources building up military strength to respond to the military spending of their adversary. If only we could find ways to move to the cooperative situation! Solutions to these problems include cooperation, binding agreements, rules, and laws. Some of these options are discussed in chapter 8 about trade agreements, in chapter 9 about common property, and in chapter 12 about fishery management.

Recommended Readings and References

Additional general discussions of market failures and externalities are found in most intermediate microeconomics textbooks such as those listed at the end of chapter 2. See also textbooks on environmental and natural resource economics, including Barry Field, *Natural Resource Economics*, 1st ed. (Boston: McGraw-Hill/Irwin, 2000); Barry Field, *Environmental Economics*, 3rd ed. (Boston: McGraw-Hill/Irwin, 2001); Eban Goodstein, *Economics and the Environment*, 4th ed. (Hoboken, NJ: John Wiley and Sons, 2004); and Tom Tietenberg, *Environmental and Natural Resource Economics*, 6th ed. (New York: Addison-Wesley, 2002).

On the problems associated with common pool resources, see Garrett Hardin, "The Tragedy of the Commons," *Science* 162 (1968): 1243–1248; and Scott Gordon, "The Economic Theory of a Common Property Resource: The Fishery," *Journal of Political Economy* 62, no. 2 (1954): 124–142. A standard, though advanced, reference is Richard Cornes and Todd Sandler, *The Theory of Externalities, Public Goods, and Club Goods*, 2nd ed. (Cambridge: Cambridge University Press, 1996). For a fascinating introduction to cooperation and the Prisoners' Dilemma, see Robert Axelrod, *The Evolution of Cooperation* (New York: Basic Books, 1984). For a textbook on game theory, see Robert Gibbons, *Game Theory for Applied Economists* (Princeton, NJ: Princeton University Press, 1992). References on policies and other approaches to correcting market failures and externalities are found in the chapters of part 2.

6

Sustainability: Stocks and Flows

Sustainable development is development that meets the needs of the present without compromising the ability of future generations to meet their own needs.

—World Commission on Environment and Development, 1987

We ought to define a man's income as the maximum value which he can consume during a week, and still expect to be as well off at the end of the week as he was at the beginning.

—Sir John Hicks, 1939

The terms "sustainability" and "sustainable development" have become as well known for the controversy surrounding their meaning as they have for the ideas underlying their advocacy as guides for social policy. There is probably agreement that sustainability has something to do with maintaining some thing or things for the future. Beyond that, there seems to be little consensus on what is to be sustained, how best to go about it, and whether or not sustainable development is oxymoronic. This situation has led many observers, including economists, to be puzzled by the staying power of such a confusing and ambiguous concept. Still, sustainability has been a pervasive watchword for nearly twenty years and shows no signs of becoming passé.

Hicks's classic definition of income implicitly measures income only in terms of the level of income that could be sustained indefinitely: living off the interest rather than the principal, which is the source of our future income. The applicability and simplicity of Hicks's definition, however, becomes much more difficult as we try to apply it to more realistic and complex situations. To see this, let's take it one step at a time.

Stocks and Flows

One major source of confusion about sustainability comes from failing to recognize the distinction between "stocks" and "flows." Any notion of sustainability rests on these two concepts and the relationship between them. A stock, of course, is just a quantity of something (measured in tons, gallons, calories, or dollars) or the "quality" of something (e.g., air pollution levels in parts per million). A flow involves a quantity that "flows" during a period of time (e.g., tons per year or gallons per minute). It can flow in or out and will often be added to or subtracted from a stock. Hicks recognized this distinction and focused on a flow, the amount that could be consumed during a week.

Environmental resources typically involve both a stock and a flow, and there is generally some relationship between the two. For example, the amount of water in a bathtub (in gallons) will be a function of the "inflow" (gallons per minute) from the tap and the "outflow" (gallons per minute) to the drain. If the inflow is greater than the outflow, the stock is increasing over time. If the outflow is two gallons per minute, what must the inflow be in order for the stock in the tub to remain constant? Clearly, two gallons per minute will sustain the tub's fill level.

So can we relate stocks and flows to the idea of sustainability? In the case of a bathtub, what is it we want to sustain? Is it the stock (fill level) of the tub? Is it the inflow or outflow? If it is the fill level we want to sustain, do we care whether that stock is thirty gallons or one gallon, as long as we sustain it? Already we can see complications. In this particular case involving bathing, it is the stock or fill level that is essential. But we want more than just sustainability. We want the stock to be sufficient for the bather to be able to wash, soak, and rinse.

What about the case of a well where the outflow is the water we draw from the well for use, say, to irrigate a garden. The inflow is a function of the groundwater that seeps from the walls of the well, and the stock of water in the well is the amount available for irrigation at any one time. If we talk about sustainability in this case, is it the stock or flow we want to sustain? Is the answer the same as in the bathtub case? No, in this case, the amount of water we can withdraw from the well is what we want to sustain, and this will depend on the natural seepage inside the well. What matters is whether or not the withdrawals (outflows) for the garden can be sustained.

For these two examples, then, each involving a simple stock-flow relationship for water, we can see that sustainability needs to be applied differently. In the case of a bathtub used for bathing, sustaining an adequate fill level is probably our goal for purposes of bathing. By contrast, in the case of the well, what we want to sustain is our ability to irrigate our garden. So it is a sustainable outflow that is directly important to us: our ability to withdraw the needed quantity of water per week for irrigation. Of course, if the stock of water in the well is declining when in use, we cannot count on a sustainable outflow. What will allow us to achieve sustainability? The inflow must equal the outflow so that the stock of water does not change. Is the stock of water in the well important? In this case, not really. As long as we can dip our bucket into the water, whether the water level is high or low, our ability to water the garden sustainably is not affected. Of course, the stock can be important, for example, if the well goes dry or overflows, flooding our garden.

For most resources, the flow depends on the stock. The bathtub outflow may be higher when the tub is filled due to the added water pressure on a leak or at the drain. This is also true for an important class of resources where the "inflow" is generated from within the resource itself. A fishery grows from within as a result of biological reproduction, and this growth rate (which we can think of as its inflow) is "density dependent" or varies depending on the stock of fish. Biological resources, including forests and wildlife populations, tend to have growth rates that are density dependent. At relatively low stock levels the growth rate may be higher than at high stock levels because of increased competition among fish, trees, and wildlife at higher population densities.

For comparison, consider sustainability of a bank account. It will provide a sustainable *flow* of services (withdrawals) so long as the inflow (deposits or interest earned) is greater than or equal to the outflow. If we care only about sustainability, then the bank balance is not of direct concern. However, if the inflow is accumulated interest, and the interest is paid as a percentage of the bank balance, then we again have a case where the sustainability of the outflow is dependent on both the stock (bank balance) and the interest rate, which combine to determine the inflow. This relationship comes closest to the one that Hicks had in mind in his definition of income at the start of this chapter: our income from a bank account or other financial asset is only the interest accrued, not the principle. Way back in 1939, when Hicks defined income, he had in mind a definition that implicitly required sustainability.

Okay, at this point the idea of sustainability seems pretty straightforward once we've recognized the importance of stocks and flows and when we're looking at a single resource. But what happens with more than one resource?

Multiple Resource Systems

Let's think now about a system with two or more interconnected resources. Consider a forest, a stream, a lake with a fishery, and farmland—and one person, Robinson Crusoe, who uses them. The farmland, which used to be covered with forest, is now irrigated from the stream and produces food. The forest, which provides wood for cooking and heating, helps maintain a reliable and timely flow of irrigation water in the stream (a smaller forest would mean less water flowing at the time of year it is needed). The stream feeds into the lake of fish. The larger the farmland, the smaller the forest. The smaller the forest, the lower the flow of water during the irrigation season (and the smaller the available fuelwood for heating and cooking).

If Crusoe wants to live sustainably, his food needs determine the amount of land he needs for farming and the amount of water he needs for irrigation, and his heating and cooking needs determine the amount of wood he needs from the forest. If he notices that his woodcutting (outflow) in the forest is not sustainable (given the forest's growth rate), he could let some of his farmland return to forest (increasing the forest stock). He could make up for the smaller farm area (reduced stock) by irrigating more, but that would require diverting more water (outflow) from the stream. But Crusoe also catches fish from the lake, and increased irrigation will lower the inflow into the lake, reducing the growth rate of the fishery below sustainable levels given his current harvest.

Crusoe wants to live sustainably, but how does that translate into action? He can sustain each resource at a certain level, but each level is influenced by the levels of the other interconnected resources. In fact, there are an infinite number of different levels of farmland, forestland, irrigation level, and fish harvests that are sustainable. So, how does a commitment to sustainability help him decide what he should do? In the situation described, it should be clear that too much farmland could be a bad thing because it reduces the stream flow. This could limit irrigation and fish, while at the same time make his fuelwood use unsustainable. Too much forest could provide plenty of water and fish, but the farmland might be insufficient to keep him fed.

What this hypothetical situation suggests is a balancing act, or trade-off, and a need to find the best balance of stocks and flows for a set of resources that are interconnected. From any given starting point, a careful examination of these trade-offs might show that the stocks of some resources are too high or too low and that lowering one is needed in order to bring another one up to its desired levels. Our previously straightforward way of thinking about sustainability seems to be breaking down. Interdependent stocks and flows among resources mean that we have to choose between different things, all of which we might want to sustain. In the end, we have to make trade-offs.

Irreversibility and Substitution

At this point, you might want to throw up your hands in despair. We appear to have no clear basis for choosing from an infinite number of sustainable arrangements for a given set of resources.

(One approach would be to base these choices, or trade-offs, on the marginal value of each stock and flow—which is the economics approach described in chapters 2 and 3.) When somebody advocates sustainability, which stocks or flows do they mean? What, in particular, is being promoted with sustainability?

What seems to be missing is a basis for differentiating among resources: which ones are prime candidates for sustainability consideration and which ones are not. One way to distinguish between resources would be to consider (a) the irreversibility of the losses and (b) the uniqueness of that particular resource. Often, when sustainability is raised as an issue, there is a concern about regret, that the loss of a particular resource will be regrettable because it will not be possible to restore or recover from the loss of the resource, and because there are no close substitutes; no other resources can serve its purpose well. If species

BOX 3
Sustainability with Exhaustible Resources

Can exhaustible resources be used sustainably? The answer is yes if other renewable resources are also available. Think of an exhaustible resource as you would a bank account that earns no interest; there is no "sustainable rate" at which it can be drawn on indefinitely by living off the interest rather than the principal. The same is true for economies that depend on mineral or oil deposits. But if some of the income from an exhaustible resource can be invested in productive forms of capital, then a forward-looking strategy could be used to achieve sustainability.

Here's how it works. Consider a lucky individual with a trust fund annuity that will pay her $20,000 each year for twenty years and then it's finished. To use this "exhaustible resource" sustainably would require reinvesting some of these proceeds in a "productive" form of capital, such as a bank that pays interest on deposits. If some of the income from the trust fund were deposited in the interest-bearing account each year, then by the end of twenty years, a sustainable flow of interest could continue to be withdrawn from the new account.

How much needs to be invested? What level of income can be sustained? The key to sorting this out is to consider the present value of the trust fund, and become extinct, if soils become permanently degraded, or if climates change, these resources can't be restored. By contrast, if a building is destroyed, either it can be rebuilt or a different building can serve a similar purpose.

In these cases, then, the inference being made when waving the flag of sustainability is that some particular resources—those relatively unique resources vulnerable to irreversible loss—should be protected at the expense of other kinds of resources. In the case of Robinson Crusoe, if forests that have been cleared for farming can never be restored to forests, or if the fish population in the lake is the only one there is and it risks extinction, then invoking sustainability would place added weight to protecting the forest and fish stocks, and Crusoe would adjust the mix of other stocks and flows in order to protect them. For an example of how this can be done in the case of an exhaustible resource, see box 3.

what must be done so that the present value of the combination of the trust fund and the new account doesn't decline. For a 6% interest rate, the present value of the trust fund before the first year is $230,000. If the trust fund itself could be sold for that amount, and if that amount could be deposited in an interest-bearing account at 6%, then the annual interest would be $13,764, and this could be withdrawn each year forever without diminishing the principal. This calculation tells us that the difference between the trust fund annual payment of $20,000 and the sustainable income the trust fund could potentially provide ($13,764) is $6,236. This difference represents the depreciation that would occur if the entire $20,000 were spent. So, if each year $6,236 is invested in an account earning 6% and only $13,764 is spent, then when the trust fund runs out after twenty years, the holder of the new account will be able to continue to withdraw and spend the same amount, $13,764, in perpetuity.

This same basic analysis can be applied to an oil-exporting country or a mineral-rich nation. A forward-looking strategy to shift from an exhaustible to a renewable source of income can be achieved without a decline in income, but it requires a willingness to consume less today in order to provide for sustained consumption in the future.

This sounds somewhat promising. Recognizing uniqueness and irreversibility can help prioritize the candidates for sustainability. These considerations may not be captured in conventional economic approaches, in part because people, when making individual decisions, may not give these considerations much thought. But what if people have differing views about what is unique, valuable, and irreversible?

Multiple Users

Let's add more people to the Robinson Crusoe story to make it a community of individuals, some who practice farming, some forestry, and some fishing. They all understand that sustainability is about stocks and flows and that their resources are interconnected. But they also have the idea that, for them, sustainability means sustaining their ability to practice what they know.

If we look at the current allocation of resources and determine that changes are needed in the stocks or flows of these interconnected resources, any change in farmland, forests, or stream flow will likely pose a threat to the livelihood of some individuals who will not be able to continue doing what they now do. One might be tempted to argue that these individuals could switch from farming to fishing or to logging as opportunities arose, and that the preferred allocation of land and water would also be the one that generated the greatest income potential. But forced relocation and retraining are costly and often undesirable. Sustaining communities, and the less tangible values associated with them, is often cited as part of the sustainability agenda. Built capital, human capital, and social capital are also valuable assets.

Thus, the sustainability of people's livelihood may come into conflict with choosing the "preferred" balance of stocks and flows among natural resources (if we could assume that individuals could shift from one source of income to another). This complicates sustainability even more, since natural resources are only a part of what people want to sustain. They also want to sustain a flow of income, the use of their income-earning skills, and the communities and friends they are attached to. As a result, the status quo, or existing set of stocks and flows, will be difficult to alter because individuals see sustaining the stocks and flows that affect them as an important part of what sustainability means to them. And in some cases, sustaining the flow of income to one group involves reductions in the stock of a resource important to another group.

In some of the literature on sustainability, a distinction is made between "weak sustainability" and "strong sustainability." Weak sustainability refers to a nondecreasing total stock of capital. Strong sustainability separates natural capital and emphasizes protecting these stocks from further decline. Both definitions are problematic. The first presumes we have a satisfactory way of weighting and adding together the total amount of capital stocks, including built assets, natural resources, and human and social capital. The second definition is problematic because it would seem to allow no substitution between natural and other forms of capital. Even if we qualify this rigid interpretation of the rule by allowing modest or acceptable drawdown of critical natural resources, who and how is it decided what is "modest" and what is "critical"? How might we conclude that now is the time to invoke nondeclining natural capital, as opposed to one hundred years ago or one hundred years from now?

Social Indicators

Discussions about sustainability goals frequently expand to include concerns such as the equitable distribution of income, civil and political liberties, democracy, or the extent of malnutrition and infant mortality. Indeed, a number of attempts have been made to create indexes of sustainability, and these indexes typically include measures of these kinds of social issues, combined into a weighted-average index.[1] There may be general agreement that these are all social issues deserving attention, but in what sense do they measure or involve sustainability? Are they stocks or flows? What weights should they be given relative to ecosystem functions? How might we compare their substitutability with, say, that of the ozone layer?

[1]See, for example, the country-level Environmental Sustainability Index of the World Economic Forum (http://www.ciesin.columbia.edu/indicators/ESI).

An alternative approach would be to establish separate measures of progress toward these other goals, ones that could be considered alongside measures or indices of sustainability. This would allow each index or measure to be tracked and judged separately, and it would also allows individuals with different priorities to consider how much weight they would give to sustainability versus other social goals, as the example in box 4 illustrates.

Sustainability and Growth

One way to overcome the social and political obstacles facing any proposed change from the status quo use of resources would be if improvements in resource productivity could be made, ones that make it possible to achieve a desired increase in a specified stock or flow without reducing some other stock or flow. For example, if irrigation water could be applied more efficiently so that less water was required, or if trees were pruned and thinned so that they grew faster, or if only the largest, nonreproducing fish were caught so that the overall population of fish grew faster, then some changes in Robinson Crusoe's use of land and water could be accommodated with little or no reductions in food, wood, or fish.

These possibilities, of course, represent forms of technological change. Technological change can also be thought of as an increase in the "stock" of technology or knowledge. Knowledge is just another resource, a form of capital that, like natural resources, involves stocks and flows. A given stock of knowledge generates a certain flow of services for those who make use of it. In the same way that the available flow of irrigation water affects the productivity of farmland, so too does the flow (use) of technology affect the productivity of other resources.

However, unlike most natural resources, an increase in the use of knowledge does not diminish the existing stock. This is because knowledge is a "pure public good" (see chapter 5), so that the consumption of the good or service does not diminish the amount available for others to use. Not so for fish or water.

This discussion is leading us in the direction of examining productivity improvements in general. Increased productivity means that more goods valued by individuals can come from a given resource or that the same goods can be produced with

BOX 4
Sustainability in Context: Logging versus Fishing and Tourism

Can the notion of sustainability sketched out in this chapter be applied to a real-world situation like the one facing a region in the Philippines? Let's see.

Bacuit Bay, on the island of Palawan in the Philippines, is known for its rich marine life, clear water, and productive fishery. But in the hills above the bay, logging operations threaten the bay's natural resources and economy. The logging causes soil erosion and runoff into the bay, which kills coral, reduces the local fish catch, and threatens the new and growing diving-based tourism business.

So a trade-off exists between income from logging on the one hand and income from marine resources and tourism on the other. So far, this is nothing new since such trade-offs are what economic analysis is all about. Why do we need a new concept of sustainability?

We observe that the logging operations produce high profits that benefit a small number of people (mainly those living outside the region) over a short period of time. Once the hills are cleared of trees, it will be a very long time before income from logging will return to the region. Also, the adverse impact of logging on the marine resources could be essentially permanent: the loss of fish and tourism could force the locals to abandon the region and move elsewhere.

On the other hand, fishing and tourism may produce lower benefits annually, but those benefits affect a larger number of people and can continue indefinitely if the natural resource base is maintained. If we bring equity into the equation, the village fishing industry has a broader distribution of benefits, and those benefits affect more low-income people than does the capital-intensive timber industry.

In this situation, standard benefit-cost analysis (see chapter 15) might conclude that timber is more valuable than fishing and tourism: the net benefits, even over the long term, are higher for timber even after subtracting the losses that would be created for fishing and tourism. With sustainability as one of several criteria, however, the analysis might lead to a different conclusion. It might find that for these two interconnected resources, the added weight given to sustainability of the marine resource, in addition to distributional equity for the low-income villagers, favored a ban on logging to protect the resource-dependent communities over the long term.

Source: John Dixon and Louise Fallon, "The Concept of Sustainability: Origins, Extensions, and Usefulness for Policy," *Society and Natural Resources* 2 (1989): 73–84.

fewer resource stocks or flows. We are now talking about economic growth, an increase in the overall level of goods and services available to individuals. Economic growth is commonly seen as conflicting with the idea of sustainability because of a presumption that economic growth necessarily means increasing the stocks and flows of "built assets" at the expense of natural resources. In principle, this need not be the case (e.g., if growth is due only to improved technology). Moreover, it should come as no surprise that many people who are in favor of sustainability also want to improve their own standard of living or quality of life. Sustainable natural resource flows may be one source of quality of life, but an increase in the flows of some other kinds of goods and services, whether market commodities, enjoyment of the arts, or spending time with family, may also be a part of that desire.

Much more needs to be said about the process of economic growth and its relationship to sustainable development, and the next chapter takes up these issues in more detail.

Recommended Readings and References

The World Commission on Environment and Development first popularized sustainability and sustainable development in *The Bruntland Report: Our Common Future* (Oxford: Oxford University Press, 1987). Using the *Journal of Economic Literature* CD-ROM, ECONLIT, you can find more than 3,400 hits when searching for the keyword "sustainability," several hundred of these are books. For information on how to obtain this CD-ROM, visit http://www.econlit.org.

Some notable contributions from the economics literature about sustainability and sustainable development include John R. Hicks, *Value and Capital: An Inquiry into Some Fundamental Principles of Economic Theory* (Oxford: Oxford University Press, 1939); Richard B. Norgaard and Richard B. Howarth, "Sustainability and Discounting the Future," in *Ecological Economics*, ed. R. Costanza (New York: Columbia University Press, 1991), 525; Bryan G. Norton and Michael Toman, "Sustainability: Ecological and Economic Perspectives," *Land Economics* 73 (1997): 553–568; David W. Pearce and Giles D. Atkinson, "Capital Theory and the

Measurement of Sustainable Development: An Indicator of 'Weak' Sustainability," *Ecological Economics* 8 (1993): 103–108; Robert M. Solow, "The Economics of Resources or Resources of Economics," *American Economic Review* 64 (1974): 1–14; Clem Tisdell, *Biodiversity, Conservation, and Sustainable Development: Principles and Practices with Asian Examples.* New Horizons in Environmental Economics (Cheltenham, UK, and Northampton, MA: Edward Elgar Publishing); and Michael Toman, "Economics and 'Sustainability': Balancing Trade-offs and Imperatives," *Land Economics* 70, no. 4 (1994): 399–413.

7

Economic Growth and Development

[Economic development is] a generalized process of capital accumulation in which capital includes not only plant, equipment and other forms of physical capital and exploitable natural resources, but also capital embodied in human resources and capital in the form of economically useful knowledge and skills and effective organizations, both public and private.

—Harry Johnson, 1964

To understand economic growth and development, we need, once again, to distinguish between stocks and flows. In the previous chapter we defined flows of goods and services as the quantities of those items available for consumption, use, or enjoyment during a given period. Stocks are the assets, the forms of "capital" that makes these flows possible. Capital is used here to refer to any valuable stock, and consumption refers to the flow of benefits that the stock makes possible (including environmental benefits). Economic development involves an increase in the level of benefits (commodities, services, and intangibles), and this increase is generally the result of an increase in the stocks of capital. For an economy to grow, we need to augment the capital stock: a larger stock of factories, more educated people, abundant fisheries or forests, and healthy ecosystems will make it possible to consume more of the goods and services they provide—without drawing down the stock.

There is a distinction often made here between economic growth and economic development. Economic growth is sometimes used to refer only to an increase in the scale of the market economy, the level of those goods and services produced and measured as part of gross domestic product (GDP). By contrast, economic development is frequently understood to imply a broader concept, one that acknowledges how our standard of living can increase qualitatively and in ways other than by increasing the gross domestic product. However, when economists talk about "optimal growth," they have in mind maintaining the optimal mix of flows of goods and service from all forms of capital, tangible and intangible.

Deferred Consumption and Capital Accumulation

Let's consider the story of Robinson Crusoe, or at least a version of it. We find Monsieur Crusoe all alone on his island where he is able to live without too many complaints because he can hunt, fish, and gather food from the forest. These tasks take up most of each day, however, leaving almost no time for leisure, to relax and enjoy his paradise. If he wanted to, he could continue this routine indefinitely, and sustainably.

Crusoe, however, might want to make his daily tasks easier, faster, and more efficient, so that he could relax—or perhaps write that novel he's been talking about. For example, he might build a ladder for harvesting coconuts, or a spear for hunting, or a net for fishing. He might research the migratory patterns of the island's wildlife or fish so that he could improve his fishing and hunting success. If he did these things, his labor productivity would eventually increase, and he would finish his daily chores sooner or with less physical effort, and he would have more time for hobbies and other leisure activities.

But to build a ladder, a spear, or a net would take time, and he currently has no time to spare. He would have to give something up in the short run (sleep, a meal) in order to raise his productivity in the long run. He would need to defer consumption (save) while he builds a ladder or makes other improvements (investments), with the future payoff (return on investment) being less work and more goods and services. This is what economic growth is all about—the process of capital accumulation described by Harry Johnson at the beginning of the chapter.

Before we venture too far into the study of economic growth, we should consider a simple but useful model of the relationship between consumption and growth that relates income, Y, to capital, K, and investment ΔK. This model is from the old classical development economics literature. The essential relationship is $Y = (1/k) \times K$, where k is the "incremental capital-output ratio," or the amount that capital must be increased to cause an increase in output of one unit. If it takes two units of capital to raise output by one unit, then $k = 2$. We can define the growth rate, g, as the percent change in income, or $g = \Delta Y/Y$. We can also define the savings rate as the portion of income saved, or $s = S/Y$. With these two relationships we can come up with a key relationship: $g = s/k$, which says that the growth rate of the economy will rise with the savings rate and decline with the capital-output ratio, k. If k is lower, income will increase faster. If s is higher, income will also rise faster. So higher savings, or more productive investments (ones where less capital is needed to produce a unit increase in income), will produce a higher growth rate. The basic insight is a simple but important one: income (a flow) is a function of capital (a stock), and increases in income are made possible by saving and investment that increase these stocks. Keep in mind that investment includes R&D, which promotes growth through technological change and increased productivity, and this kind of growth may not require increasing the use of natural resources and other inputs.

Investment in Different Kinds of Capital

The kind of growth that occurs will depend on the kinds of capital that are maintained or increased, including environmental resources, human capital, and institutions. To foster economic development or optimal growth, we want to choose the right mix of investments among the different kinds of capital in order to promote improvements in human well-being, not just increases in market commodities.

We can characterize the problem with a production possibilities frontier (PPF) for an economy with two kinds of capital, one for the flow of market goods and services and the other for the flow of nonmarket goods (such as clean air, water, fish, ecosystem services, and cultural amenities). Economic growth occurs when investing in one or both kinds of capital. The PPF will expand outward in one or both directions depending on these investments (see figure 7.1, panel A), with the allocation of resources moving, for example, from point A to point B. If the kinds of capital that produce market goods are increased at the expense of the capital that produces nonmarket goods, we would see a contraction of the PPF on one side as it expands in the other direction (figure 7.1, panel B), and the allocation of resources might move from point A to point B, implying a large decline in nonmarket goods.

What is efficient growth? Efficiency in this dynamic sense means the most desirable path of growth over time, and this involve three requirements: (1) efficient use of resources in each period (operating on the PPF), (2) the maximum net benefits from resource allocation (finding the best possible point on the PPF), and (3) achieving the optimal rate of growth or shifting out of the PPF (finding just the right level of savings and investments in each kind of capital stock).

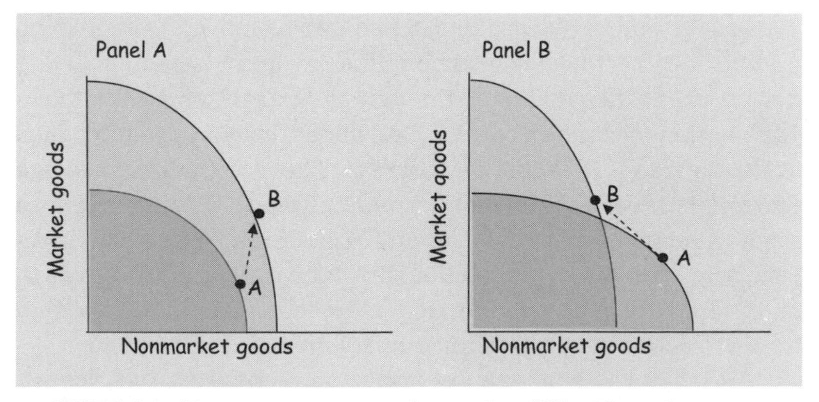

FIGURE 7.1 Alternative patterns of growth in PPF with market and nonmarket goods

If we recognize qualitative improvements and nonconsumptive kinds of capital (institutions, social capital, and productivity improvements that allow us to increase the flow of goods and services from a given stock), then, in principle, improvements in quality of life can continue without limit, even while there may be physical or technological limits to the increases for some kinds of goods and services.

Limits to Growth and the Environmental Kuznets Curve

Many observers believe that continued economic growth will only lead to worsening environmental problems as production of more commodities uses up the earth's natural resources, and as the economy generates ever-increasing amounts of waste byproducts and pollution. Other, more optimistic observers expect solutions for scarcity to be found in human ingenuity and technology. One line of reasoning has been the argument that poverty is an important cause of environmental degradation, and that as income per capita increases, the willingness and ability of society to confront and solve environmental problems will also increase.

This split between environmental pessimists and growth optimists has been around for centuries. Beginning in the early 1990s, however, a new angle on this debate emerged. Data collected from countries around the world appeared to show some tentative evidence that environmental degradation first increased, and then decreased, as countries moved from poor to middle income to high income. This evidence set off a lively debate about the validity of the evidence itself, about the likely explanations for such a pattern, and about the policy implications of the pattern if in fact it was correct. The issue quickly became known as the environmental Kuznets curve (EKC), referring to the development economist Simon Kuznets, who long ago hypothesized an "inverted U" relationship between economic growth and inequality. The new version is an inverted U relationship between economic growth and environmental degradation.

Although the dust has definitely not settled on this debate, some important ideas have emerged. First, there does appear to be evidence of an inverted U pattern for some kinds of environmental damage (urban air pollution where high-income cities have experienced improved air quality in recent years; deforestation where high-income countries have recently seen actual increases in acreage forested), but definitely not for others (CO_2 emissions, solid waste).

Second, the absence of evidence of an EKC for some environmental indicators should not be construed as proof that the EKC notion is invalid. There is no reason to expect that evidence of an inverted U should be observable for all types of environmental damage within the same range of income per capita levels. Depending on the underlying cause of the inverted U pattern, the "turnaround point" may differ greatly from one environmental resource to another.

What explains this EKC evidence? In the past few years, attention has focused on several explanations based on economic theory, including ones that are simple, straightforward, and not particularly controversial. The basic idea revolves around the relative abundance of consumer goods compared with environmental goods at different levels of per capita income. In a very poor economy, there is an absolute scarcity of consumer goods such as food, clothing, shelter, and other necessities. This same economy may also have an abundance of natural resources, forests, clean air, and pristine watersheds. Think of Robinson Crusoe on a large tropical island or a small village in the middle of the Amazon. If we think about the production possibilities frontier that would characterize the trade-offs they face between market goods and nonmarket goods, what would it look like?

Actually, it will look quite different from the PPF we looked at in chapter 3, which assumes we are beginning with small amounts of two kinds of factors of production (e.g., labor and capital) and use them to produce either of two goods. In reality, however, a poor economy at an initial stage of development may begin with an endowment of natural resources and environmental quality—sometimes in great abundance such as in Canada or the western United States 150 years ago. The PPF will look like the one in figure 7.2, panel A, where all the production possibilities are at the top of the vertical axis like a flag up a flagpole. Why is the PPF "hinged" to the top of the vertical axis this way? Well, it's partly because the society doesn't have to "produce" environmental quality: it's an endowment of natural resources that generates environmental services at a high level. In addition, the society's capacity to degrade its own environment as a by-product of producing commodities is limited, primarily because its capacity to produce goods and services is limited (not enough factories or earthmovers). The most it can do is damage the environment to the level at point A.

What would a poor society prefer? Well, let's start at point A where the production of market goods is maximized (without

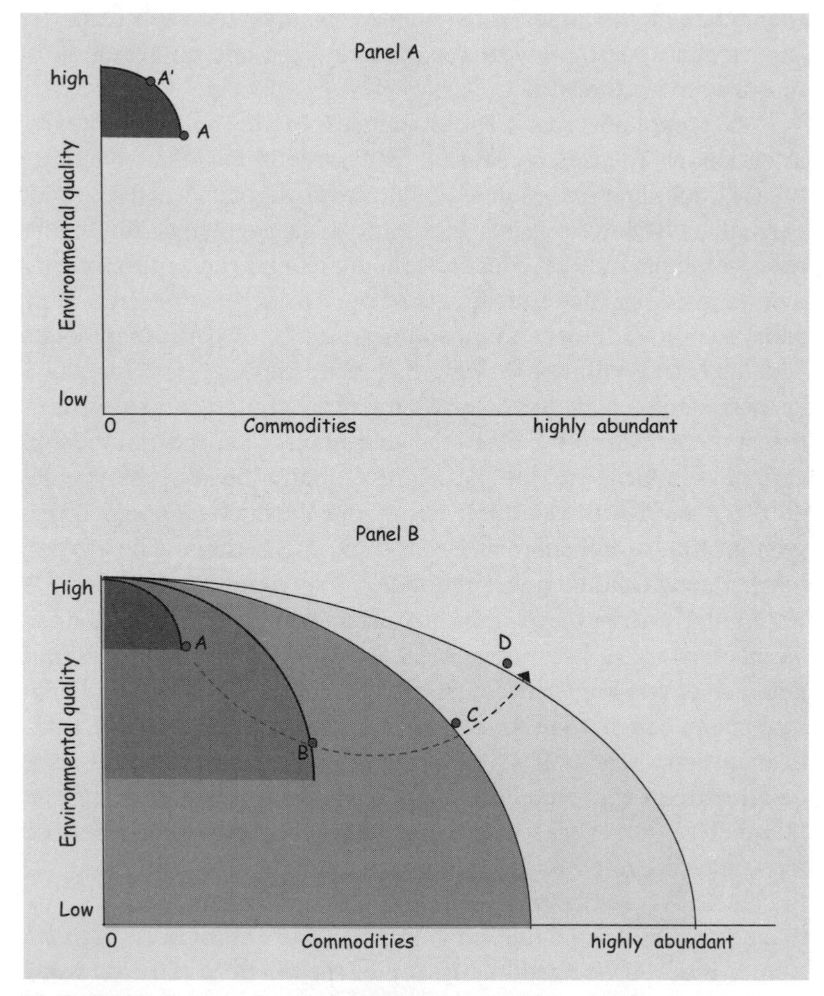

FIGURE 7.2 Expansion of the production possibilities frontier between commodities and environmental quality

regard to the environmental side effects). We can ask ourselves whether there would be an incentive or preference to moving from A toward A′, up the PPF by giving up some commodities in order to have (even) more environmental quality. Given the very low level of consumer goods available, and with an already high level of environmental quality, a poor community is unlikely to want to give up *any* market goods. If raising environmental quality means giving up even a small amount of market commodities such as food, shelter, or clothing, poor societies are unlikely to make that choice, so they would prefer to stay at point A.

Would these preferences change at higher levels of income, when commodities are more abundant but environmental quality has declined? In figure 7.2, panel B, we represent an expanded PPF that would reflect some economic growth relative to the first figure, with the PPF shifted out to an intermediate level. Here we might begin to see people's willingness to trade off consumption in the form of low-cost ways to protect the environment. The chosen allocation might be at point B, which is not at the bottom edge of the PPF but still reflects a strong preference for consumer goods over incremental improvements in the environment.

By the time income per capita has grown to the third and fourth PPFs containing points C and D, the capacity to produce commodities has grown dramatically compared with the first PPF in panel A, and the capacity to degrade the environment has also expanded (or damage may be cumulative if we have in mind an environment that does not regenerate). At these stages, there is a capacity to produce an abundance of commodities. But presumably people also place considerable value on the environment, in part because it is now degraded, and in part because they now have such high levels of commodity consumption that they *would* be willing to give up some of those abundant consumer goods to protect or restore environmental quality. This situation suggests that society will prefer an intermediate point on the PPF, one that offers them some of both kinds of goods, environmental goods and commodities. At these higher-income levels, however, we see that point C is higher than point B, and point D is higher than point C, indicating a U-shaped path, like the dotted arrow in the figure where environmental quality first declines and then rises with increases in per capita income.

If this theoretical explanation is what underlies the evidence of an EKC, then what does it mean? Well, it does *not* mean that we can just relax and sit back because environmental problems will take care of themselves. There are two reasons for this. First, some kinds of environmental damage are essentially irreversible like species extinction and climate change. (Even though some of these changes can be reversed over eons, the time period involved is so great that for all practical purposes they can be considered virtually irreversible.) In cases where irreversible damage occurs, if we move from A to B, no matter how rich we get, we will not be able to reverse these changes to move toward C and D.

Second, the ideas behind this EKC story do not suggest that the environment takes care of itself. It seems to suggest that as people begin to want an improved environment more than they want still more consumer goods, they find a way to overcome the forces of free riding and market failure that characterize many environmental problems. Societies can be expected to introduce policies and other mechanisms to limit further environmental degradation and encourage environmental improvements. Evidence backs this up: the level of environmental regulations in rich countries is much higher than in poor countries.

For concerned citizens and environmentalists, there is reason to see this EKC story as good news (even though some observers seem to see it as a threat). It suggests that environmental quality is a "normal good," meaning that as people's incomes go up they want more of it. The evidence of less air pollution, less water pollution, and more forest in the United States and other high-income countries in Western Europe is consistent with these ideas, as is the growing interest in the United States toward removing dams in order to restore free-flowing rivers after many years of damming up the country's rivers and streams. One cautionary note, however. Changing policies to reflect society's changed priorities is relatively easy for a homogeneous country with strong institutions. For global problems such as climate change and biodiversity, the disparity in income levels and international free riding problems will make it much more difficult to turn the corner on the U-shaped path for the global environment.

Recommended Readings and References

The quotation at the start of this chapter is from Harry G. Johnson, "Towards a Generalized Capital Accumulation Approach to Economic Development" in *The Residual Factor and Economic Growth*, OECD Study Group in the Economics of Education (Paris: Organization for Economic Cooperation and Development, 1964). For a textbook on the economics of developing countries, see Dwight H. Perkins, Malcolm Gillis, Steven Radelet, Michael Roemer, and Donald Snodgrass, *Economics of Development* (New York: W. W. Norton, 2001). See also Amartya Sen, *Development as Freedom* (New York: Anchor Books, 1999). An advanced, seminal work on the relationship between poverty, population, economic growth, and the environmental resource basis is Partha Dasgupta, *An Inquiry into Well-Being and Destitution* (Oxford: Oxford University Press, 1993).

Other references on economics, growth, and the environment include Edward B. Barbier and Anil Markandya, "The Conditions for Achieving Environmentally Sustainable Development," *European Economic Review* 34, no. 2–3 (1990): 659–669; Graciela Chichilnisky, "What Is Sustainable Development," *Land Economics* 73 (1997): 476–491; Gene M. Grossman and Alan B. Krueger, "Economic Growth and the Environment," *Quarterly Journal of Economics* 110, no. 2 (1995): 353–377; David W. Pearce and Giles D. Atkinson, "Capital Theory and the Measurement of Sustainable Development: An Indicator of 'Weak' Sustainability," *Ecological Economics* 8 (1993): 103–108; and David W. Pearce and Karl-Goran Maler, "Environmental Economics and the Developing World," *Ambio* 20, no. 2 (1991): 52–54.

8

International Trade

In many ways trade between countries is no different from exchanges in markets between individuals, cities, or states, where voluntary transactions represent gains from trade—unless of course there are externalities. There are also important differences between local markets and international markets, and recent debate and protests over globalization makes clear that those differences are of public concern. It's not possible to address all aspects of trade and globalization issues in these few pages, but we can lay out some of the basic ways to frame trade issues in economic terms.

Trade affects the allocation of resources, the efficiency of how goods and services are produced and distributed within and between countries, and all this has an effect on people's well-being, the distribution of benefits and costs, and the environment. One of the bedrock principles in all of economics is that **gains from trade** between two countries, and the specialization in production that this exchange makes possible, will tend to make both countries better off. Opportunities for gains from trade arise when there are differences between countries in the costs of different goods. These differences are generally due to differences in the scarcity and productivity of specific factors of production. Differences in climate, land, labor, and capital create opportunities for mutually beneficial trade. There are also important differences in natural resource abundance (e.g., minerals and agricultural potential) and differences in human capital, institutional capital, technology, and tastes. If there were no differences in any of these things so that all prices were the same, then there would be no reason for, or benefit from, trade.

Key Concept: *Gains from trade, comparative advantage* 

Even if one country can produce all goods cheaper than another country, there are still likely to be gains from trade. Trade will be mutually beneficial so long as there are differences in the *relative* prices or costs of different goods. This fundamental insight is called **comparative advantage,** and it is one of the most well-known and widely agreed-upon ideas in economics.

Let's take a simple example in a world with only rice and airplanes. If the United States can produce rice at a cost one-third lower than in China, and the United States can also produce airplanes at a cost two-thirds lower than in China, then the United States has an "absolute advantage" in producing both goods, but a comparative advantage in producing airplanes. The cost advantage in producing airplanes in the United States compared with that in China is twice the cost advantage in producing rice. It is easy to show with a simple numerical example that, with trade, if the United States specializes in the production of airplanes and China specializes in rice, both countries can consume more of both goods, because of gains from trade.

Many research studies have demonstrated evidence of the gains from trade by comparing the experiences of "open" versus "closed" economies and using statistical methods for data from many different countries and over many years. These analyses show strong support for the prediction from the theory of comparative advantage: countries that have pursued more open trade policies have experienced higher rates of economic growth than those with more closed policies.[1] What about the role of capital flows (e.g., direct foreign investments) in gains from trade? Research on direct foreign investment in developing countries, for example, also indicates a positive effect on growth in per capita income.[2]

Two key caveats need to be recognized in discussions of trade and changes in trade policy. First, any change in trade policy between countries will make some people better off, but it will also likely make some people worse off. This will be true, however, whether trade barriers are lowered or raised. For example, a lowering of U.S. restrictions on sugar imports will benefit sugar consumers and U.S. candy makers, but it will make U.S. sugar producers worse off. By contrast, raising U.S. restrictions on sugar imports will benefit U.S. sugar producers and harm U.S. sugar consumers and U.S. candy makers. It is important to keep this point in mind, that reducing trade barriers cannot be assumed to make everybody better off, even though a great deal of evidence suggests that over the long term, the gains by those who are made better off will be larger (in measurable terms) than the losses to those who, at least temporarily, are made worse off by opening up an economy to trade.

The second caveat is that the promise of gains from trade may be partly offset or even completely outweighed if there are other inefficiencies in the economy, such as insecure property rights or uncorrected externalities that may be exacerbated by trade flows. For example, in the absence of government controls on logging, open trade could lead to increased deforestation for export markets compared with the rates necessary to satisfy domestic demand. These kinds of unexpected side effects are reminders of what economists call the theory of second best, a problem discussed in chapter 13. The specific ways in which market failures can be corrected is the subject of part 2 of this book.

---

[1]See, for example, Jeffrey Frankel and David Romer, "Does Trade Cause Growth?" *American Economic Review* 89, no. 3 (1999): 379–399. Also see L. Alan Winters, Neil McCulloch, and Andrew McKay, "Trade Liberalization and Poverty: The Evidence So Far," *Journal of Economic Literature* 42, no. 1 (2004): 72–115.

[2]See, for example, Marcelo Soto, *Capital Flows and Growth in Developing Countries: Recent Empirical Evidence*, OECD Development Centre Technical Paper No. 160 (Paris: Organization for Economic Cooperation and Development, 2000).

The effect of trade on people's well-being becomes more complicated in the presence of externalities, public goods, and common pool resources. To get a handle on these issues, let's start with a simple model of a small country with the option to trade with the rest of the world. As in earlier chapters, to evaluate these issues we contrast the net benefits (economic surplus) with and without trade, considering the effects this would have in the market for an exported good and then for an imported good.

Gains from Trade

Figure 8.1 represents a country that does not trade. The (domestic) market equilibrium is given by the quantity demanded, which equals the quantity supplied ($Q_D = Q_S$) at price P_D. The net benefits from the rice market (i.e., the net social value to the economy) is the shaded area, which can be divided up into the benefits to consumers, the consumer surplus triangle CS, and the benefits to producers, the producer surplus triangle PS.[3]

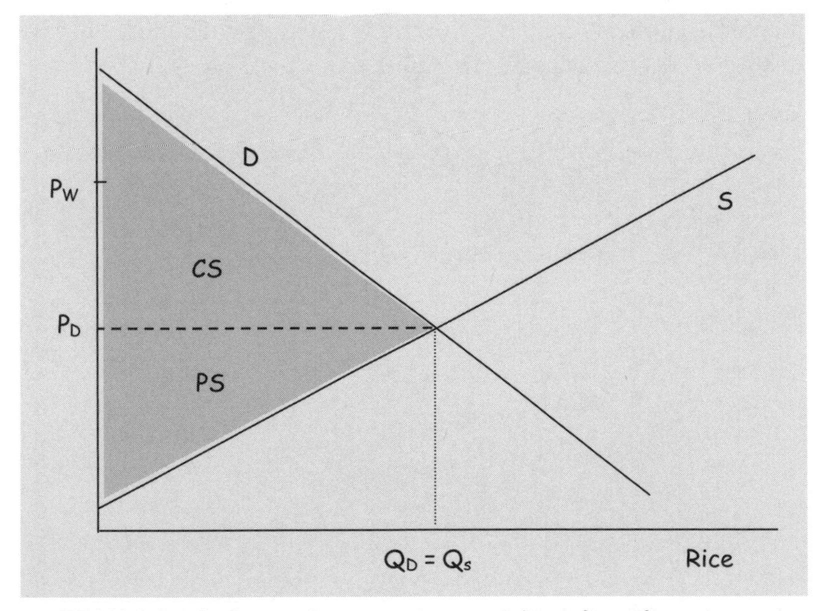

■ FIGURE 8.1 Market equilibrium and net social benefit with no rice trade

[3]See chapter 2 if these terms are unfamiliar.

The domestic market price in this case, P_D, is below the world price P_W. This means that this country is a potential exporter: at P_W producers would be willing to produce more than domestic consumers would be willing to buy. Looking at figure 8.1, we might expect to hear producers complaining that they could get a higher price if they could only export rice at P_W. Consumers, on the other hand, would prefer to keep the market domestic, so that they don't have to compete with foreign rice consumers who would pull the price up to P_W. When foreign demand is included, the demand curve becomes the "kinked" line DD_W in figure 8.2.

If unrestricted trade is allowed in this case, the demand for rice will include foreign demand, which is assumed to be "perfectly elastic" (horizontal) at the world price P_W, as shown in figure 8.2. This assumption of perfectly elastic demand is reasonable if the country is small relative to the size of the foreign market. Trading opportunities mean that rice production will rise to meet the foreign demand at P_W, which will raise the incomes of producers. Domestic consumers will have to pay more for rice, however, and will therefore consume less (the quantity demanded domestically will now be Q'_D while production will rise to equal domestic consumption plus exports, $Q'_D + Q_X$).

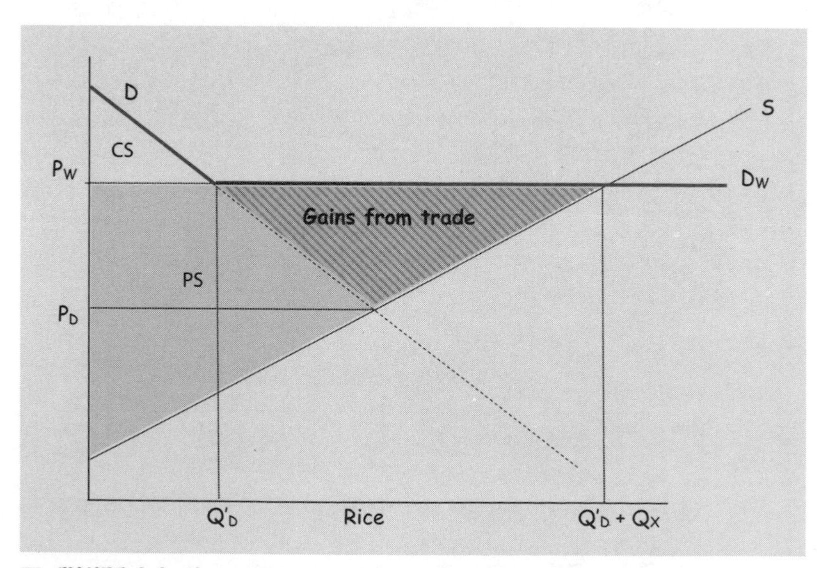

■ **FIGURE 8.2 Change in net social benefit and gains from rice trade**

In this simple case there are three effects of trade. First, producers are made better off because the (shaded) area of PS has increased. Second, consumers are made worse off because the area of CS has been reduced. And third, there are gains from trade because the gains by producers are larger than the losses by consumers. The net benefit or change in total economic surplus is equal to the striped area in figure 8.2 when compared with the original net benefit in figure 8.1.

Now let's look at an example of a country that is a potential importer. In the absence of any trade, the situation will look just like the one in figure 8.1, except that P_W will be below P_D rather than above it. Let's take the example of trade in bicycles, depicted in figure 8.3. What will happen if the borders are opened and trade is allowed in this case? The effects are similar to the export case, except that this time the winners are the consumers and the losers are the producers. We still expect to see gains from trade: the increase in CS will be greater than the decrease in PS, so that overall economic surplus or net benefits will increase, as indicated by the striped area in figure 8.3.

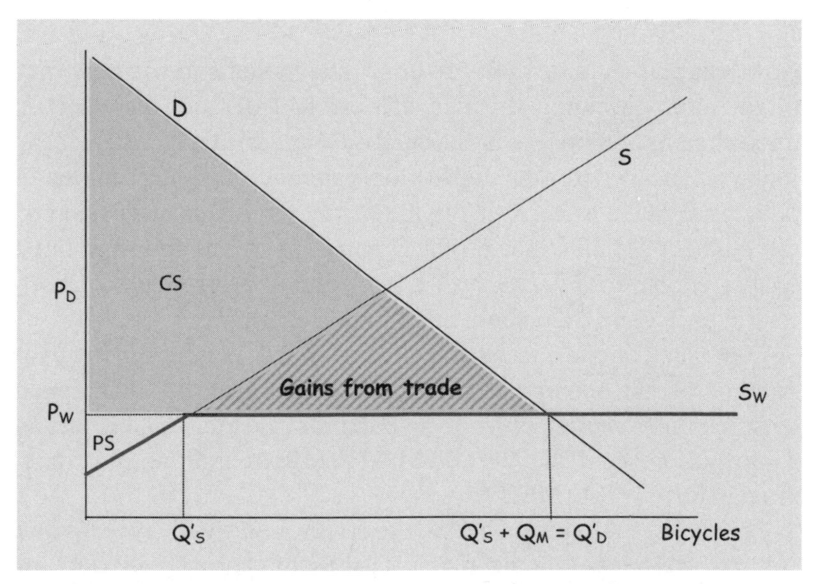

■ **FIGURE 8.3 Domestic market for bicycles with and without imports**

In the importing country, trade lowers the price for consumers, allowing them to consume more bicycles, Q'_D, and to spend a smaller share of their income on them. Consumer surplus grows larger. By contrast, domestic producers must now compete with foreign bicycle suppliers, meaning that prices drop and some producers leave this industry or reduce the scale of production (moving to Q'_S).

Based on these two simple models, the analysis suggests that eliminating barriers to trade will increase net benefits overall, but that for individual markets there will be winners and losers. There is an important realization in this: even if the elimination of trade barriers will generate gains from trade in each of one thousand markets for different goods, there are potentially one thousand interest groups representing either producers or consumers that will have reason to oppose the elimination of trade barriers. Even though trade represents an enlarged range of opportunities for consumers and producers, these added opportunities for some individuals represent threats to other individuals who must now compete with foreigners. Therein lie the incentives for trade barriers and protectionism.

Environmental Side Effects of Trade

Now let's add an externality to our trade model and see how that might alter our analysis. The effects will depend on whether environmental damage is associated with trade in exports or imports, and it will also depend on whether there are domestic policies in place to correct the externalities. A full discussion of the kinds of policies that might accomplish this is found in later chapters. Some readers may want to skip ahead to look at chapters in part 2 and then come back to this chapter.

Let's look at one case where an externality occurs during production of an exported good. We represent the difference between the marginal private cost and the marginal social cost as a marginal cost (MEC). We add MEC to MPC to get the total, marginal external cost (MEC).

In figure 8.4 we can see what effect trade will have. When exports are allowed, output will rise from Q_D to $Q'_D + Q_X$. But what will the net effect be? In this example we assume no controls on pollution (producers do not pay for these external costs), so production will increase to $Q'_D + Q_X$. There are gains from trade (the increase in producer surplus will exceed the reduction in consumer surplus), but there will also be an increase in environmental damage, and these may be small or large depending on the magnitude of marginal environmental damages. The increased inefficiency or deadweight loss (DWL) due to the environmental externality will equal the triangle DWL_E.

If, however, the country decided to ban trade, this would also result in inefficiencies and deadweight loss. The environmental damage would be reduced, but there would be no gains from trade. In this case the deadweight loss from no trade, DWL_{NT}, is indicated as the triangle above the domestic equilibrium point. Now, given the way it has been drawn, DWL_E appears to be slightly larger than DWL_{NT}, but the reverse could just as easily be true. The inefficiencies of either outcome (trade without environmental protection or no trade) could be very large or very small depending on the nature of the commodity and the magnitude of the environmental damages. The efficient outcome to the situation is at point A, with trade, but also with effective institutions to control environmental damage that align the private and

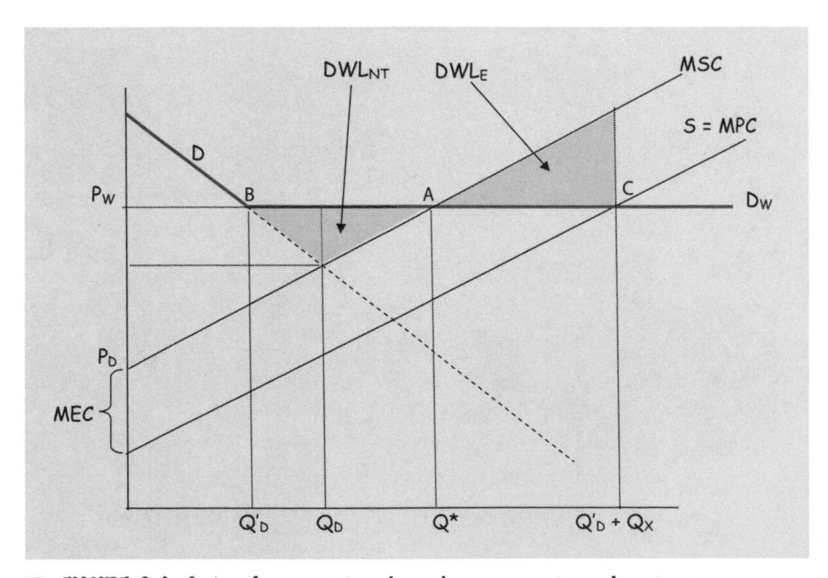

■ **FIGURE 8.4 Gains from trade when there are external costs**

social cost of the good being produced at MSC. If these policies were in place, then the supply of the good would fall along the MSC curve, and the equilibrium outcome with trade would be the optimal one, at point A, where P_W equals MSC and $Q = Q^*$.

We can represent the three allocation possibilities in figure 8.4 (A, B, and C) on a production possibilities frontier (PPF) as shown in figure 8.5. Point A is the efficient and optimal point that is on the production possibilities frontier. Points B and C are not optimal in terms of the allocation between market and nonmarket goods, and they will generally not be on the PPF. Point C could represent trade-induced excessive deforestation, overfishing, or highly polluting industries that have large health effects and reduce the productivity of the labor force. Market goods are produced at higher levels than at point A, but environmental quality and other nonmarket goods are available at much lower levels. Point B could represent trade restrictions that reduce job opportunities and lower income: environmental quality is high, but at a high cost in forgone market opportunities.

Of course, the optimal balance of market goods and environmental quality is something that people will disagree strongly

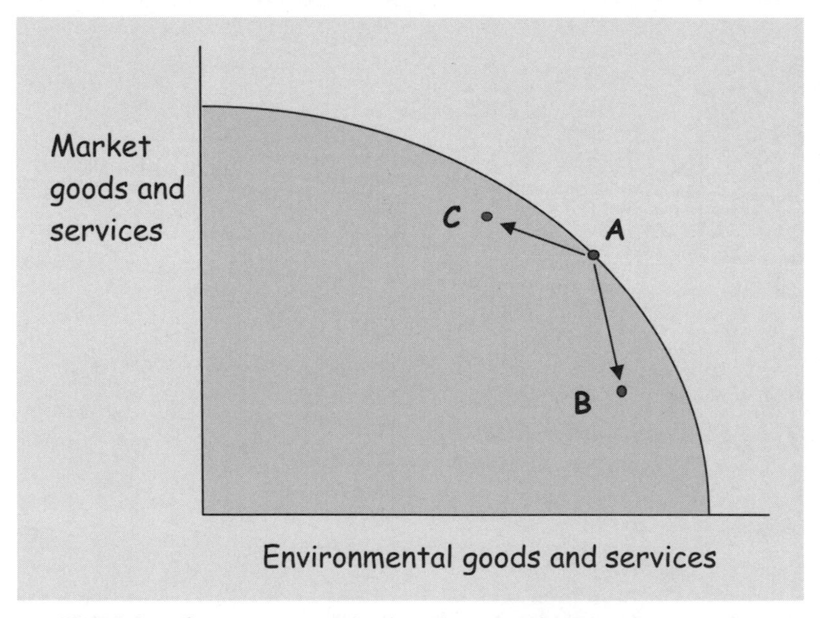

■ **FIGURE 8.5 Production possibilities with and without trade**

about. Some may prefer A, others B or C. Later in this book, in chapter 14, we discuss methods for environmental valuation and how this would help estimate social preferences.

Strategies and Interest groups

Even if markets within every country were perfectly competitive, it's unlikely that trade between countries would be perfectly competitive. Why? Recall that perfect competition will not occur with a monopoly, because a monopolist can manipulate prices and increase profits at the expense of consumers, and this will be inefficient. A country's government can do the same thing, acting like a monopolist by imposing trade barriers that manipulate trade flows and the prices of imports or exports in ways that benefit domestic groups at the expense of foreign groups.

Each country can try to take advantage of the other with tariffs, quotas, and other trade restrictions. Because these measures inflict costs and inefficiencies in both countries, this will make them both worse off. The payoffs for different trade policies can be characterized as a Prisoners' Dilemma game (see chapter 5). Each government may want to influence the market price for a particular commodity on behalf of the producers or consumers. Within a country there can be thousands of individual firms and consumer groups, none of which can influence price individually, but if their government weighs in to control exports or imports, perfect competition and efficiency can give way to highly distorted barriers to trade. This creates a situation where countries can either cooperate (low trade barriers) or defect (high trade barriers), much like a Prisoners' Dilemma game describing the tragedy of the commons. The situation can look like this:

Payoffs with and without trade barriers between countries

		Canada	
		Cooperate	Defect
United States	Cooperate	10\10	5\12
	Defect	14\3	7\6

Given these payoffs, the dominant strategy for both countries is to "defect." The United States is better off defecting no matter what Canada does (14 rather than 10 and 7 rather than 5). The same is true for Canada. Defecting is intended to represent high trade barriers; the payoffs for cooperating represent the gains from trade. The dilemma here is that if both countries act independently, then their incentive is to defect, and the likely outcome will be the bottom-right payoff (7\6), with payoffs below what could be achieved with cooperation (10\10).

Using game theory for models of this kind is now an important part of research in international economics. Defection represents the case where trade barriers are erected to protect a particular domestic interest group. Producers of lumber, steel, food, clothing, shrimp, fossil fuels, airplanes, and a multitude of other commodities have incentives to lobby their government to use trade restrictions to give them an advantage over foreign competition. Consumer groups and organized labor will also see potential gains from restricting trade in ways that manipulate the price or availability of goods in the market. Even if there were only two countries in the world, we would still need to think in terms of hundreds or thousands of Prisoners' Dilemma situations, one for each traded commodity and each interest group. In a world with about 189 countries, the number of potential strategic dilemmas becomes vast. By the 1940s, countries had mostly given in to these interests, and trade barriers between countries were very high. It is not surprising that it has taken more than fifty years of negotiations under the General Agreement on Tariffs and Trade (GATT) to reduce or eliminate most of those trade barriers, a difficult and painstaking shift from defection to cooperation requiring thirty thousand pages of rules!

Even with these thirty thousand pages of rules, all countries protect some parts of their domestic economies with trade restrictions. Many of these restrictions are allowed under the GATT and World Trade Organization (WTO) rules, in part because many of them have to do with legitimate social goals such as ensuring domestic food security, ensuring health and safety, or protecting globally endangered species. Generally speaking, these rules do not prohibit or conflict with domestic environmental laws or regulations, provided that foreign and domestic sources are subject to the same standards.

Still, governments constantly face strong pressures to impose protectionist trade restrictions despite signing on to these international agreements. The temptation to "defect" in a Prisoners' Dilemma game is unrelenting. How do they get around these agreements? Increasingly, governments try to "disguise" protections of domestic interest groups, sometimes citing insincere health, safety, or environmental concerns to justify thinly veiled protectionism. One of the current dilemmas facing the world's trade agreements, and the dispute resolution process of the WTO, is how to distinguish between legitimate and devious trade barriers.

Using these kinds of trade barriers to block competition is often defended as job protection, but estimates of the cost for the United States run as high as $170,000 per job saved.[4]

We can characterize three kinds of interests when we look at how trade issues and environmental (and other social) issues interact, especially in relation to negotiated agreements like the rules governing the WTO. First, there are domestic concerns: using trade barriers to limit domestic opportunities in order to further one group's domestic interests or to promote a goal such as food security or energy self-sufficiency. Second, there are foreign concerns: using trade barriers in order to further one's interests in a foreign issue. These include sanctions, boycotts, retaliatory trade barriers, and so on to influence foreign policies (such as human rights, labor standards, etc.). And third, there are global concerns: using trade barriers (or their removal) as a penalty (reward) for compliance by other countries in the use of a global resource (e.g., whaling ban, ban on trade in endangered species, Montreal Protocol, nuclear weapons agreements, or climate change agreements).

We can see each of these, potentially, as a legitimate use of trade barriers, depending on the issue, the justification, and the social choice process by which a policy is chosen. However, in all

[4]Gary Clyde Hufbauer and Kimberly Ann Elliott, *Measuring the Costs of Protection in the United States* (Washington, DC: Institute for International Economics, 1994).

cases, it must be recognized that domestic collective choice is only a part of what is going on here. In this setting, collective domestic decisions to introduce trade barriers are not independent of what other countries do. The use of trade barriers to influence the behavior of other countries (e.g., to impose sanctions on other countries) raises the possibility of retaliation from these other countries. In this setting, social choices become interdependent internationally.

Individual states in the United States often disagree with constraints placed on them by the federal government: there are benefits and costs to being part of the federation. In the same way, international interdependence, international markets, and international agreements like those imposed on members of the WTO bring a similar kind of trade-off into play. Trade is a two-way street. These realities of compromise and cooperation at the international level are not that new, but there appears to be a newfound awareness of how important they are, and there is an understandable level of anxiety and mistrust about these changes and how they will affect our lives now and in the future.

Globalization and the Race to the Bottom

There are many issues related to trade and globalization that have economic dimensions, but many of these topics go beyond economics. One issue frequently raised is the concern that globalization, trade, and foreign investment lead to a "race to the bottom" for both environmental protection and the wages of workers. In the case of environmental protection, this idea is also referred to as the "pollution havens" hypothesis, suggesting that as poor countries try to attract foreign investments they compete by relaxing their environmental standards for fear that more stringent regulations will deter firms from investing in their countries. Numerous studies have examined data on environmental policy and trade and investment flows between countries, and the weight of the evidence suggests, first, that trade liberalization has a positive effect on economic growth,[5] and second, that rising

[5]Winters, McCulloch, and McKay, "Trade Liberalization and Poverty: The Evidence So Far."

per capita incomes can often affect the environment in positive ways—consistent with the idea of an environmental Kuznets curve discussed in chapter 7. Among these studies, there is very little evidence of "pollution-havens-driven" trade, although there may be small effects that are difficult to detect.[6] Some researchers have concluded that the cost of compliance with environmental regulations is a small portion of production costs, and that low labor costs and the political stability of the country are much more likely to affect these investment decisions.[7]

In the case of workers' wages, the claim is that foreign investors contribute to a race to the bottom by encouraging countries to compete by lowering their wages so that the "winner" is the country that lowers its wages the most. Not only is this view unsupported by evidence, it is hard to square with a simple analysis of supply and demand.

Let's look once again at the market for labor where supply and derived demand interact. Figure 8.6 characterizes a labor market in a developing country where demand, D, and supply, S, lead to an equilibrium wage W_1. This wage may be very low by the standards of high-income countries, but this is due in part to having a large and willing labor force (causing the supply curve to be relatively low and to the right), and because the scarcity of capital (physical and human) means the productivity of labor is low (causing the demand curve to be relatively low and to the left).

What can we expect when foreign firms, like Nike or computer electronics manufacturers, set up production facilities in this country? This creates additional demand for labor, shifting the demand curve to the right (from D to D′). This shift will put upward pressure on both wages and employment, toward W_2 and Q_2, and these would appear to be welcome changes for the workers in this country.

---

[6]Brian R. Copeland and M. Scott Taylor, "Trade, Growth and the Environment," *Journal of Economic Literature* 42, no. 1 (2004): 7–71.

[7]See Adam Jaffe, Steven Peterson, Paul Portney, and Robert Stavins, "Environmental Regulation and the Competitiveness of U.S. Manufacturing: What Does the Evidence Tell Us?" *Journal of Economic Literature* 33 (1995): 132–163; and David Wheeler, "Racing to the Bottom? Foreign Investment and Air Pollution in Developing Countries Source," *Journal of Environment and Development* 10, no. 3 (2001): 225–245.

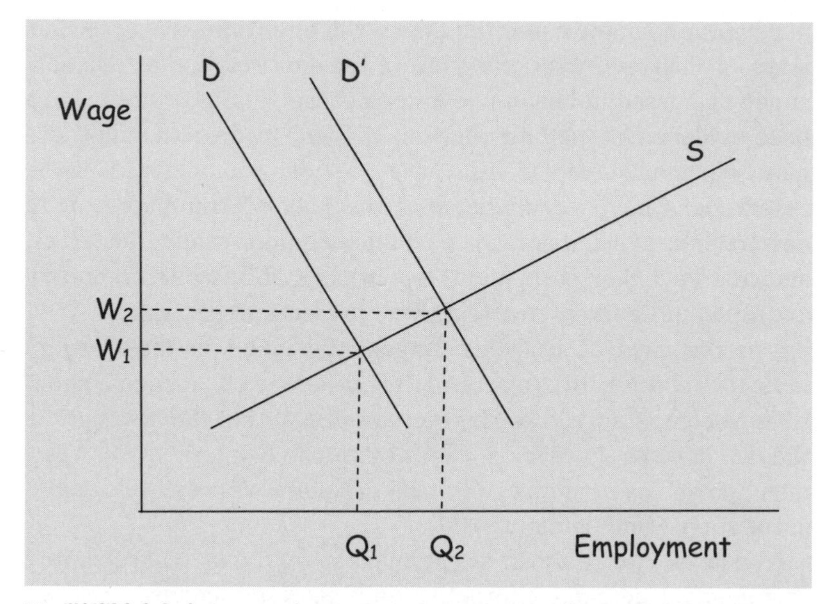

■ **FIGURE 8.6 Labor markets adjustments to direct foreign investment**

Indeed, the implications from this simple market analysis are consistent with the evidence found in numerous country studies. Recent research that has looked at manufacturing wage data across all plants in low-income countries has found, in every case, that foreign-owned plants pay higher wages than locally owned firms. This may be due in part to better technology that makes their workers more productive, or because they try to attract the best workers. This evidence does not mean that multinational firms could not be asked to do more in terms of wages, working conditions, or safety standards, but the evidence strongly suggests that, in general, these workers are better off with foreign investors than they would be without them.

Still, it is certainly true that firms that want to invest in other countries are looking for the best deal and the lowest cost, but that kind of motivation tends to underlie consumer and producer behavior in any market. In that sense, a race to the bottom in labor markets is just like any other efficiently functioning market. Gains from trade occur when countries exploit their own comparative advantage, and a large workforce willing to work at relatively low wages is one such comparative advantage.

People's willingness to work for low wages and their demand for goods and environmental quality depend on many things, including their income. As income rises, we expect to see changes in the demand for market goods, education, health care, and sanitation. In the context of many global issues, such as the fair wages, labor standards, or environmental quality in low-income countries, it is useful to recognize just how different the perspectives of people in low-income countries may be from the perspectives of people in high-income countries. Figure 8.7 offers a reminder of the magnitude of those differences.

In this chapter on trade we have presented the basic theory and central principles, but we have just scratched the surface of the many important issues where market efficiency, country sovereignty, and environmental issues intersect. When most economist's talk about "free trade" they really mean "efficient trade," trade that recognizes how externalities and some protectionist tendencies can cause trade to be inefficient and distortionary in ways that can encourage environmental degradation. Efficient trade, therefore, presupposes that governments have used effective policy tools to correct for those kinds of market failures. And it is those policy tools that we now turn our attention toward in part 2.

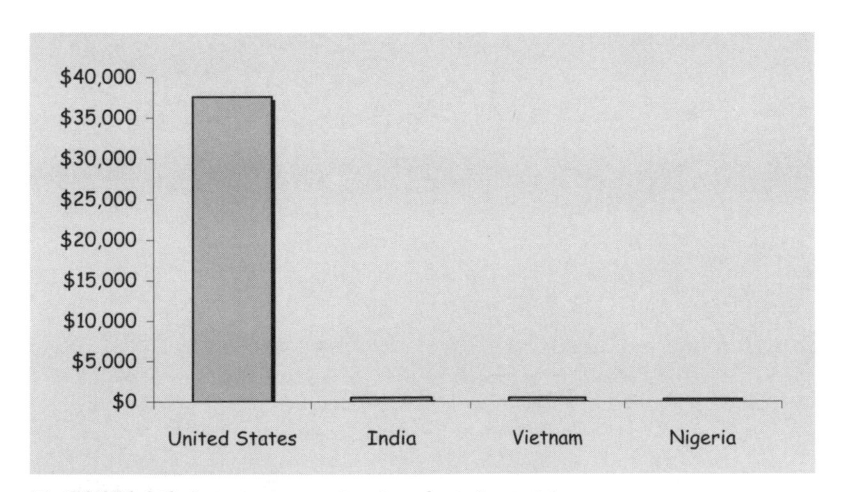

FIGURE 8.7 Income per capita in selected countries
Source: World Bank Group, *World Development Indicators 2005* (Washington, DC: World Bank Group, 2005). Available at http://www.worldbank.org/data/wdi2005/index.html.

Recommended Readings and References

An introduction to international trade can be found in many intermediate microeconomics textbooks like those mentioned at the end of previous chapters. For an international economics textbook, see Paul R. Krugman and Maurice Obsfeld, *International Economics: Theory and Policy*, 6th ed. (Reading, MA: Addison-Wesley, 2002).

For recent surveys of evidence on the relationship between trade liberalization and economic growth, see L. Alan Winters, Neil McCulloch, and Andrew McKay, "Trade Liberalization and Poverty: The Evidence So Far," *Journal of Economic Literature* 42, no. 1 (2004): 72–115. On trade, growth, and the environment, see Brian R. Copeland and M. Scott Taylor, *Trade and the Environment: Theory and Evidence* Princeton, NJ: Princeton University Press, 2003); and Brian R. Copeland and M. Scott Taylor, "Trade, Growth and the Environment," *Journal of Economic Literature* 42, no. 1 (2004): 7–71.

For a useful primer on trade and the environment, see *Environment and Trade: a Handbook*, a joint product of the International Institute for Sustainable Development and the United Nations Environment Programme. It is available at http://www.iisd.org/trade/handbook/.

PART II
Institutions and Policy Approaches

9

Rules of the Game

For somebody like Robinson Crusoe, alone and isolated on an island, allocating resources would not require a book about economics. Presumably, in a world with only one person, that individual would make choices and allocate resources based on his or her preferences and priorities. This would likely involve making trade-offs at the margin, weighing the present against the future, and doing so in a more or less rational and efficient way. While we might wish to examine these choices and subject them to economic analysis, what would be the use of doing so?

Institutions

In a world with more than one person, conflicts arise when the choices of one individual conflict with those of other individuals. For these more realistic situations, some way to minimize or avoid conflicts is needed: rules or other mechanisms that resolve the conflicts and achieve the desired level of coordination among people. Economists refer to these kinds of mechanisms or rules of the game as **institutions, meaning any humanly devised mechanism or tool that influences individuals' incentives and choices by either constraining, guiding, or encouraging certain kinds of actions.**

Take, for example, a sidewalk. It's a resource that can be used by many people to get from one place to another. At a given point in time, one pedestrian is using only a small portion of the sidewalk, but conflicts arise when pedestrians going in both directions want to use the same piece of sidewalk at the same time. Clearly, this is a problem of resource allocation, and a number of different mechanisms could be proposed to coordinate use of the sidewalk. For example, a "central planner" could assign individuals to specific portions of the sidewalk at specified times. But this seems absurdly impractical, especially since there is a simple rule that works amazingly well: "stay to the right."

This stay-to-the-right rule is an elegant example of a mechanism or institution that solves a coordination problem by bringing order to the use of the sidewalk. It is also a self-reinforcing rule. There is little incentive to violate the rule because, if you do, you will likely slow yourself down by bumping into more people. This attribute of self-reinforcement is important because, if the rule were not self-enforcing, we might need sidewalk police to enforce it, which could become very costly.

Unfortunately, similarly simple, elegant, and self-enforcing institutions are not readily available to solve many of the coordination problems we face in society, so more complex and more costly approaches to coordinate are necessary. These approaches will have different attributes, advantages, and disadvantages. Given a menu of alternative institutions to choose from, we will want to consider how effective and how costly each is likely to be. As we will see, large differences in the costs of different approaches can give one mechanism important advantages over others.

Key Concepts: *Formal and informal institutions* 

Let's start by making a distinction between formal institutions and informal institutions. **Formal institutions are established by governments and enforced by them. These include property rights, regulations, and criminal laws. Informal institutions include social norms, culture, etiquette, ethics, and moral rules.** Informal institutions can be extremely important in affecting how people behave and how they allocate resources. The formal rules tend to be more apparent and in some cases easier to change. Informal institutions in a society tend to be more subtle and often evolve and change slowly. However, the social norms, etiquette, and ethics affecting people's behavior and interactions are probably just as important as formal institutions for social coordination.

One important kind of institution is the market, although markets actually reflect the interactions of several institutions. We talked earlier about the strict set of conditions that would need to be satisfied for markets to be perfectly competitive and Pareto efficient. But the idea of efficient markets presupposes efficiency of property rights. Property rights are what's really being traded in a market. Markets are where we transfer ownership for goods and services from one person to another. Government plays a key role in establishing, monitoring, and enforcing these property rights, and we will want to distinguish private property from common property. This is important because many environmental issues involve problems of ownership and property rights. Let's take a closer look.

Private Property

Just as in the case of markets, where certain conditions must be satisfied in order for markets to be efficient under perfect competition, there are four conditions that ensure efficiency with respect to private property. And just as in the case of markets (where they never really live up to the ideal of perfect competition), the ideal conditions for unattenuated, or complete and efficient, private property rights also run into complications in the real world. **The four conditions for efficient property rights are that they be (1) individually owned, (2) completely specified, (3) secure and fully enforced, and (4) transferable.**

Key Concept: *Conditions for efficient property rights*

As we will see, it is often the characteristics of different kinds of property that determine the success or failure of a given form of ownership. But let's start with a very broad perspective. The fundamental way that economists interpret the benefits of property rights is to say that they reduce uncertainty. The idea is that we can all make better choices and allocate our resources more efficiently the more certain we are about what to expect from people around us. For example, if I own a car (i.e., if I have the rights associated with car ownership), I am more certain about being able to drive to work each day. If I own land, I may consider planting an apple tree with the confidence that I will be able to enjoy its fruits at some time in the future. A ticket to a concert assures us of having a place to sit and enjoy the performance, and so on.

As legal experts are quick to explain, however, ownership of something does not imply the right to do anything you want with it. Ownership entitles you to a limited set of rights. You cannot torture your pets, burn your book inside my piano, or drill for oil in your urban backyard. Each of these examples involves an externality of some kind, and externalities are precisely what create the uncertainties that make property rights valuable: they help eliminate externalities or at least make them more predictable. If ownership of a car did not mean that you had a right to control its use, then ownership would not help reduce the uncertainty about whether the car would be where you left it when you needed it. Uncertainty about the security of ownership for agricultural land can have adverse effects on the land's productivity.

We'll come to enforcement in a minute, but first let's consider a world in which all private property is secure with no concern about theft or trespassing. Would this eliminate all uncertainty problems? No. One of the main reasons for this has to do with proximity, with the benefits from your property rights when enjoyed in the proximity of others who may be enjoying their own property rights and who are doing so in ways that create unanticipated externalities. A theater ticket guarantees you a seat, but it does not guarantee that the person behind you will keep quiet. You may reserve a campsite at a national park, but that does not protect you from loud neighbors during the night. These examples may represent only temporary annoyances, but when it comes to ownership of land or house, externalities can be disastrous and last a very long time when incompatible or conflicting activities are within the rights of neighboring property owners. Externalities related to land use and land use policy are taken up in chapter 11.

Let's return to those four conditions for efficient property rights. The first condition is individual ownership, which eliminates many coordination problems. Anytime more than one person has rights to use property, coordination becomes an issue (just ask a car-owning parent with teenage children old enough to drive). This will be a central issue when we discuss common property later.

The second condition about completely specified rights is more complex than it appears. To be truly "completely specified," we would need to establish rules for all contingencies, including those involving noisy neighbors at the theater or campground; whether home owners can build additions on their homes that block the neighbor's view of the mountains or plant a tree that will cast a shadow on the neighbor's vegetable garden; whether I can play my tuba in a public library or sell my gun to a child. Unless the rights related to every possible contingency are specified, then this second condition does not hold.

The third condition—secure and fully enforced rights—says nothing about the costs of enforcement. In many cases this cost is *the* central issue when comparing different property rights arrangements. And the fourth condition—transferability—is necessary for efficiency because it enables goods and services to find (via markets) their highest-value use. Of course, exchange in markets is costly, for example, when consumers are trying to find what they want at the best price, and when suppliers are trying to find the buyer who will pay the most. (Reducing this kind of transaction cost is precisely what has made e-Bay so successful.)

Yes, private property and market exchange can be a highly efficient way to allocate many kinds of resources. The problem is that the ideal conditions for efficient private property and market exchange do not come close to reality in most cases. One of the reasons for this has to do with situations where monitoring and enforcement are very costly or just plain impossible. Pencils, shoes, and umbrellas do not pose major problems in terms of satisfying these four conditions, but what about the air, rivers, whales, populations of migratory seabirds, and the ozone layer? Individual private ownership is just not a practical way to allocate many kinds of resources much as it is not practical to have a central planner allocate space on the sidewalk.

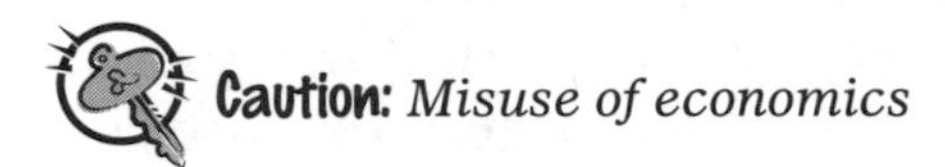

Some committed advocates of private property rights argue that essentially all resources would be better allocated with private ownership and market allocation, including environmental resources. In some cases these advocates will point to anecdotal evidence from unique situations as evidence that proves their point. This "one-size-fits-all" view, however, is frequently driven by ideology—such as libertarianism or the free enterprise/ property rights movement—rather than the result of a thorough examination of the evidence, or a recognition of how monitoring and enforcement costs differ greatly for different kinds of resources and in different circumstances. Indeed, the four conditions for unattenuated property rights (and also elements of the Coase Theorem described next) are frequently cited as "proof" that private property and markets are *always* better than approaches involving government. Well, that's just silly.

The question should not be, which institution is always best, private property (and markets) or public ownership (and government)? The more useful question is, which institution will do the best job of promoting social objectives at the lowest cost in a given situation? But before we delve into more detail about the alternatives to private property (common property and open access), we need to make a detour of sorts to discuss some important ideas about property rights and externalities, specifically the often misunderstood and misused Coase Theorem.

The Coase Theorem

Key Concept: *Reciprocal externalities* 

The Coase Theorem refers to an important point made by Nobel laureate Ronald Coase in a 1960 paper called "The Problem of Social Cost." The most important point Coase made is not particularly controversial. Coase points out that from an economic perspective, **externalities are reciprocal;** they can go either way—from A to B or from B to A—depending on how the property right (or liability) is defined. He uses an example of a doctor's office located next to a confectioner, where the confectioner's noisy equipment makes it impossible for the doctor to examine patients. Coase's point is that while the noise may physically travel in one direction, the direction of the externality (in economic terms) can go either way depending on the prevailing property rights or liability rules. If a confectioner has a right to make candy at this location, then she does indeed impose an externality on the doctor. But what if the doctor has a right to a certain level of quiet (meaning the confectioner is liable for disturbing the doctor's work)? In that case, the doctor is imposing an externality on the confectioner because the doctor's right to quiet imposes a cost on the confectioner: she must either shut down the confectionary or install noise proofing.

Coase recognizes how property rights, liability, and the burden of proof related to an externality can be defined either way in the law. This is not just a trivial theoretical point. For example, most people would assume that if a rancher's cows wander into someone's flower garden and damage it, the rancher is liable for his cow's damage. Well, in Wyoming, it's the other way around: the gardener is responsible for keeping cows out of the garden. Forty years ago smokers in the United States had a right to smoke wherever they pleased, imposing an externality on the nonsmokers who would have to go outside to avoid second-hand smoke. Nowadays, society generally supports the rights of nonsmokers to clean air, so the "property right" (the prevailing institution) has been reversed and smokers, now on the receiving end of the externality, must go outside to smoke. Indeed, in some cases the direction of the externality changes with the time of day. Typically, urban residents have the right to play music or be noisy in their homes except during designated quiet hours (e.g., from 11 P.M. to 6 A.M.) when the property right or liability is reversed so that neighbors have a right to quiet.

Key Concept: *Precautionary principle*

Coase's central idea is also relevant when external damages are uncertain. Who has a right to impose risks or "potential damage" on others? If the risks are uncertain, who should bear the burden of proof? The liability for uncertain damages can shift as the degree of uncertainty diminishes (as in the case of smoking where, between the 1960s and the present, the health risks from smoking have become accepted as fact). But even when risks are highly uncertain the liability and the burden of proof can be established either way. Here there are sharp differences between the United States and the European Union on environmental issues. In Europe, the **precautionary principle** seems to be widely accepted. It means that actions that have uncertain, but potentially damaging, effects on the environment should not be allowed unless it can be shown that the risks are low or the harms are small. In the United States, the precautionary principle has much less influence on policy. The precaution or burden of proof tends to run in the opposite direction: the actions of individual entrepreneurs should not be constrained unless it can be shown that they are harmful. Indeed, the different approaches taken by the European Union and the U.S. government toward climate change appear to reflect these differing perspectives, as does their approaches toward genetically modified (GM) food. In the case of GM food, the implications of the Coase Theorem and burden of proof can be quite surprising, for example, when windblown genetically modified pollen "contaminates" a farmer's crop, yet that same farmer is then held liable for stealing the patented genetically modified product (see box 5).

The second major point from Coase's paper is more controversial, in part because it is often misinterpreted. Under certain assumptions, Coase observed, it doesn't matter who gets the

BOX 5

Property Rights and Liability with Genetically Engineered Crops

Percy Schmeiser, a canola farmer in Saskatchewan, found in the mid-1990s that some edges of his fields had become contaminated with Monsanto's Roundup Ready canola from either pollen drift or truck spillage from a neighbor. Nobody knows for sure. Schmeiser was unhappy about this contamination because he had been saving and developing his own disease-resistant canola for fifty years, and Monsanto's varieties were inferior to his in this regard.

To Percy Schmeiser's surprise, Monsanto sued him in 1998 for illegally growing its Roundup Ready canola without a license, violating Monsanto's patent on the gene. Monsanto wanted Schmeiser to pay damages and legal costs that could reach several hundred thousand dollars.

To many people's surprise, the courts agreed. In June 2000 the Federal Court of Canada ruled that it didn't matter how the pollination occurred, it still infringed on Monsanto's patent, and that any cross-pollinated canola on Schmeiser's fields was the property of Monsanto so the corporation could confiscate his crop. Essentially, the patent and property rights laws were found to override the rights of farmers in this case.

That wasn't the end of the story, however. In May 2004 the Canadian Supreme Court ruled on the case, also finding that Schmeiser infringed on Monsanto's patents. The court prohibited Schmeiser from using Monsanto's technology in the future and required him to turnover any contaminated seed. The court found, however, that Schmeiser did not intentionally make use of the benefits of the patented technology (by spraying the crop with Roundup), and so no financial damages were awarded to Monsanto.

This kind of ownership law and involuntary liability is a very new phenomenon. It's unclear where future rulings will lead. Laws and court interpretations may change as the scope and potential costs of rulings of this kind become more apparent—in terms of the social efficiency of the outcomes (as discussed later in this chapter).

This ruling may not be all good news for Monsanto, however. Percy Schmeiser's wife, Louise, has since filed a claim seeking $140 in damages from Monsanto for the costs of removing Roundup Ready canola plants from her organic garden. She claims that Monsanto owns and controls the gene, so the liability issue now follows the flow of the gene, making Monsanto liable for contamination and pollution of anybody's field with its product.

property right related to an external effect (e.g., either full liability or no liability for the confectioner), the outcome could still be efficient. The reason for this is that, assuming zero bargaining or transaction costs, the two parties could bargain. If the confectioner is liable for her noise, she can offer to pay the doctor to let her operate her machinery. If the confectioner is not liable, the doctor could offer to pay the confectioner to halt operating the machinery. This part of Coase's analysis is interesting theoretically, but it's largely irrelevant to most real-world problems because transaction costs are usually prohibitively large. It's also just a restatement of a familiar point about market efficiency, applied to new kinds of "commodities": noise, pollution, or other external effects.

But this is where free market enthusiasts jump up and say, "Ah ha! No need for government; private actions like bargaining can solve environmental problems, and Coase proved it." Well, not so fast. If there are no transaction costs, then Coase is correct, an efficient outcome will occur no matter who is given the initial property right. It seems plausible that one doctor and one confectioner might actually bargain this way, but what about more realistic examples involving more than two people? What about two neighbors being affected by a third noisy neighbor late on a rainy night? What about an upstream factory and a few downstream fishing communities? What about Canadians being impacted by acid rain from Midwest power plants? As the number of individuals involved increases beyond two or three, the assumption that independent bargaining will occur becomes highly dubious. While Coase understood this, some current enthusiasts for this idea do not.

A third key point related to Coase's ideas (but not directly part of his analysis) involves just these kinds of situations where transaction costs are very high and direct bargaining just isn't going to happen. In the absence of some kind of government regulation or other policy, can we say anything about which property right (full liability versus no liability) is preferable or which is more efficient?

To answer this, we need to revisit the distinction between Pareto efficiency and social efficiency. Pareto efficiency, as explained in chapter 2, refers to a situation with an existing set of property rights, endowments, and other institutions; it assesses whether the allocation of resources in that situation could be altered in a way that would make at least one person better off without making anyone worse off. If the answer is no, then the allocation is said to be Pareto efficient *for those specific initial conditions*. Social efficiency, by contrast, compares different institutional arrangements and evaluates them from the perspective of net social benefits.

Let's look at an example. Consider the case of an upstream farming community whose cattle and irrigation practices reduce the water quality and river flows to downstream portions of the river. A community downstream relies on fishing, including salmon that spawn in the stream and are harmed by the upstream farming practices. The situation is depicted in figure 9.1. We want to compare two alternative property rights: full liability (FL), meaning that the party creating the physical externality (upstream) is liable for the damages they cause, and no liability (NL), meaning that the party bears no liability for those damages.

Let's assume there is no possibility of direct bargaining between the two communities, and there are no government polices such as regulation. This means that under no liability, the farming community will be unconstrained and will choose Q_{NL} since the cost to them of polluting is zero. The deadweight loss at

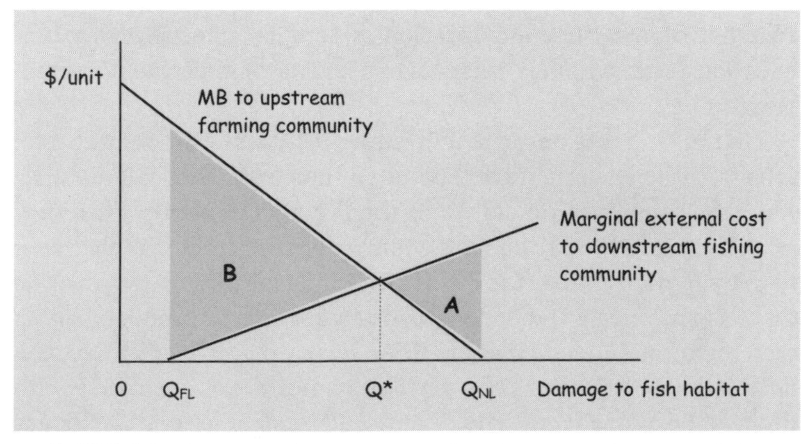

■ **FIGURE 9.1 An externality between a farming community and a fishing community**

Q_{NL} (net benefit compared with the optimal allocation at Q*) is the shaded area A. If, instead, there is full liability, then the farming community will be constrained at Q_{FL}. In this situation the deadweight loss is the difference between net benefits at Q_{FL} and at the optimum, Q*, or the shaded area B.

Beginning at full liability, no Pareto improvement is possible by switching to no liability, because it makes somebody worse off. The same is true going the other direction from no to full liability. Which situation is Pareto efficient? These two property rights situations are considered "Pareto incomparable." Neither can be said to be "Pareto superior" to the other. You may notice, though, that the deadweight loss for full liability is larger than at no liability. This means that the net social benefit is greater for no liability than for full liability. So, using the criterion of maximizing net social benefit, we can say that social efficiency is higher with no liability than with full liability.

Is there a connection between the Pareto criterion and social efficiency? The connection can be made by referring to a "potential Pareto improvement." A potential Pareto improvement is a change with winners and losers, but if the winners compensated the losers for their losses, no one would be worse off and at least one person would be better off than before. If no liability has a higher net social benefit than full liability, then it has to be the case that a switch from full liability to no liability would satisfy the criterion for a potential Pareto improvement. Whether or not the compensation is actually paid is a separate question from whether the social benefits of the change would be positive.

In the example described in figure 9.1, area A is smaller than area B. If the reverse were true, as in figure 9.2, then full liability would be socially efficient. Does the social efficiency of the situation have anything to do with which property right is most likely to exist in the real world? This is an important question, and one that has spawned a lively debate. One view is that property rights tend to be established, and modified over time, in ways that maximize social welfare. This view is sometimes associated with Richard Posner, a legal scholar and U.S. federal judge. The idea is that our laws are made and modified in ways that seem to promote social efficiency. For example, if, at some time in the past, a situation looked like that in figure 9.1, we would expect no liability to be the established legal rule. If, over time, population increased downstream, or the value of fish increased relative to agricultural products, the situation might change to one that looked more like the situation in figure 9. 2.

If our laws are responsive to opportunities for increasing social welfare, then we would expect the laws to change from no liability to full liability. But it would be naive to think that these changes just happen automatically to maximize social welfare, especially when those who stand to lose the most will fight to retain the status quo. Smoking is an example where the liability changed as public understanding of the health costs of secondhand smoke changed. But U.S. mining law offers a counterexample, where rights and liability have not shifted much in light of changing demographics and environmental concerns. One reason has to do with the vested interests that will resist change if they are not compensated. For example, tobacco companies spent huge sums over several decades to halt or slow the erosion of smokers' rights. And oil-exporting countries, oil companies, and industries dependent on fossil fuel industry are currently waging a global campaign to undermine the science and policies to slow

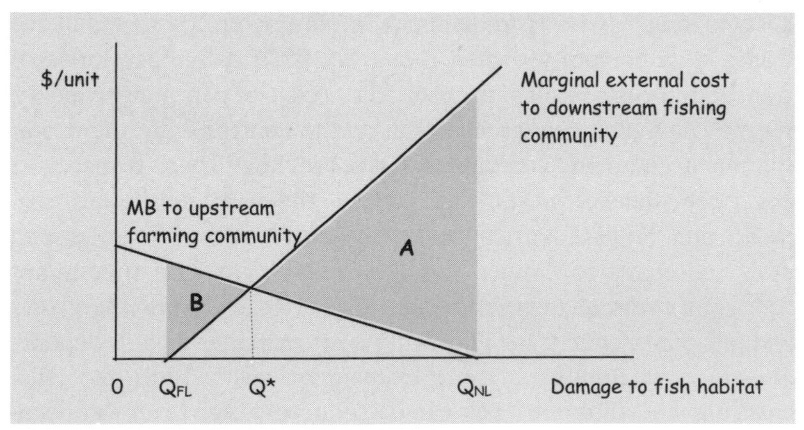

FIGURE 9.2 An externality between a farming community and a fishing community

climate change. These efforts can be seen as examples of "rent seeking," a topic discussed more in chapter 13.

Common Property

Although private property is probably the most basic institution affecting the allocation of resources, common property, with multiple owners or users, is an alternative that is also prevalent and can have advantages over private property in some cases. Given the importance of these two basic kinds of property rights, we'll start off by comparing the two and asking which one makes the most sense in different kinds of situations.

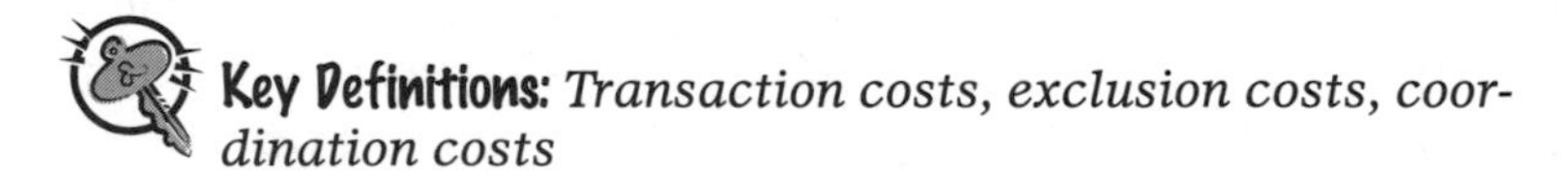

Key Definitions: *Transaction costs, exclusion costs, coordination costs*

Just as efficient private property involves costs, so does common property. When considering whether private property or common property is preferable for a given resource, we would like to know whether these costs are relatively large or small. **Economists call these costs transaction costs, to refer to all the costs associated with a particular institutional mechanism, including monitoring and enforcement, administrative costs, waste, and so on.** In the case of private property, the owner incurs costs to keep others from using or infringing on the rights of the owner of a privately owned resource. We'll call these kinds of transaction costs **exclusion costs.** In the case of common property, we also have transaction costs related to coordinating the use of the resource among a group of users. We'll call these transaction costs **coordination costs**, and include the monitoring, enforcement, and administrative costs (meetings, dispute settlement, etc.) necessary to control the free rider problems that tempt users of a common property. Choosing between common property and private property for allocating a given resource will depend, among other things, on these transaction costs. Both exclusion costs and coordination costs can be relatively high or low depending on a variety of factors. If the exclusion costs for private property are lower than the coordination costs for common property, then private property would be preferable (if there are no other reasons to favor the high-cost arrangement over the low-cost arrangement). If the costs of exclusion are higher than the costs of coordination, then common property should prevail.

In figure 9.3 we can represent a particular resource in a specific kind of setting (e.g., a pasture in fourteenth-century Spain, a well in an African village) as a point that reflects the transaction costs that would result under either private property or common property. The coordinates of each point represent the coordination costs that would exist under common property (the value on the *x* axis) and the exclusion costs that would exist under private property (the value on the *y* axis). Either type of transaction cost may be relatively high or low depending on the characteristics of the resource, the characteristics of the group of users, and the larger socioeconomic setting in which they reside.

For a sidewalk, we might indicate this as point A on the graph, where the costs of coordination are very low relative to the costs of exclusion under private property. The property rights institution in this case is just the self-enforcing, informal stay-to-the-right rule. For wristwatches, we might find that private property costs (individual ownership including protecting your wristwatch from theft) are lower than under common property (some

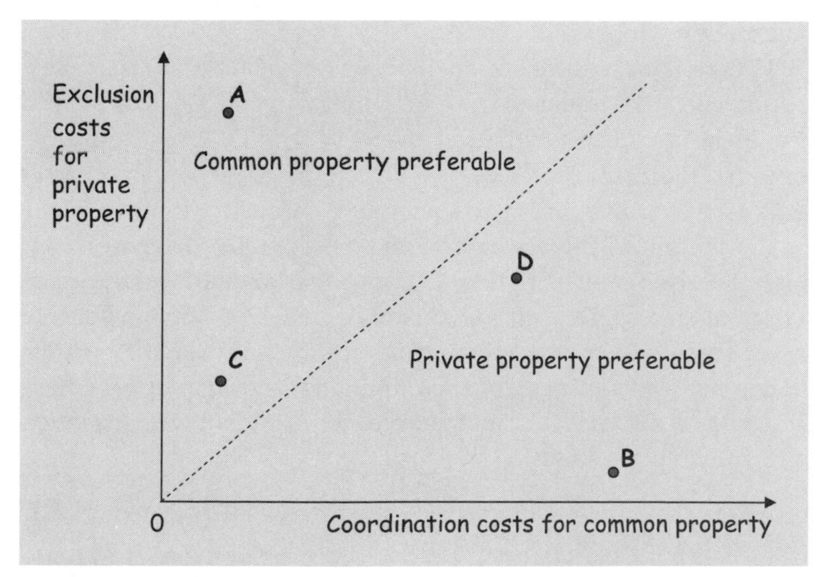

■ **FIGURE 9.3 Transaction costs for private property and common property**

arrangement whereby wristwatches are shared among a group of people). We might represent this example as point B. Depending on the region or country in question, timber resources might be situated at either point C or point D; the same could be true for elk or buffalo herds, or an aquifer.

The coordinates depicted in a graph like this for a given kind of resource would vary by location and would also change with changing circumstances such as population or social cohesion. Presumably, a common property wristwatch could be shared among members of a small family at lower coordination costs than among all residents of a town. Neighbors sometimes adopt common property for ladders or other yard tools, or even a trailer or pickup truck, which are normally seen as private property. Although many people think of industrialized countries as dominated by private property, common property arrangements abound, often managed by a more formal common property institution: government. Our air, water, public lands, and forests are all forms of common property allocated under a set of government rules and regulations. For some resources, such as migratory seabirds, whales, and the global atmosphere, national government institutions are not adequate. Forms of international common property are reflected in treaties such as the Law of the Sea and the Montreal Protocol.

There is a third choice, open access. In some cases the transaction costs for either private or common property will exceed the benefits of establishing property rights. This could be because the resource has a low value, or because establishing effective coordination or exclusion is very costly (think of rocks at the bottom of the ocean, or lunar real estate). In these cases open access (no effective institution) can actually be the most efficient choice, leaving the resource available for anybody to use. In many other cases, though, open access is the outcome popularly known as tragedy of the commons (see chapter 5), where institutions are absent or ineffective, resulting in the degradation of a valuable resource.

An Unfortunate Dualism

Regrettably, comparisons of the advantages of private versus common property have become entangled in an ideological debate between the merits of free markets (private property and free enterprise) on the one hand and the role of government on the other hand. What is unfortunate is that these issues are framed as an "either/or" choice between free markets and government regulation. In reality, neither choice can be said to always be better than the other. Some resources can go either way, private or common property, depending on the circumstances and especially depending on the influence of other institutions. Bank accounts are normally private property, but marriage or membership in a club can produce circumstances when a common property bank account makes sense. The privacy of one's "own backyard" is a familiar right, but increasingly, common property landscaping has become widespread in residential gated communities. Aren't the books in a library just the common property of a city? Aren't corporations owned collectively by the stockholders? The rules for using library books in a city are no different in principle from the common property rules found to exist in many parts of the world for pastures, forests, fisheries, or water. What may surprise some readers is the evidence that in many cases these common properties were being used efficiently, perhaps more efficiently than if they had been allocated on the basis of private property institutions (see box 6). Some reflection on the workings of a typical household should make this point clear. Some items in a household tend to be individually owned; others tend to be common property.

Institutional Teamwork

To complete this picture, we need to recognize that property right institutions, whether private or common, rarely function in isolation. Typically, resource allocations are influenced by a mix of overlapping and interacting institutions, including private property rights, government regulations and policies, and local rules or informal social norms. "Free markets" don't exist. What economists sometimes mean when they refer to a free market is an efficiently functioning market, one where private property rights are defined and enforced by government, where contracts and exchanges are monitored and validated with the aid of government, and where government facilitates the smooth functioning of markets by setting standards for weights, measures, safety, and quality and disseminating information helpful to reducing market

BOX 6

The Maine Harbor Gangs

Many case studies demonstrate that under the right conditions, common property or common pool resource management can be efficient with informal institutions that prevent free riding and the "tragedy of the commons." Along the Maine coast, the lobster industry has been managed for many years in large part by "harbor gangs" that informally control lobster fishing, and there is convincing evidence that they are doing a better job than in many government-managed fisheries. The Maine lobster fishery is one of the world's most successful. Harvests were stable from 1947 to the late 1980s and have risen in the 1990s to all-time highs, just as most fisheries are declining. You need a state license to catch lobsters in Maine, but that is not enough. You also need to be a member of a local harbor gang, which controls lobster fishing in its own territory. Competing harbor gangs maintain control of their territory by occupying it, by warning interlopers who violate its boundaries, and in some cases by vandalizing the intruder's gear—but rarely turning to other forms of violence.

The Maine harbor gangs represent a striking example of how an informal common property system can work efficiently. In recent years they also have provided an example of how formal and informal institutions can work together. In the mid-1990s the state of Maine passed legislation to limit the number of lobster traps used but did so with a zone management law that divides the coast up into zones and creates local councils composed of lobster fishers elected by the license holders of that zone. These councils have the power to establish rules for their zone, such as the number of traps and the time of day when lobster fishing is permitted. More recently, these councils were given the formal authority to limit entry into their zone by establishing rules for the number of retirements that must occur before a new entrant is allowed in.

These changes provide a successful example of a transition from management primarily with informal institutions to a hybrid management regime that balances state-level legislative control with local-level informal institutions that continue to be highly effective.

Source: James M. Acheson and Jennifer F. Brewer, "Changes in the Territorial System of the Maine Lobster Industry," in *The Commons in the New Millennium*, ed. Nives Dolsak and Elinor Ostrom (Cambridge, MA: MIT Press), 37, 59.

transaction costs. Since information is a public good, enforcement involves economies of scale, and transaction costs can be lowered by standards and rules that reduce uncertainty. Markets that function efficiently do so *because* of government not in spite of government. Corporations are private enterprises, held in common by their stockholders; Ducks Unlimited buys up wetlands and marshes, intended for (common) use by its members. Protection of watersheds and other complex resources often involves private landowners, state and federal policies and regulations, local watershed associations, city governments, and local customs. Maine's harbor gangs (box 6) involve all these kinds of institutions.

Recommended Readings and References

The best accessible introduction to the "new" institutional economics is found in Douglas North's *Institutions, Institutional Change and Economic Performance* (Cambridge: Cambridge University Press, 1990). For additional readings on institutional economics and social coordination, see Robert Axelrod, *The Evolution of Cooperation* (New York: Basic Books, 1984); Albert Hirschman, *Exit, Voice, and Loyalty* (Cambridge, MA: Harvard University Press, 1970); and Mancur Olson, *The Logic of Collective Action* (Cambridge, MA: Harvard University Press, 1965).

On common property institutions and environmental resources, see Daniel Bromley, ed., *Making the Commons Work: Theory, Practice and Policy* (San Francisco: Institute for Contemporary Studies Press,1992); Elinor Ostrom, ed., *Governing the Commons: The Evolution of Institutions for Collective Action* (Cambridge: Cambridge University Press, 1990); and Susan Hanna, Carl Folke, Karl-Goran Maler, and Asa Janson, *Rights to Nature: Ecological, Economic, Cultural, and Political Principles of Institutions for the Environment* (Washington, DC: Island Press, 1996).

The pioneering theoretical work on commons problems is found in Scott Gordon, "The Economic Theory of a Common Property Resource: The Fishery," *Journal of Political Economy* 62, no. 2 (1954): 122–142; it was later popularized by Garrett Hardin, "The Tragedy of the Commons," *Science* 162 (1968): 1243–1248. Ronald H. Coase discussed his so-called theorem in "The Problem of Social Cost," *Journal of Law and Economics* 3 (1960): 1–44.

10

Pollution Policies

In this chapter we begin to talk about policy, by which we mean the specific actions that governments take to address an environmental problem like pollution or other kinds of externalities. We examine various kinds of policy instruments that can be used to address externality problems, and we focus on the advantages and disadvantages that each may have in different contexts. One potential difference among policy instruments is their cost, and while other considerations are also important to society, cost can be very important. Environmental objectives are chosen based to some extent on the cost of achieving them. If the costs differ based on the policy instrument, then this will likely affect the chosen objective.

Key Definitions: *Command and control versus economic incentives*

Economists tend to emphasize the distinctions between two main types of policy instruments used to control pollution and other externalities. The first is regulatory standards and controls, what economists have traditionally referred to as **command and control,** or **CAC,** policies. The second type involves **economic incentives,** or what we will call **EI** policies. These policies are also sometimes referred to as market-based approaches. What we want to do here is to explain how these approaches work and point to some of the differences between them. Later, we will talk about some additional types of policies and point to some innovative ways that specific externality problems might be addressed.

Regulatory Standards and Controls

The most commonly used type of policy instrument continues to be direct control or regulation by government of the actions of firms or individuals. In some cases these CAC regulations limit the quantity of emissions but leave the method of control up to the firm or household; in other cases these regulations require the use of a particular or "best available" technology. Many land use regulations such as zoning are examples of CAC controls to limit externalities.

In order to compare and contrast CAC with EI policies, we want to use a common, and simple, analytical framework. To do this, we begin with a very basic pollution problem as represented in figure 10.1. An externality occurs when waste is generated as a production by-product (e.g., smokestack emissions from a wood products plant). The producer could reduce the amount of pollution by adjusting the production process, but these actions are costly (and these costs would be passed on to the consumers of the product being produced). The marginal benefit curve (for polluting) reflects the benefits to the producer of being able to get rid of these waste products in the cheapest way possible (moving left to right in the figure). If the producer cannot pollute, and must abate, then the cost of abatement amounts to forgoing the marginal benefits of polluting. This means that the marginal benefit (MB) curve (moving left to right) is the same as the **marginal abatement cost** (MAC) curve (moving right to left).

Key Concepts: *Marginal abatement benefit, marginal abatement cost*

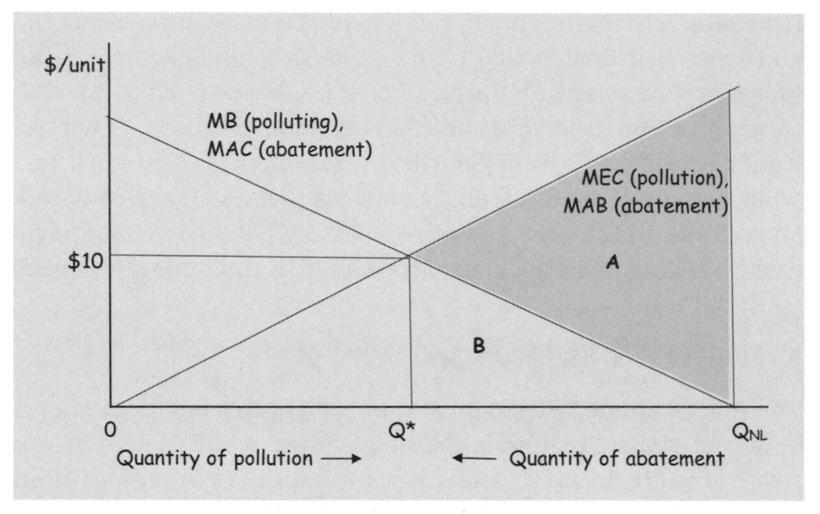

■ **FIGURE 10.1 Externality and CAC regulation**

The externality is reflected in the marginal external cost (MEC) curve, which in this case rises as the pollution level increases. Once again, however, we will want to consider changes going from right to left when pollution is reduced, in which case reducing pollution will generate a **marginal abatement benefit** (MAB) that will have the same magnitude as the marginal external cost (MEC) of pollution. In the absence of any policy, pollution will occur at Q_{NL}, which is inefficient because MEC > MB at that level. Prohibiting pollution (zero emissions) would also be inefficient because MB > MEC at Q = 0. The efficient level of pollution is Q*, where marginal benefits equal marginal costs. A CAC policy is straightforward: restrict emissions to a level of Q*. Compared with a starting point of no control (Q_{NL}), the benefits of a CAC regulation at Q* is the cumulative MAB from Q_{NL} to Q*. These benefits add up to the areas of the two triangles A + B. There are costs, too. The firm must find some way to reduce pollution, and these costs are reflected in the MAC curve going from Q_{NL} to Q*. These costs add up to the area of the triangle B. The net benefits, then, of controlling pollution at Q* compared with Q_{NL} is A + B − B = A, the shaded area. CAC has the advantage of being relatively exact in terms of the amount of pollution that will be permitted. There are other aspects of CAC to consider and discuss, but for now we just want to lay out the basic idea.

Economic Incentive Policies

An alternative to the regulatory, or CAC, approach is an economic incentive, or EI, policy. Unlike the more rigid CAC approach, EI instruments discourage pollution with monetary incentives (penalties and rewards) such as taxes, user fees, or subsidies. Firms and households are not told how much they can pollute or what technology they must use, but their choices will have financial consequences and this will influence the choices they make.

Let's begin with a simple example of a pollution charge or tax. From the perspective of the polluter, a pollution tax would raise the cost of pollution by the amount of the tax (e.g., \$10/ton of emissions). Compared with a situation of "no policy" where pollution has zero cost to the firm, a pollution tax introduces a cost curve in figure 10.1. Normally, we think of this as a fixed price per ton that does not change with the pollution level, so it is a horizontal marginal cost (tax) curve.

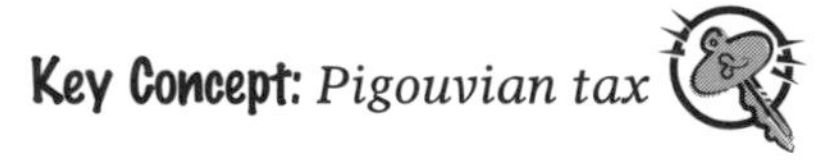

In figure 10.2 we have added a dashed line to represent the tax. Polluters will not want to pay the tax, but they will also not want to pay the costs of abatement. Given a choice between the two, polluters will likely do whichever is cheapest. At Q_{NL} abatement is cheaper than paying the tax (MAC < \$10), so they will reduce pollution. At some point, however, after they have used up the low-cost abatement actions, abatement becomes more expensive. At the point where MAC is equal to the tax, they will become indifferent to paying the tax or abating. Where the MAC curve is higher than the tax, they will choose to pollute and pay the tax rather than abate. From figure 10.2, we expect that with a \$10 tax, polluters will abate until the level of pollution is reduced to Q*. This, in fact, is the optimal level of pollution, the point where the marginal benefits from reducing pollution (MAB) is just equal to MAC. When a pollution tax is set equal to the value of marginal environmental damage at this optimal level, it is sometimes called a **Pigouvian tax,** after the economist Arthur C. Pigou who proved in *The Economics of Welfare* (1920) that a tax on an externality set equal to the marginal external cost will be optimal.

One important difference between these two approaches is that in addition to the abatement costs under CAC, there is a "transfer" under the pollution tax. Under the CAC policy, all polluters have to do is reduce pollution to Q*. With a pollution tax, polluters will lower pollution to Q* at a cost equal to area B but then will still have to pay pollution taxes on Q* equal to C + D or $10 × Q*. Does this make the pollution tax more costly to society? From society's perspective the answer is no, assuming those revenues are used efficiently and not wasted. The tax payments do not represent a social cost; we refer to this as a transfer from polluters to government (see key concept page 59). Funds change hands, but no "real cost" is incurred such as using up resources or buying capital equipment. Of course, firms can't be expected to view it that way. To them, paying taxes is as costly as abatement: they don't like either one. In fact, firms will tend to prefer the CAC approach because the only costs they face are the abatement costs (area B in figure 10.2). Firms can be expected to pass all of the cost on to their customers in the form of higher prices, which could reduce demand. Also, if their competitors (including

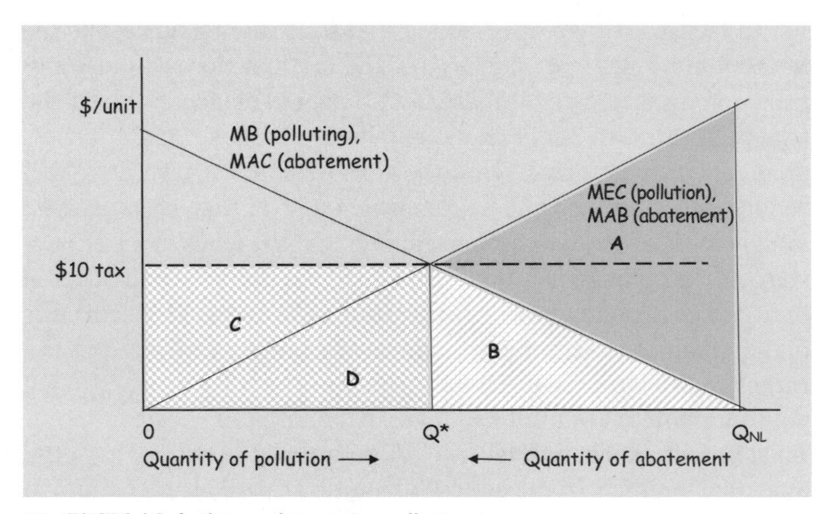

FIGURE 10.2 Externality and a pollution tax

foreign producers) do not face these same costs, this could affect their competitiveness.

The net social benefit of the pollution tax, at least as depicted in this figure, appears to be the same as under a CAC approach, A + B − B = A, the shaded area. If the net benefits are the same for both CAC and a pollution tax, as in figures 10.1 and 10.2, why are economists so smitten with EI policies? The problem is with the figure, not with the economics. The figure suggests that the MAC curve is the same for each polluter. If that were true, or even approximately true, then the differences between CAC and EI may be very small. But if abatement costs differ significantly across polluters, then an EI approach lets individual firms make individual decisions that reflect those differences in cost. Faced with a given pollution tax, each firm (knowing its own situation best) can make its own "decentralized" decisions about whether to pay the pollution tax or to find ways to reduce pollution, and this can reduce the overall cost of reducing pollution.

So how do differences among polluters affect the social costs of pollution control? Usually a pollution problem involves numerous polluters who face different costs or have different capacities to reduce pollution. When this is the case, the pollution tax or other EI policies such as tradable pollution permits, discussed later in this chapter, will have a lower overall cost.

We can prove this point graphically. Consider a situation in figure 10.3 involving two polluting firms, firm 1 and firm 2, with different marginal abatement costs (MAC^1 and MAC^2, respectively). Each firm currently produces 100 tons of pollution per day, so a total of 200. Policymakers want to reduce pollution to a total of 120 tons/day. A CAC approach would simply require each firm to reduce pollution from 100 to 60 tons/day. The cost of this policy would be the sum of the cost for each firm. For firm 1, the area under MAC^1 is A + B + C + D + E. The cost for firm 2 is the area under MAC^2, or A + C. If we used a pollution tax, T, instead of a CAC approach, would the firms respond differently? Yes! Each firm would reduce pollution up to where MAC = T. Firm 1 would reduce pollution to 70 given its relatively high (steep) MAC curve. Firm 2 would reduce pollution to 50 given its relatively flat MAC curve. The new level of total pollution would be the same, 120 tons/day, but the firm with the lowest cost will do more of the abatement, and this lowers the overall cost of achieving the policy goal.

We can see this precisely by adding up the costs under the tax and comparing them to the costs under CAC. The total cost for firm 1 (the area under its MAC curve) would be A + B, and for firm 2 the total cost would be A + C + F. Let's subtract the total abatement cost (TAC) for the tax from the TAC for CAC, or:

$$\begin{aligned} TAC_{cac} - TAC_{tax} &= (A + B + C + D + E + A + C) - (A + B + A + C + F) \\ &= 2A + 2C + B + D + E - (2A + B + C + F) \\ &= C + D + E - F \end{aligned}$$

We can see that C + D + E is the area of the trapezoid between 60 and 70, and F is the area of the trapezoid between 50 and 60. Given the added height of C + D + E, the geometry tells us that the cost of using a CAC is greater than for a tax. Why? Because the tax provides incentives that equalize the marginal abatement cost among polluters, and this ensures efficiency. By contrast,

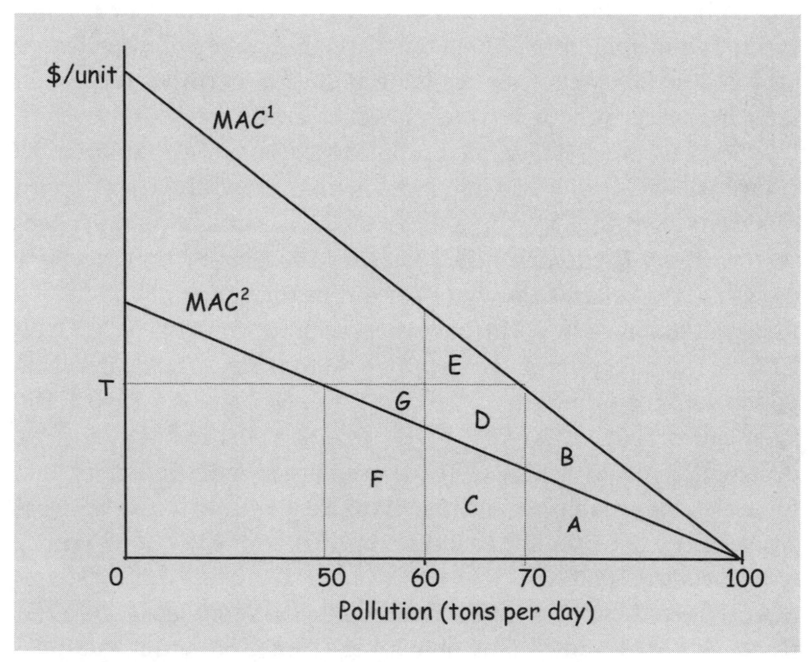

FIGURE 10.3 Cost differences between CAC and EI policies

the CAC approach treats every polluter the same, regardless of any differences in their abatement costs.

The greater the differences in abatement costs among polluters, the greater will be the social cost advantages of a tax policy compared with pollution standards. These differences can be huge (or in some cases they may be small). Estimates of these differences have been made for a number of U.S. pollution policies, indicating that, compared with CAC approaches, the cost may be reduced by 30 to 95 percent if an efficient, EI approach is taken (see table 10.1).

One aspect of both policies that deserves some attention is how to choose the level of pollution and how to choose the pollution tax. Regulation requires setting the level of pollution. We can consider it to be somewhat arbitrary since we can never really know exactly what the MAC and MEC curves look like. We often estimate them, but there is always a high degree of uncertainty (and probably disagreement) about their actual position and slope. If we set the standard at a very low pollution level, firms may be forced to incur unnecessary costs and reduce pollution below the level that is really justified. Pollution taxes, however,

Air	Location	Cost savings compared with CAC
Particulates	St. Louis	87%
	Baltimore	76%
	Lower Delaware Valley	95%
Sulfur dioxide	Lower Delaware Valley	44%
	Four Corners (AZ, NM, CO, UT)	76%
Nitrogen dioxide	Baltimore	83%
	Chicago	93%
Water		
Dissolved oxygen	Delaware River	30-60%
	Fox River, WI	28-56%

SOURCE: Tietenberg, *Environmental and Natural Resource Economics*, 4th ed. (New York: HarperCollins College Publishers, 1996).

TABLE 10.1. Estimated cost savings for EI policies compared with CAC policies

are also arbitrary—policymakers must set the price. If they set it too low, then excess pollution may occur. If they set it too high, then excess abatement may occur. So although some critics may point to the difficulty of choosing a pollution level, or a pollution tax rate, this arbitrariness is similar for both: in the absence of full information about MAC and MEC, there will always be some guesswork in addressing environmental problems. Depending on where the uncertainty lies, there is an argument for choosing one over the other. It goes like this: If the cost of being wrong about marginal damages is very high, then there is a strong argument for preferring to set the quantity. If the cost of being wrong about the marginal abatement cost is very high, then there is a strong argument for preferring a tax.[1]

One additional advantage of a pollution tax, though, is that the policy itself will generate useful information; setting a pollution standard does not do this. When we set a pollution tax, firms will respond by reducing pollution by an amount of their choosing. That response may confirm the MAC curve estimated by the policymakers, but it may reveal something quite different. It may suggest that abatement is more, or less, costly than previously believed. In any case, the response of the firms reveals a point on the MAC curve, and that can be very useful information for policymakers. This advantage is significant, but the general public may not be particularly impressed. The public generally tends to be more concerned about the certainty of the policy in terms of the level of pollution and less interested in certainty about the marginal cost. There is one policy, however, that both reveals information about costs and ensures a prescribed level of pollution: tradable pollution permits, discussed next.

Tradable Pollution Permits

Tradable pollution permits, also referred to as emissions allowances, represent an important innovation with a number of potential advantages over other approaches. In some respects tradable permits are like a CAC approach because emissions are

[1]Martin L. Weitzman, "Prices vs. Quantities," *Review of Economic Studies* 41 (1974): 477–491.

limited to a predetermined quantity (permits are issued for only a limited level of emissions), but they also have the advantages of a pollution tax because the permits can be bought or sold in markets, which creates incentives at the margin very similar to a pollution tax.

To illustrate how a tradable pollution permit scheme would work, consider again a situation with two polluters, firms 1 and firm 2, who pollute 100 tons of SO_2 per day in the absence of any controls or incentives. The two firms have different abatement costs, as indicated by their marginal abatement cost curves in figure 10.4. If a limit of 120 tons of pollution is desired, government can issue permits for that amount. Both firms will need to either reduce pollution or acquire permits. We can evaluate what would happen by recognizing that this situation would create market forces that tend to move toward equilibrium. The supply is fixed and so the supply curve can be represented as a vertical line at Q = 120. The demand curve is the (horizontal) sum of the demands from each firm. Since firms would rather not incur abatement costs, their demand (or willingness to pay) for permits is identical to their MAC curve. If we add the two firm's demand (MAC) curves, we get the "kinked" demand curve for permits indicated by the dotted line.

If permits were free, each firm would want permits for 100 tons, or a total demand of 200. With only 120 available, excess demand would push up the price until demand equals supply. In figure 10.4 this will occur at price P, where demand equals the predetermined supply of 120 tons. Also from the diagram we can see how many permits each firm will acquire by looking at the individual demand curves. At a price of P, the demand by firm 1 is 70 and the demand by firm 2 is 50. Why do we expect firm 1 to end up with more permits? The reason is that firm 1's MAC is higher, and so it is more willing than firm 2 to pay for permits rather than incur its somewhat higher abatement costs. This is how the permit scheme achieves efficiency; the cost of buying a permit or the opportunity cost of not selling a permit generates the same kind of decentralized incentives as an emissions tax.

Tradable permits differ from pollution taxes in several important respects. Unlike a pollution tax, the quantity of pollution under a permit scheme is predetermined and fixed. The marginal

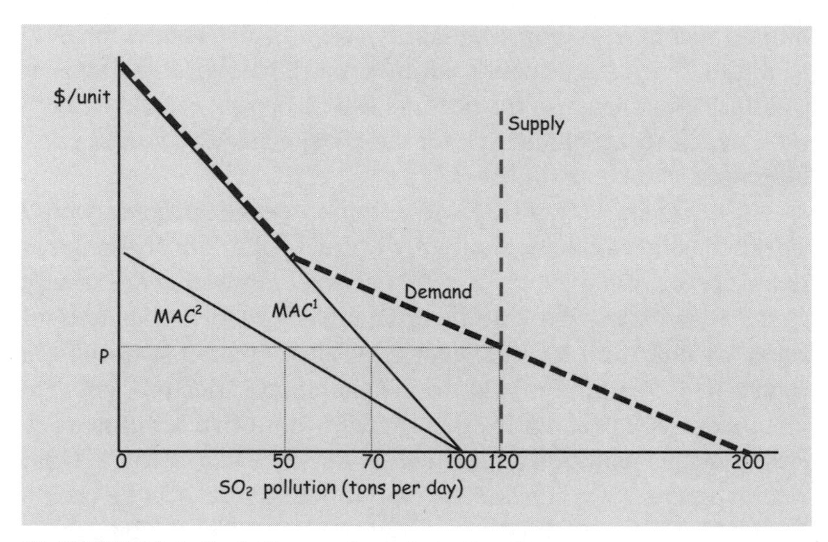

■ **FIGURE 10.4 Tradable permit market allocation**

cost of polluting (the permit price) is not set but is instead determined by market forces. In this sense tradable permits substitute price uncertainty for quantity uncertainty.

Another attribute of permits is that they can be much less costly to firms than a pollution tax if government decides to given them away for free rather than auction them off. One of the main objections of polluting firms to pollution taxes is that in addition to incurring abatement costs, they also have to pay a tax on the remaining pollution they produce. As was indicated, these transfers from polluters to government do not represent social costs, but they do represent private or industry costs, which can affect the competitiveness of firms, for example, in international markets. With pollution permits, government has the option of just giving the permits away (e.g., equal amounts to each firm, or based proportionally on each firms historical emissions). Firms, of course, have a strong preference for a permit giveaway, and you will not be surprised to learn that there are few examples where firms are required to bid for permits from government.

Two additional aspects of tradable permits should be mentioned here. First, in a dynamic economy, we want policies that adjust to economic changes in a way that will maintain the initial policy goal. For example, in an inflationary economy, a nominal pollution tax may lose its incentive effects if the real (inflation adjusted) tax rate declines to levels that do little to discourage pollution. By contrast, a fixed number of pollution permits will let market forces push prices upward in response to inflation so that the market will always clear at the same pollution level. In a growing economy, too, the number of polluting firms may increase. Under a pollution tax policy the amount of pollution will also increase if a larger number of firms respond similarly to the pollution tax. By contrast, with a pollution permit scheme, the amount of pollution will stay the same. An increase in the number of polluters will bid up the price of permits, which in turn will encourage more abatement by each firm in order to keep emissions at the fixed level.

Finally, however, tradable permits often raise concerns that can be raised for any market: will the market be competitive, or will there be opportunities for one of a few firms to exert market power in a way that will be distorting or unfair? This is a real concern, and one that should be examined carefully, especially in cases where a small number of firms may be competing for permits. Indeed, in the case of a growing economy as just discussed, if permits are allocated (given away annually) on the basis of historical emissions, then new firms will be at a cost disadvantage because the pollution policy has created a barrier to entry.

Tradable permit policies are still relatively new, but the success of the SO_2 tradable permit program in the United States (see box 7) has raised awareness and expectations for them in the future. Already there are a number of other emissions trading programs in Canada, the European Union, Chile, Singapore, and the United States for other air pollutants, ozone-depleting substances, particulates, and nitrous oxide.[2]

Policy Instrument Comparisons

So far we've pointed out just a few of the differences between CAC and EI policies, including the potentially large cost advantages

[2]Robert Stavins, *Experience with Market-based Environmental Policy Instruments*, Discussion Paper 01-58 (Washington, DC: Resources for the Future, 2001).

BOX 7

Acid Rain and Tradable SO_2 Permits in the United States

The 1990 Clean Air Act Amendment created the first large-scale tradable permit program in the United States. Its goal was to reduce sulfur dioxide emissions by 10 million tons below 1980 levels. The program was implemented in stages, beginning in 1995 and with more stringent limits imposed beginning in 2000. For those polluters covered under the program, tradable allowances were issued based on a percentage of their 1986 pollution levels.

Because it was the first large program of its kind, this program has been watched and evaluated by economists and others. It has even been referred to as the grand policy experiment. Some observers had doubts that the program would work, that emissions would be reduced, that many permits would be traded, or that the cost-effectiveness advantages touted by economists would be realized. Now that phase I of the program has been completed and we are into phase II, there is a general consensus that the program has been a big success.

Not only is there an active market for SO_2 allowances, but most indicators suggest that the cost advantages predicted by economists have been fulfilled. Over the past decade compliance costs have fallen dramatically to one-quarter of what they had been predicted to be. Before the start of the program, economists predicted that phase I prices for permits would be around $750/ton,

with EI approaches. There are other characteristics that may be important as well. We summarize some of these in table 10.2 and describe them here.

First, as discussed, EI approaches are expected to be more efficient because they use decentralized incentives to take advantage of differences in abatement costs among polluters. These advantages appear to be borne out in the real world, but there is also evidence that where abatement costs do not differ among polluters, or where regulations are so stringent that all abatement actions have been taken, the advantages of EI over regulations may be small.

Key Concept: *Dynamic efficiency*

reflecting estimates of the marginal abatement costs that firms would have to incur. Between 1992 and 1996, however, permit prices went from $300/ton to less than $90/ton, suggesting, among other things, that these kinds of incentives led firms to reduce pollution at lower costs than would have been possible with a uniform CAC approach. Observers are quick to point out that switching to low-sulfur coal was responsible for some of these costs savings. There is evidence that innovations at the firm, market, and regulatory levels all contributed to dramatic cost reductions compared with what was expected. Compared with analyses done in 1990 that predicted that the benefits of the program would approximately equal its costs, more recent analysis estimates that the benefits far outweigh the costs. Estimates indicate savings of more than $1 billion per year under the program (Stavins 2001).

Source: Douglas Bohi and Dallas Burtraw, *SO_2 Allowance Trading: How Experience and Expectations Measure Up*, Discussion Paper 97-24 (Washington, DC: Resources for the Future, February 1997).

Dallas Burtraw, *Innovation Under the Tradable Sulfur Dioxide Emission Permits Program in the U.S. Electricity Sector*, Discussion Paper 00-38 (Washington, DC: Resources for the Future, September 2000).

Curtis Carlson, Dallas Burtraw, Maureen Cropper, and Karen Palmer, "Sulfur Dioxide Control by Electric Utilities: What Are the Gains from Trade?" Discussion Paper 98-44-REV (Washington, DC: Resources for the Future, 2000).

Robert N. Stavins, "What Can We Learn from the Grand Policy Experiment? Lessons from SO_2 Allowance Trading," *Journal of Economic Perspectives* 12, no. 3 (Summer 1998): 69–88.

Robert N. Stavins, *Experience with Market-based Environmental Policy Instruments*, Discussion Paper 01-58 (Washington, DC: Resources for the Future, 2001).

	CAC Standards	Taxes	Tradable permits
Efficiency (static)	Lower	Higher	Higher
Efficiency (dynamic)	Depends	Higher	Higher
Certainty of control	Higher	Lower	Higher
Private cost	Lower	Higher	Depends
Self-adjusting	No	No	Yes
Revenue generated	No	Yes	Depends
"Learning by doing"	No	Yes	Yes
Administrative costs	Significant	Significant	Significant

TABLE 10.2. Expected performance comparisons for pollution policies

Second, EI policies are generally expected to have more "dynamic efficiency." **Dynamic efficiency** refers to allocative efficiency over time, including the efficient levels of saving and investment. Here we are interested in investments in research and development and the kinds of innovations that might result in less pollution or lower cost abatement technologies. Economic reasoning suggests that EI approaches provide stronger incentives for the kinds of R&D that can lead to technological change that either reduces abatement costs or lowers pollution in the long run. Under CAC regulations, firms may have little incentive to do this kind of research. Indeed, in cases where firms are required to use specific technologies, new technologies can be seen as potentially new and costly government requirements. Most of the evidence tends to support this view, but not in all cases. Some CAC approaches could also offer incentives for innovation. If a firm patents a new technology, and that technology is adopted as the CAC standard, the inventing firm can benefit from leasing or selling the technology to other firms.

Third, CAC approaches are believed to provide a more certain level of control, and this appears to be true in many cases. However, the evidence is mixed, and in some cases unrealistic CAC requirements can result in noncompliance, delays, and allowed exceptions.

Fourth, the private costs to firms tend to be lower for CAC even though the social costs tend to be higher. Taxes on emissions face objections from polluting firms, as do tradable permits schemes in which permits are auctioned. Experiences in the United States and Europe suggest that governments face strong incentives to return fees to firms. So far in the United States, tradable permits have been given away rather than auctioned.

Fifth, only tradable pollution permits will self-adjust to inflation or changes in the number of polluters over time in order to maintain the same level of pollution.

Sixth, taxes and tradable permits have the potential to generate revenue, and this can create the opportunity to use the revenues for other public goals, including "green tax reform" (discussed later in this chapter). However, experience in the United States and Europe suggests that it is politically difficult to generate revenues from pollution policies. Nevertheless, Robert

Stavins reports existing programs involving effluent or emissions fees on carbon monoxide (six countries), carbon dioxide (five countries), sulfur dioxide (sixteen countries), nitrous oxide (eleven countries), and water pollutants, including BOD (biological oxygen demand) and TSS (total suspended solids) (twenty countries).[3] Many additional indirect policies (discussed later) that also generate revenue and discourage environmental harm include user charges, insurance premium taxes, sales and value-added taxes on fossil fuel products, administrative charges, and tax differentiation.

Seventh, both taxes and permits represent an example of "adaptive management" in that they generate information that reduces uncertainty. Pollution problems are typified by uncertainty about both the benefits and the costs of abatement. These two policy options will reduce the uncertainty surrounding the MAC curve by identifying a point on the curve when a price (tax) or quantity (permit level) is put in place. Over time, this kind of information can be very useful for updating and refining policy goals and approaches. In the case of the U.S. SO_2 trading program, the market for permits demonstrated that the marginal cost of abatement was much lower than had been initially estimated (see box 7).

Table 10.2 summarizes the differences we have mentioned so far between CAC standards and the two EI approaches, pollution taxes and tradable permits. In any specific policy context, other social considerations should also be recognized such as distributional equity, fairness, and individual rights (see chapter 16).

Indirect Policy Instruments

Now it might occur to you that a tax on pollution has some very practical obstacles to overcome. Aren't there millions of automobile tailpipes in the United States, and hundreds of thousands of stove chimneys in Beijing, and thousands of miles of farm boundaries where nonpoint pollution can drain off toward a stream? How in the world can government possibly monitor, measure, and

[3]Ibid.

charge for each unit of pollution from each of these locations? Wouldn't the administrative costs be prohibitive?

Key Concept: *Indirect policy instruments—Tax a complement or subsidize a substitute*

In many cases a *direct* tax on pollution is a practical impossibility. In fact, the same is true for CAC standards limiting pollution to a prescribed level. But there is an *indirect* way to achieve pretty much the same policy goal. We refer to these as **indirect policy instruments, by which we mean doing something that indirectly causes people to reduce pollution.** If people do X every time they pollute, then if we control X, we can control pollution indirectly. And if people who do Y do *not* pollute? Then if we can encourage Y, we can also reduce pollution. In economic terms, X is a "complement" to pollution and Y is a "substitute" for pollution. The rule to remember for indirect policies is: **tax a complement or subsidize a substitute.**

Examples are the best way to make this point clear, for either CAC policies or IE policies. If it is impractical to tax tailpipe emissions directly, an indirect gas tax will have a similar effect. If we can't tax pesticide runoff from a farmer's fields, an indirect tax on the pesticide itself should discourage excessive applications. If it's too complicated to charge a congestion fee for using the highway during rush hour, a tax on downtown parking or a subsidy for public transportation may achieve some of the same goals. In the case of CAC standards, a fuel economy standard may be more practical than an emissions limit. A requirement that refrigerators be built with a non-CFC technology may be preferable to a ban on CFCs (chlorofluorocarbons). And when a ban on elephant poaching is found to be difficult to enforce, a prohibition on the trade in ivory can have a similar effect (see box 8).

Congestion Pricing

Let's put some of these ideas to work on a common externality problem, highway congestion. A highway is a congestible public good, which means that it is nonrival with low numbers of users

BOX 8

Ivory and Rhino horn

Even when direct policies are impractical, economic reasoning and market incentives can help identify creative solutions to difficult problems. Here's an example. Poachers of ivory and rhino horn kill the animals in the process, which creates an externality problem because of concerns over the possible extinction of African elephants and rhinos. Direct regulations, such as making poaching illegal, have proved costly and ineffective because monitoring and enforcement are difficult when both the animals and the poachers wander across thousands of miles of forest and grassland.

If direct enforcement at the point of ivory and rhino horn "collection" (where the externality occurs) is too costly or ineffective, might there be some other point along the market chain where intervention would be less costly and more successful? Ivory and rhino horn are generally consumed in different countries than where they are produced, so import regulations and retail markets represent a logical alternative point of intervention.

Indeed, the ban on trade under CITES (Convention on International Trade in Endangered Species) is credited with successfully reducing elephant poaching. Following the 1989 ban, and along with continued antipoaching efforts, demand declined and prices to suppliers fell along with their incentives to poach. As a result, elephant populations have rebounded in recent years. (It may also be the case that changes in social norms in some high-income countries [i.e., stigma associated with buying ivory] have helped.)

In contrast, the CITES ban on trade in rhino horn has been a disaster. The population of African black rhinos has fallen precipitously over the past twenty years, and they are now on the verge of extinction.

So why such different results? One explanation is found by looking at the economics. Demand for rhino horn is very inelastic because its main use is in traditional medicines in Asia where there are no close substitutes. Ivory demand, on the other hand, is quite elastic given its principal use as tourist trinkets and jewelry. When legal trade in rhino horn was replaced with a ban on trade, prices rose more than sixfold, making the rewards to poaching even more attractive, despite "shoot-to-kill" rules for suspected poachers in Zimbabwe and Kenya.

What can be done? One very creative solution has been proposed

(Brown and Layton 2001) that takes advantage of this inelastic demand by consumers but recognizes that there actually *is* a very close substitute on the production side for poached black rhino horn: "cropped" horn from either black or white rhinos. Governments in southern Africa could cut or crop rhino horns without killing the rhinos. The horns grow back fast enough to make this idea plausible, especially since white rhinos are much more abundant than black rhinos and the horns are undifferentiated for medicinal uses. By flooding the market, or even just threatening to flood the market, governments could manipulate the price of rhino horn, keeping it too low to attract poachers to this risky enterprise.

In essence the government would be trying to drive its competitors out of the market, forcing out a product that generates an externality (poached rhino horn), and replacing it with a different product that does not (cropped rhino horn).

Source: Gardner Brown and David Layton, "A Market Solution for Preserving Biodiversity: The Black Rhino," in *Protecting Endangered Species in the United States: Biological Needs, Political Realities, Economic Choices*, ed. Jason Shogren and John Tschirhart (Cambridge: Cambridge University Press, 2001).

(since they don't impose costs on each other), but rival at higher levels of use (as users interfere with each other, slowing them down and causing traffic congestion). It can also be evaluated as an externality problem, where motorists impose costs on each other. The magnitude of these costs can be very large where daily rush hour traffic jams cause thousands of people to spend extra time commuting. A study of seventy-five U.S. cities estimated that commuters spent 3.7 billion hours stuck in traffic in 2003, at a cost of $65 billion annually in time and fuel.[4]

In figure 10.5 we represent how the marginal private cost (MPC) diverges from the marginal social cost (MSC) at high levels of highway use. Given the demand for highway use (MB), we expect Q_0 users on the highway, which is inefficient since

[4]David Schrank and Tim Lomax, *The 2005 Urban Mobility Report* (College Station, TX: Texas Transportation Institute, Texas A&M University, 2005). Available at http://mobility.tamu.edu/ums/report/

MSC > MB, creating a deadweight loss equal to area A. The result is traffic congestion. In effect, individuals do not consider the congestion they cause for other drivers, MEC, when they decide to use the highway during rush hour. They consider only their own private cost, MPC. These external costs include time and fuel but also increased air pollution.

A single, direct EI approach could be used to address this congestion problem in the same way that a pollution tax was used to correct this pollution example. The optimal or Pigouvian tax on congestion would be a tax rate, t*, equal to the difference between MSC and MPC at Q*. The effect of the tax is illustrated in figure 10.6 as a shift up in the MPC curve by t*. Graphically, we see that with the shift in the MPC curve, the new intersection of the demand curve with MPC is at Q*, the optimal level of highway use.

A congestion tax has some advantages as well as disadvantages. One important advantage is that it lets individuals choose to use the highway (and pay the congestion fee) based on their own weighing of benefits and costs. The outcome is going to be efficient because each individual can best make that judgment. Individuals may even find that it is worth it to them to pay the fee on some days (e.g., an emergency) and not on other days.

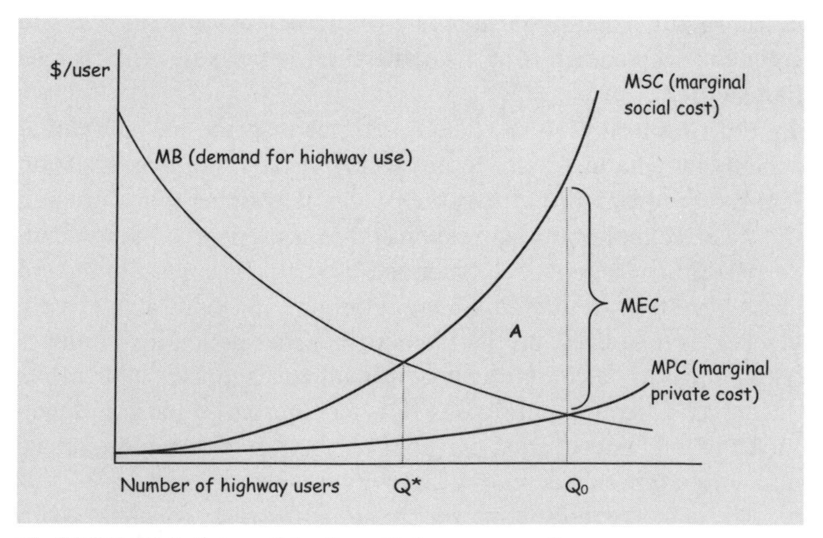

■ **FIGURE 10.5 Externalities from highway congestion**

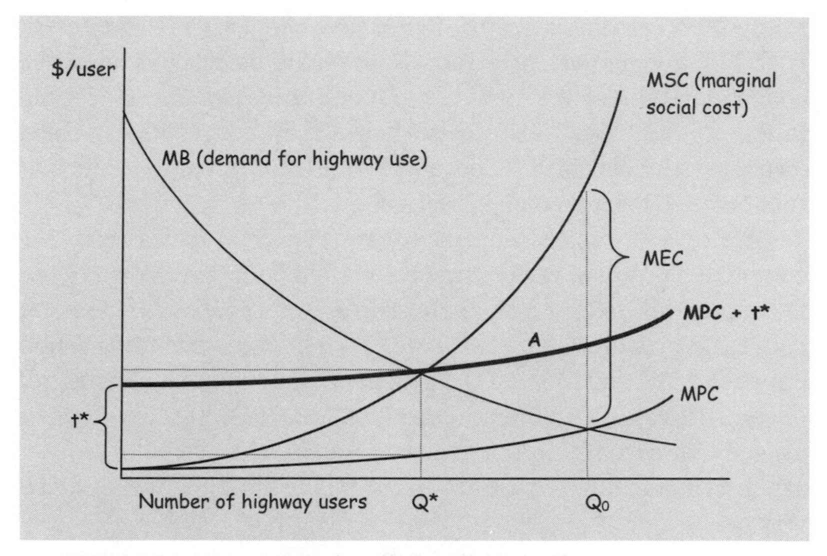

■ **FIGURE 10.6 Externalities from highway congestion**

A congestion fee scheme is likely to be met immediately with opposition, however. First, it will be viewed as inequitable since low-income people who live outside town and work downtown will have a difficult time paying a stiff daily fee. A lower congestion fee may reduce this burden, but it will also do less toward discouraging excessive use of the highway. So are there ways to solve the problem while at the same time addressing other issues like equity?

Starting in the 1970s, Singapore put in place an innovative scheme that did just that. Rather than impose a single congestion fee, the government put together a set of policies that achieved the desired goal and also responded to a number of other concerns. First, Singapore introduced a registration scheme and pricing system similar to a congestion tax but with a relatively low fee. It then drew on the ideas of indirect policy instruments (remember, tax a compliment or subsidize a substitute). It introduced subsidies for public bus service, increased park-and-ride facilities, and encouraged car pools (substitutes). And Singapore also raised taxes on downtown parking (complements).

The primary motivation for these components was the equity issue. Many people could not afford to pay a high price for highway use, and rather than force those individuals (probably low-income groups) to relocate or lose their jobs, the bus service, park-and-ride facilities, and car pools offered attractive alternatives to those unable to pay the highway fee. For example, the availability of other transportation services and higher parking costs will reduce the demand for use of the highway, shifting the demand curve to MB´, as shown in figure 10.7. If this were the only policy implemented, it would reduce demand and use of the highway to Q_1, which is not sufficient to reach the optimal level of use.

In addition to these indirect policies, Singapore introduced a modest congestion fee, raising the costs of using the highway somewhat. We represent this with the MPC + t curve in figure 10.7. The combined effect of these policies is to raise costs and to reduce demand so that the intersection of MB´ and MPC + t is at Q*, the social optimum where MB = MSC.

You might be wondering how Singapore will pay the cost of subsidizing bus services or enhancing park-and-ride facilities. Look no further than the congestion fee, which generates revenues from those who continue to use the highway. If the policy is balanced just right, the whole package could be self-financing,

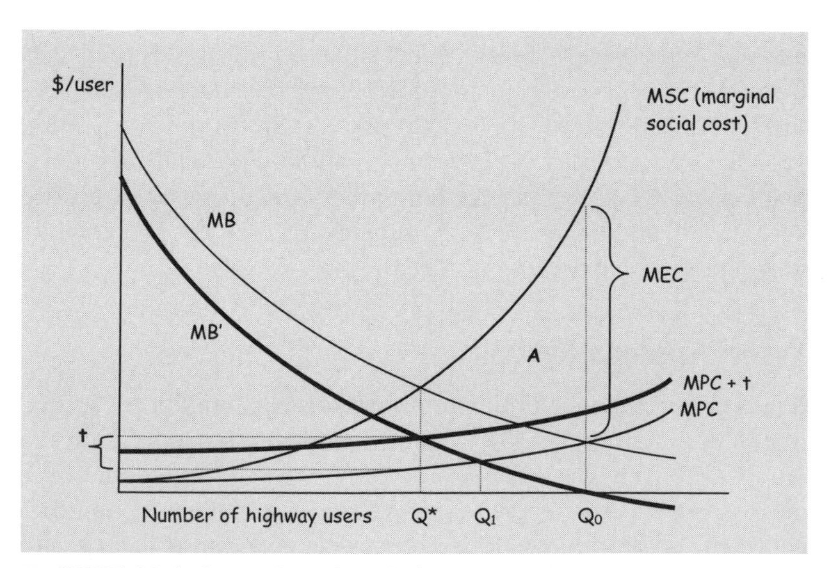

■ **FIGURE 10.7 Externalities from highway congestion**

with the fees from the highway users (a relatively higher-income group) subsidizing the public transportation of the bus riders (a relatively lower-income group). Each group makes a choice. Lower-income people who have a lower opportunity cost of time may be more willing to spend the extra time on a bus or at a park-and-ride station. Having the high-income group subsidize the lower-income group is an appealing side effect. It may not make the whole plan into a Pareto improvement (where nobody is made worse off), but it limits the negative impacts on the poor.

The analytical approach in figures 10.5–10.7 can also be used to evaluate other environmental problems involving congestion externalities. For example, in many parts of Africa, fuelwood is the main source of energy for cooking and heating, and residents of villages and cities must travel farther and farther from home to gather wood because the woodlands nearer by have been completely depleted. Each time an individual cuts a small tree near the village instead of letting the tree get large enough to grow at a faster rate, everybody pays a price by having to walk longer distances in search of wood. This type of congestion cost is analogous to highway congestion, and the range of possible fixes is, in principle, similar to those for highway congestion. In Malawi, for example, the government recognizes that it is very difficult to impose a tax on wood collection in large part because monitoring and enforcement are nearly impossible. So the government has instead turned its attention to indirect policies such as subsidizing fuel-efficient woodstoves that use less wood and subsidizing saplings for villagers to plant on private land around their compounds and farms (on lands where individual property rights are recognized and respected). A subsidy on nonwood fuels like kerosene has also been considered.

Deposit-Refund Systems

Factory smokestacks typically represent (a) a stationary source of pollution that (b) is easy to monitor and where (c) the ability to curtail airborne waste disposal is very costly. In contrast, a guy with a beer bottle represents (a) a nonstationary (potential) source of pollution that (b) is hard to monitor and (c) can easily avoid disposal of glass bottles in public spaces if he chooses. Litter patrols in all places at all hours are not feasible. If only there were a way to create incentives for "self-monitoring" that would discourage this kind of littering.

Well, a deposit-refund system does precisely that. It's like an invisible monitor that follows each bottle or can around, constantly discouraging the user from disposing of the item in places where the external costs may be high. We are all familiar with this concept for bottles and cans, and you may have seen a similar system aimed at getting travelers to return airport luggage carts to a central location. (In this case the refund process is automated so that the costs of the program are kept extremely low.)

More than twenty-five countries have programs of this kind for beverage containers, and the concept has been applied to many other products such as auto batteries (in some U.S. states and in Mexico), scrap automobiles (Sweden), and refrigerators (Austria).[5] The basic concept is really no different from setting bail for prisoners or requiring employees who handle large amounts of cash to be bonded: a financial claim is held in escrow to ensure a particular kind of behavior.

Are there other possible applications? Following the *Exxon Valdez* oil spill, the idea of a deposit-refund system or bonding program was mentioned as a way to ensure that oil companies take adequate precautions when shipping petroleum. The program would require the oil company to register the amount of oil loaded into the ship and make a deposit with a government bondholder. When the oil is delivered, the bond or deposit would be refunded to the oil company. Other uses involve private mining and logging activities to enforce postproduction land restoration, for example, in cases where small firms may otherwise have incentives to evade such obligations by moving out of the jurisdiction or even declaring bankruptcy.

Cap-and-Trade Safety Valves

Implementing emissions trading policies, like tradable carbon permits, faces many obstacles, including strong disagreements

[5]Stavins, *Experience with Market-based Environmental Policy Instruments.*

about how costly it would be for industry to comply with the desired reductions. If the marginal abatement cost curve is steep, then a higher level of permits (and emissions) would be appropriate than if the MAC curve is flat. With no solid estimates of costs, policymakers are often caught between environmental advocates who want sharp reductions in pollution and industry representatives who warn of unacceptably high abatement costs.

One solution to this dilemma is a cap-and-trade "safety valve" policy proposed in the case of carbon trading. The idea works as follows: A limited number of carbon emissions permits are issued for the desired level of emissions, Q_L, based on the assumption that abatement costs will be relatively low, as illustrated by demand (low) in figure 10.8. These permits are expected to trade at price P_L. The government, however, announces that it stands ready to sell as many additional permits as needed at a predetermined price, P_H. If demand (and marginal abatement costs) turn out to be very steep (demand [high]), then the market price for tradable permits will rise to the government's "trigger price" or "safety valve price" at which point the government will sell as many permits as demanded by the market (Q_H in this case) at P_H. The supply curve for this permit scheme forms an inverted L, adjusting the number of permits to the demand for them without any further tinkering.

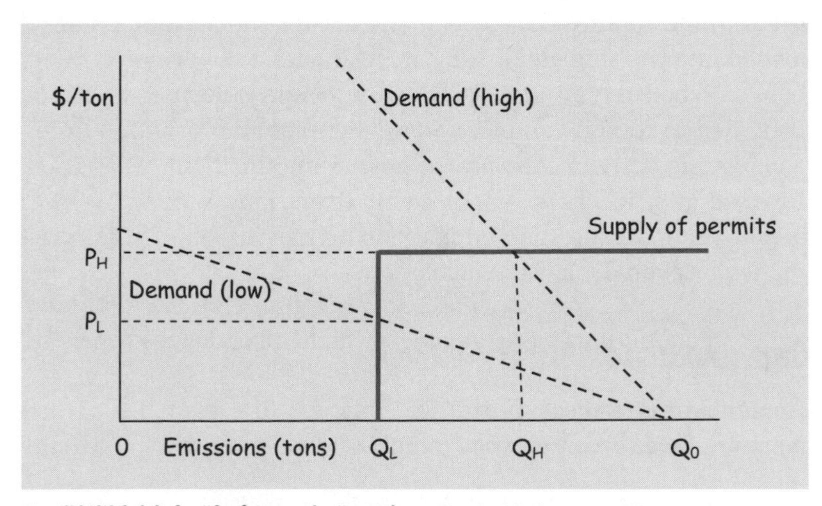

■ **FIGURE 10.8 "Safety valve" with carbon emissions permits**

This policy guarantees an upper bound on the price of permits and therefore on the actual cost of abatement (polluters would buy more permits before they would engage in abatement more costly than the trigger price). As a result, both sides—the abatement cost optimists and the abatement cost pessimists—will get what they want if it turns out they are right. If abatement costs are low, then the trigger price will never be reached and the strict emissions limit Q_L will be in force. If abatement costs are high, then emissions will be higher and the industry will be protected from having to incur costs above the trigger price. Time will tell whether this clever scheme will find its way into practice for carbon emissions limits or other pollution problems.

Green Tax Reform

An issue that comes up frequently when discussing market-based or incentive policies is whether the policy will generate revenues and, if so, what should be done with the revenues. In the example of congestion pricing in Singapore, the revenues were used in a way that addressed concern about inequities of the road-pricing scheme: the revenues subsidized public transportation. Another option that has gotten a great deal of attention is to use the revenues from a pollution tax or other revenue-generating policy to finance reductions in preexisting taxes. The idea is to use these revenues to pay for some portion of the public goods provided by government, so that distortionary taxes like income taxes or excise taxes can be reduced. An intuitive slogan for this "green tax reform" idea asks, why tax goods when you can tax bads?

Key Concept: *Double dividend hypothesis* 

There is a strong argument for taxing "bads" like pollution rather than taxing wage income—which discourages workers and distorts the economy. The tax programs that governments use to raise revenue create a deadweight loss and a distorting "excess burden" on the economy. Estimates of the marginal excess burden of taxes in the United States suggest that for every dollar of revenue there is an additional cost of 20¢ to 40¢ in inefficiencies caused by these distortions on income taxes (even higher for U.S. taxes on capital gains). It makes sense to raise revenues with taxes which also correct externalities: they serve two purposes and create two benefits by correcting the externality and generating revenue in a nondistorting way. The idea that there are two benefits here became known as the **double dividend hypothesis.**

In the mid-1990s, a different line of reasoning emerged from some highly mathematical theoretical work by several economists who questioned the validity of the double dividend hypothesis. These economists claimed to show that there is actually another negative effect when pollution taxes coexist in an economy with revenue-raising taxes. They called it a tax interaction effect. This work got a lot of attention among academic economists and among policymakers in the United States and Europe where these results were interpreted as showing that pollution policies are especially distorting to the economy, even when the revenues from the policies are used to lower preexisting taxes. For many economists, something seemed to be not quite right with their interpretations, and many remained skeptical of their conclusions because the intuition of these contrary results just didn't add up.

The problem with this tax interaction interpretation was complicated by an unconventional approach making the source of the problem with their analysis difficult to uncover.

But it turns out that the tax interaction interpretation is mistaken, having overlooked the compounding effect of double taxation in the way the economists set up their analysis. It is true that when introducing a pollution tax into a world with income taxes, the optimal pollution tax will be lower than it would be if there were no income taxes. But the reason for this is that with an income tax already in the economy, the "effective" pollution tax is actually higher than its nominal value. The pollution tax is paid out of income, and since that income has already been taxed, there is a compounding of the two tax rates, making the effective pollution tax higher than it appears to be.

Once we get that nominal versus effective tax rate issue out of the way, the double dividend hypothesis is valid and implies that revenue-generating environmental polices make it possible to increase the optimal pollution tax by about 50%, and this increases the net social benefits of the policy also by about 50%.[6]

Green Labeling

Consumers can have enormous influence over what firms produce, how firms produce it, and even on government policy. Increasingly, consumers are basing market decisions on what a product contains, how or where the product was produced, on the basis of sustainability, or other social implications. So even without regulations, without Pigouvian taxes, consumers have the potential to influence not only the goods that come to market, but also the social and environmental setting in which they are produced.

The basic idea here is nothing new. For a very long time, consumers have used their purchasing power to encourage specific interests through bake sales, car washes, and Girl Scout cookie sales, or to discourage other interests through boycotts of products from states or countries with objectionable social and environmental policies such as child or forced labor and apartheid. Boycotts have included those on ivory, fur coats, and dolphin-harming tuna. In recent years large numbers of consumers appear willing to pay a premium for products that are grown organically, sustainably, or consistent with standards of fair wages and social equity. Country- or state-of-origin labeling has caught on in many places, as has support for local enterprises.

What's somewhat new is that this kind of influence has increasingly gone global with the promotion of imports that are organic, sustainably produced, or produced under fair labor practices. The expansion of "consumers who care" from local bake sales to global markets has created huge information problems: how to know if the import was produced the way the label says? This problem has in turn led to the expansion of third-party certification and the creation of a variety of governmental, non-governmental, and for-profit entities that inspect and monitor

[6]William K. Jaeger, "Optimal Environmental Taxation from Society's Perspective," *American Journal of Agricultural Economics* 86, no. 3 (2004): 805–812; and William K. Jaeger "Carbon Taxation When Climate Affects Productivity," *Land Economics* 78, no. 3 (2002): 354–367.

producers to ensure compliance with their claims, for example, of sustainable forestry. The certifying organization then affirms this with a label that attaches the organizations credibility to the product being marketed internationally. As with the very old "Good Housekeeping Seal of Approval," or many other industry certifications in the United States, newer entities such as Fair Trade Certified and Quality Assurance International now lend their name to products grown organically or sustainably in developing countries.

Governments can, and have, introduced eco-labeling such as the U.S. Energy Star program to encourage use of energy-efficient appliances, the European Union's Eco-label on more than 200 products, and Canada's Environmental Choice Award granted to more than 1,400 products. Evidence suggests that, in the case of the U.S. Energy Star program, for example, government certification has had significant impacts on energy efficiency improvements by making both consumers and producers aware and sensitive to energy costs.[7] These approaches have great potential in an increasingly global economy where other mechanisms have not been particularly successful in promoting global environmental interests.

Recommended Readings and References

This is a good place to note several surveys and collections of economics articles on environmental economics and policies: Daniel Bromley, ed., *The Handbook of Environmental Economics* (Oxford: Blackwell, 1995); Anil Markandya and Julie Richardson, eds., *Environmental Economics: A Reader* (New York: St. Martins, 1992); and Robert N. Stavins, ed., *Economics of the Environment: Selected Readings* (New York: W. W. Norton, 2000).

Readers will also find many interesting studies produced by Resources for the Future (www.rff.org) and World Resources Institute (www.wri.org). An excellent survey is found in Maureen Cropper and Wallace E. Oates, "Environmental Economics: A

---

[7]Richard G. Newell, Adam B. Jaffe, and Robert N. Stavins, "The Induced Innovation Hypothesis and Energy-Saving Technological Change," *Quarterly Journal of Economics* 114, no. 3 (1999): 941–975.

Survey," *Journal of Economic Literature* 30 (1992): 675–740). And a standard reference for those familiar with calculus is William J. Baumol and Wallace E. Oates, *The Theory of Environmental Policy*, 2nd ed. (Cambridge: Cambridge University Press).

Other notable sources include Curtis Carlson, Dallas Burtraw, Maureen Cropper, and Karen Palmer, *Sulfur Dioxide Control by Electric Utilities: What Are the Gains from Trade?* Discussion Paper 98-44-REV (Washington, DC: Resources for the Future, 2000); Winston Harrington, Richard D. Morgenstern, and Thomas Sterner, eds., *Choosing Environmental Policy: Comparing Instruments and Outcomes in the United States and Europe* (Washington, DC: Resources for the Future, 2004); Richard D. Morgenstern and Paul R. Portney, eds., *New Approaches on Energy and the Environment: Policy Advice for the President* (Washington, DC: Resources for the Future, 2004); Organization for Economic Cooperation and Development, *Economic Instruments for Environmental Protection* (Paris: Organization for Economic Cooperation and Development, 1989); Arthur C. Pigou, *The Economics of Welfare*, 4th ed. (1920; repr. London: Macmillan, 1932); Paul Portney, ed., *Public Policies for Environmental Protection* (Washington, DC: Resources for the Future, 1990); Robert Stavins, *Experience with Market-based Environmental Policy Instruments*, Discussion Paper 01-58 (Washington, DC: Resources for the Future, 2001); and Tom H. Tietenberg, *Emissions Trading: An Exercise in Reforming Pollution Policy* (Washington, DC: Resources for the Future, 1985).

11

Land and Forest Policies

Land is a pretty basic resource. Its supply is fixed, more or less, and we can't move it around. We use land for housing, farming, factories, roads, parks, forestry, and wilderness. In addition to these direct human uses, land supports and protects biodiversity, hydrological systems, and a wide range of other ecosystem functions in a variety of ecosystems, including forests. Partly because of these special characteristics, land use policy and forest management are among the most complex issues facing society. Unlike some externality problems, like air pollution that can be spread fairly uniformly across an entire city's population, the positive and negative externalities between and among many different types of land uses are spatial, temporal, directional, visual, auditory, aesthetic, and seasonal. Past land uses can cast a long shadow on the future, both because it affects the feasibility of different future uses (i.e., owing to alterations such as construction, mining, erosion, and infrastructure) and because current property rights holders have strong vested interests to protect or enhance.

Homeowners in residential areas are keenly aware of how vulnerable their quality of life is to changes in nearby land uses, such as new buildings that block views, noise from commercial activity, or a change in traffic patterns. Everybody understands NIMBY (not in my backyard) concerns over the location of landfills, prisons, factories, and highways. The location and uses of forests can also have profound effects on nearby communities, creating visual and recreational amenities and pure water supplies. Or they can be eyesores and create threats of fires and mudslides.

These issues all have to do with the proximity of one kind of land use in relation to other kinds of land uses. In the case of forests, the issues often pertain to the multiple uses and services possible for a single forest and conflicts among those different uses or ecosystem services. The institutions that influence land use decisions typically include a complex mix of private ownership rights and several levels of government rules and controls. Local governments frequently have a wide array of ways to affect land use decisions, including taxes, zoning, conservation regulations, and the ability to purchase land outright. In the case of public lands, multiple and competing uses often create conflicts. Some conflicts can be minimized by segregating conflicting uses by location, time, or season. Given the broad scope and complexity of these issues, our approach here is only to provide a few observations from an economic perspective and to highlight insights that economics can offer about resolving land conflicts and promoting efficiency.

Land Rents

When land (or any resource) has unique attributes (location, view, fertility), the effect of market forces on its value will differ from other kinds of goods. To illustrate, what happens in an industry that uses a unique kind of land as an input and experiences positive profits? Normally, we expect new firms to enter the industry, which increases supply and pushes prices down until profits are zero again. But in an industry that relies on a unique input, the only way for a new firm to enter is to buy some of that input from another firm. In the case of land, this process will bid up the price of land as entrants try to gain access to these positive profits. Where will it end? Profits will go to zero.

Economists refer to this as a case where the profits were "capitalized" into land values. If you owned the land before profits rose, then you earned a windfall profit, an increase in the **land rent**, or premium on the price of land because of its unique characteristics. Economists don't refer to this as a positive profit from owning the land. Rather, they recognize that since you could sell the land for a new, higher price, the opportunity cost of the land being used is now higher, implying that the costs of using the land yourself are now higher. This situation is illustrated in figure 11.1 for high-value agricultural land. Profits shift the derived demand for land up and to the right, which will bid up the price of land. But it will not affect the supply of this particular kind of land, because its supply is fixed.

This result has important implications for certain kinds of policies. For starters, it was recognized long ago that this situation means that a tax on land rent will not create any distortion or deadweight loss since the supply of land will not change. If we were starting at D_1 in the figure and introduced a tax that shifted the demand down by the amount of the tax, t, to D_2, the price would drop by the amount of the tax. But there would be no deadweight loss, because the supply curve is vertical. No deadweight loss triangle appears because the tax does not distort the supply of land. This advantage of a direct tax on land rents was recognized long ago by the economist Henry George as an efficient, nondistorting way for government to raise revenue. In the case of commercial land, a land tax less than or equal to land rents would simply transfer those rents from landowners to government, without affecting the use of the land. While it's a great idea on efficiency grounds, it doesn't seem to have much political traction.

The same adjustment process has implications for other kinds of policies. For example, U.S. farm programs are motivated at least in part to raise the incomes of farm families. These programs raise crop prices and make farming more profitable, but these profits are quickly capitalized into the land prices and rental rates. Since a majority of U.S. farmers either rent land or

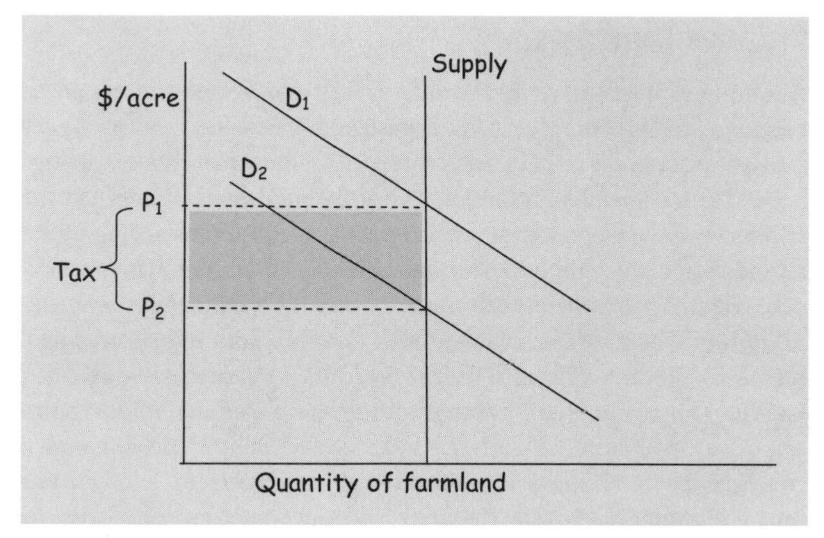

■ **FIGURE 11.1 Derived demand for farmland with environmental regulations**

bought their land after these programs began, they did not benefit from the one-time windfall land rent. Instead, they are just barely getting by as our zero profit competitive model would predict.

What if there are environmental regulations—such as prohibiting the use of chemicals, requiring erosion controls, or fencing streams—that raise the costs of farm production? The same reasoning may apply. The price of the crops cannot go up to cover these costs if they are sold in competitive national or international markets. And farmers who currently rent land would *not* be willing to rent at the same rate because they would not be able to cover their costs. With no other land use option, landowners would lower their land lease rates or prices because of reduced demand: land rents would decline. This scenario might be similar to the shift from D_1 to D_2. Land prices would be lowered to an extent that offset the increased cost of production, and this would return profits to zero. Output might be lower if the regulations affected yield, but employment and income paid to farm workers would likely be the same. Only the landowner would see a drop in income.

Creative Contracts

A number of creative legal and policy tools have emerged in response to the complexity surrounding land uses, the property rights associated with landownership, and the uncertainties about future changes in land uses and regulations. One tool is the **conservation easement.** An easement is a legal contract in which a landowner gives up one or more of her property rights to a person, organization, or government. Typically, a conservation easement involves giving up the right to develop land in order to protect a resource, such as a forest, wetland, historic site, or open space. These kinds of arrangements help reduce uncertainty about future land uses and can help governments and conservation groups take steps to reduce fragmentation of ecosystems and open spaces. Often, because the conservation objective is very long term, whereas some landowners' interests in using land may be only for their lifetime, conservation easements or gifts to land trusts are often made as bequests.

Key Concept: *Conservation easement*

Uncertainty is a key issue for landowners who plan to put their land to specific uses in the future, but who face the risk that land use restrictions, like those involving the Endangered Species Act, will block them. To protect habitat while at the same time reducing uncertainty for landowners, **habitat conservation plans** (HCPs) were devised. HCPs are legal agreements whereby the landowners agree to take certain actions to protect species and habitats, and in exchange the government assures the landowners that no new regulations will be imposed on them in the future. Some arrangements of this kind have been controversial, with interest groups on both sides claiming they got the bad end of the bargain. But the principle of asking landowners to make land use concessions in exchange for future reductions in uncertainty would appear to have merit as a mutually beneficial exchange: trading habitat protection for reduced uncertainty.

Key Concept: *Habitat conservation plans*

Another approach addresses the very difficult task of guiding the direction of land use changes over time. The externalities for a given land use mostly affect nearby plots of land, and these externalities can sometimes be very large (e.g., residential, farming, industrial, wetlands, mining, feedlots, bombing range). Arranging land uses to minimize negative externalities and maximize positive ones has got to be one of the most complex and difficult policy problems facing governments and their planners. This is true, not just because of the many types of land uses and the spatial complexity of their proximities and external effects, but because past and present land uses and property rights create huge obstacles to change, even when changes are sorely needed. Rights and equity issues often add yet one more difficult dimension.

So, exerting effective guidance and control over a dynamic process of land use changes and economic growth is enormously difficult—as evidenced by the many failures where we see jumbled suburban sprawl and mishmash development. When emerging land use conflicts arise, governments cannot just go back to the drawing board, choose a preferred arrangement, and then shuffle factories, farms, and open spaces around to new, more appropriate locations. They often even have trouble guiding the current forces of change that are propelling development in the near future. In this kind of situation, **transferable development rights** (TDRs) can give governments some leverage to influence the direction of change.

Key Concept: *Transferable development rights* 

Like the tactics in martial arts where the attacker's momentum is redirected and used by the defender to his own advantage, transferable development rights can take advantage of existing development pressures to promote the protection of farmland, open space, historic areas, or other natural resources. Instead of rearranging land or people, government can create an incentive mechanism to transfer rights. Since property ownership amounts to having a "bundle of rights," a TDR involves a mechanism for transferring one of those rights from one property to another, such as the right to develop the land for residential or industrial uses in one location rather than in another. For example, in order to develop additional land in the development zone, a contractor must purchase an equal-size lot in the conservation zone, which then becomes protected from future development. The government identifies a "sending" zone or district from which these development rights can be transferred, and a "receiving" zone or district where the development rights can be used.

Rather than allow development to proceed helter-skelter, a TDR program can guide development to the receiving district, for example, by permitting higher-density development to occur *if* the landowner obtains development rights from the sending district. By transferring development rights, landowners in the sending zone give up the right to develop their parcel of land, which may currently be a wetland, open space, or agricultural land. The development incentives are used to achieve more protection in the sending zone.

The beauty of the TDR comes from attracting development to a particular area by making landowners in the receiving district eligible to undertake specific kinds of desired development, but only if they first do something for the community: purchase a development right from the sending district, which removes the threat of development by transferring it away from that district.

Forests and Tree Growing

Forest policy provides an opportunity to apply and highlight some important economic concepts such as opportunity cost and positive externalities. It is also a great example of a resource where private objectives will often differ from social objectives, because the "resource" in question is a complex one with multiple dimensions and several competing kinds of value. It's also a resource where the uses and values to local communities may diverge from those of more distant interest groups.

Let's start by looking at efficiency from a private perspective, where the owner of a forest manages the planting and cutting of trees for wood products as a productive investment (i.e., to maximize profits). From the date of planting, the stumpage value of a forest (V) will increase for a time, then flatten out before leveling off as a mature stand. The forest's stumpage value, V, will look something like figure 11.2. To keep things simple, we assume that the price of wood products is constant and that this producer is small relative to the market, so that when this plot of land is harvested, it will not affect the market price. Also, stumpage value is intended to reflect the value of the forest net of the harvesting costs, so it's the amount the owner can expect to clear.

Given the shape of V_t, what is the optimal time to harvest? To answer the question, we need to consider the opportunity cost of the payment the owner would receive at harvest. At the time of harvest, the owner can put the money in the bank and earn interest on it. If he lets the forest grow one more year, he doesn't earn that interest. Viewing the forest as an investment, the owner will want to compare the return on the growth of the forest with the return on money in the bank. If he can get 7% each year by putting the stumpage value in the bank, then he should only be willing to let the forest grow for an additional year if V_t is growing at 7% or more.

Each year, the owner faces a choice between harvesting the forest (in which case he can put the money in the bank at an

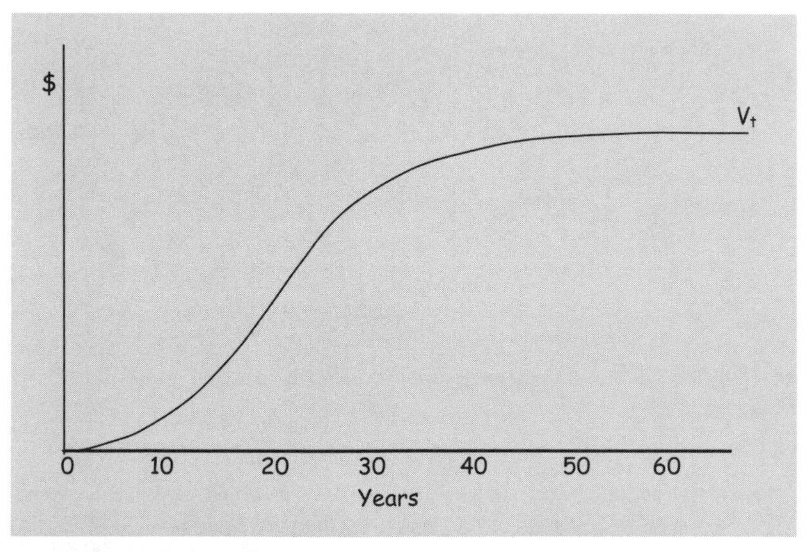

■ FIGURE 11.2 Growth of a forest's stumpage value

interest rate, r, and earn rV_t), or he can let the forest grow one more year (in which case the stumpage value will increase by the amount $\Delta V_t = V_{t+1} - V_t$). So long as ΔV_t is greater than rV_t, letting the forest grow one more year makes sense from the perspective of maximizing the value of the investment. Based on figure 11.3, the owner should let the forest grow until about year forty before harvesting.

Since initially ΔV_t will be greater than rV_t, the harvest rule can be stated as $rV_t = \Delta V_t$. Another intuitive way to state this same rule is as $r = \Delta V_t / V_t$, which just says harvest when the growth rate of the forest is equal to (and no longer greater than) the interest rate. This harvest rule will maximize profits for the owner, minimize the cost of wood products to consumers, and produce an efficient use of resources—unless, of course, there are externalities.[1]

In this example, we want to frame the issue in terms of the positive externalities associated with a standing forest rather than in terms of the negative externalities of cutting it down. These are just two ways of looking at the same thing. The basic

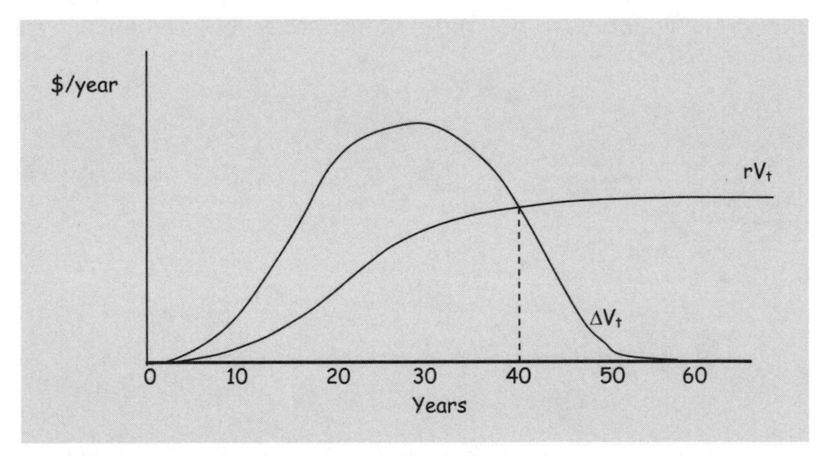

■ **FIGURE 11.3 Annual earnings from forest revenues and growth in stumpage value**

[1]The optimal harvest point will actually be a bit sooner than what we have suggested here owing to the opportunity cost of the land (the sooner the trees are harvested, the sooner the owner can replant), but in the interest of simplicity we will leave this issue aside.

problem is that standing forests often provide important public goods in the form of wildlife habitat, watershed protection, ecosystems for biodiversity, and recreational opportunities. These social values from the forest also vary with the age of the stand of trees and are lost when the forest is harvested. We'll denote the social value of the standing forest (per year) as S_t, which will vary with the age of the forest and look something like the depiction in figure 11.4.

When the value of a standing forest includes both its stumpage value for wood products and its nonwood social value, we will want to compare the sum of the private value (ΔV_t) and social "external" value (S_t) of the standing forest to the value of harvesting. When we compare the opportunity cost of the standing forest, rV_t (the forgone interest that could be earned at the bank), with the sum of the private and social (external) value of the standing forest ($S_t + \Delta V_t$), we see in figure 11.5 that the socially optimal harvest age is higher than when only private values are taken into account: it increases from forty to about fifty-five years. It's also easy to see that if the social value of the standing forest (including both private and external values) is somewhat higher than this, as in the example of $S'_t + \Delta V_t$, then the value of the standing forest will *always* be higher than its harvest value, indicating that the forest should never be harvested.

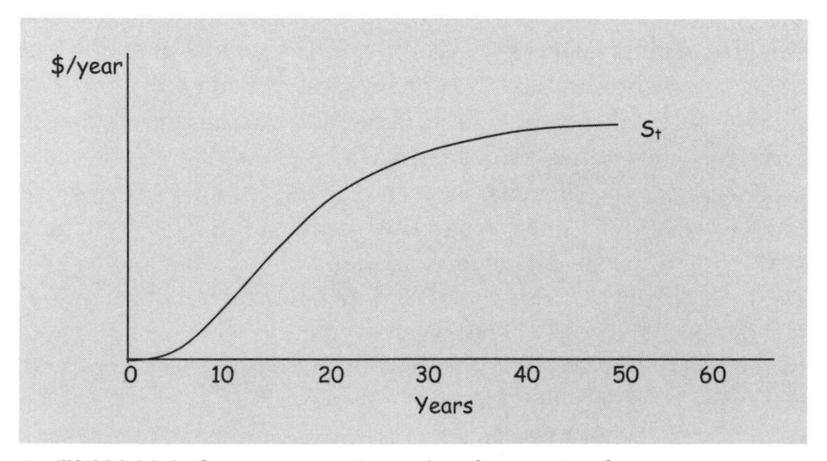

■ **FIGURE 11.4 Positive externality value of a standing forest**

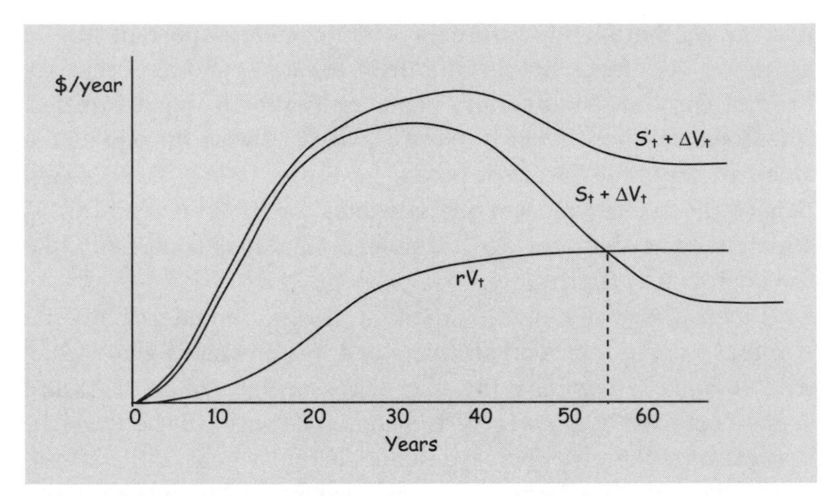

FIGURE 11.5 Potential values from a standing forest versus harvested forest

Forest Policy

Forests are a resource where the simple, even elegant, economic prescription of a market-based Pigouvian tax, intended to internalize externalities, seems quite impractical. The Pigouvian tax approach tries to align the private and the social cost of cutting a standing forest by introducing a charge or "stumpage fee" equal to S_t for cutting the forest—essentially a tax per acre or per tree. The private owner's profit-maximizing decision with this tax would lead him to harvest when $rV_t - S_t = \Delta V_t$, which is equivalent to the social optimization rule of harvesting when $rV_t = \Delta V_t + S_t$.

The forest owner, of course, is not responding directly to the positive externalities associated with the standing forest, he is responding to the financial incentive of the stumpage fee, which is a transfer of funds from the owner to the government. Landowners can be expected to strongly oppose this kind of policy. Even on public lands like U.S. national forests, where timber companies have been able to harvest under government permits or contracts, increases in the cost of obtaining these contracts are strongly opposed by industry.

There is another reason why Pigouvian stumpage fees are not only unpopular, but also impractical as a primary forest policy tool. Forests are complex, and the social value of a standing forest may vary mile by mile, acre by acre, or even meter by meter in some locations, making it very difficult to apply a direct, uniform incentive approach of this kind. The external benefits of standing forests vary with the type and ecological complexity of the forest, when trees near a stream provide important habitat protections of fish, or when trees are on steep slopes vulnerable to erosion and sliding. Recreation and aesthetic benefits also vary greatly depending on the location, accessibility, and attractiveness of a forest. And a clear-cut that is visible from a high-volume highway can have a large effect on the value of a standing forest and on public opinion about logging.

Because of these complexities (and the difficulty of imposing fees on politically influential industries that provide jobs in rural areas), forest policy tends to rely on regulations rather than market-based incentives. The array of potential approaches has become broad and increasingly creative. In cases where the nonharvest values are judged to always be higher than the harvest value, we find wilderness areas or national parks. Where there is potential for mixing harvest and nonharvest benefits, we may find national forests with limited logging and a range of recreational uses limited by location or time of year (e.g., hiking, biking, motorized recreational vehicles, and hunting). On public and private lands, riparian buffers are sometimes established to prohibit cutting trees within a certain distance of a stream. Harvesting on steep slopes is sometimes prohibited, as is harvesting in the vicinity of certain endangered species (e.g., the northern spotted owl). Many other approaches have been tried to reduce the conflict between harvest values and standing forest values by regulating the ways in which forests are harvested. These approaches include banning clear-cuts, requiring some trees to be left in a cleared area for animal habitat, and thinning tree farms to more closely replicate the structure of natural forests.

Global Interests and Local Control of Forests

One of the difficult realities of forest policy is that the communities that live in or near a forest may have different values or incentives than communities that live farther away. In the United States, local communities often rely on forests for jobs and local tax revenues from logging, whereas the values associated with the standing forest (recreation, aesthetics, wildlife, and "nonuse values" [see chapter 14]) are reflected in the preferences of a public that mostly lives at some distance from the forest. Promoting local control of resources is sometimes advocated on equity grounds, or to counter concerns about the power of large, sometimes multinational companies. However, local control can also conflict with protecting standing forests when a local community benefits primarily from wood products and when local institutions are inadequate to monitor and enforce harvest limits.

While these kinds of problems are evident in conflicts over forest policy in many parts of the United States, they are particularly acute in developing countries. The short-term needs of the poor lead to unsustainable fuelwood collection and forest clearing to make way for farming, sometimes in areas where the national and global value placed on these forests appears to be very high. Given the immediacy of the needs of the poor (and also because of the lack of a banking system or borrowing opportunities), the rate of discount that effectively guides private decisions is very high: the poor cannot afford to wait for future payoffs. This difference implies a higher discount rate, r', so that $r'V_t$ is greater than in the preceding figures, resulting in an even earlier harvest decision. If locals make harvest decisions based on equating $r'V_t$ to ΔV_t, then this makes the harvest date even earlier, less than twenty years in figure 11.6. At the same time, national and/or global values for the standing forest may be very high, as in the case of $S_t + \Delta V_t$. This kind of situation presents a dilemma where equity, local property rights, and social efficiency conflict.

Since the 1980s recognition of this problem has led to a range of development projects aimed at one of several solutions. One solution is to offer local communities alternative sources of income so that they will not be dependent on forest products for their livelihood. A second solution is to promote markets for nontimber forest products (latex, nuts, berries) as a way to live off the forest without cutting down the trees. A third solution has tried to create local institutions that give the local communities

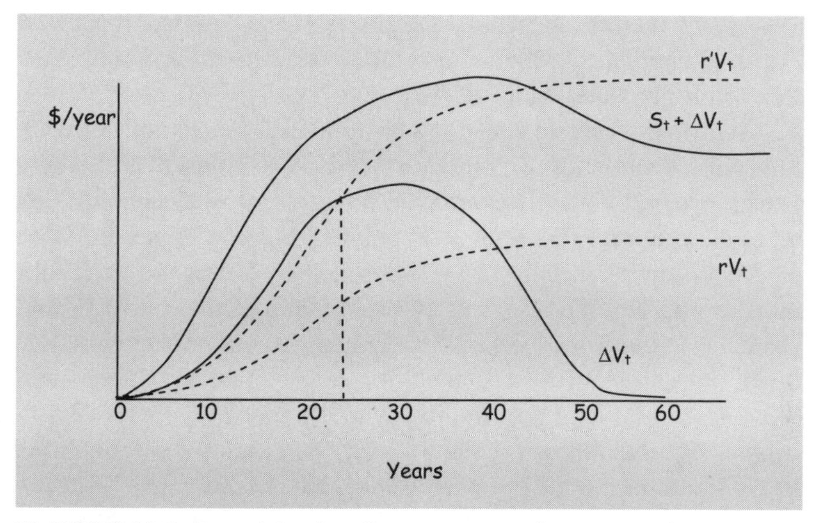

■ **FIGURE 11.6 Potential values from a standing forest versus harvested forest**

stronger incentives to protect the resource. One well-known program of this kind is the Campfire Program, promoted in southern Africa and elsewhere, to give local villagers an incentive (a tangible payoff) to protect wildlife and even to mount antipoaching patrols.

Recommended Readings and References

Many excellent sources cover land and forest issues in developed and developing countries. These include Michael D. Bowes and John V. Krutilla, *Multiple-Use Management: The Economics of Public Forestlands* (Washington, DC: Resources for the Future, 1989); Robert T. Deacon and Martin B. Johnson, eds., *Forestlands: Public and Private* (San Francisco: Pacific Institute for Public Policy Research, 1985); John Loomis, *Integrated Public Lands Management: Principles and Applications to National Forests, Parks, Wildlife Refuges, and BLM Lands* (New York: Columbia University Press, 2002); Colin Price, *The Theory and Application of Forest Economics* (Oxford: Basil Blackwell, 1989); Robert Repetto and Malcolm Gillis, *Public Policies and the Misuse of Forest Resources* (Cambridge: Cambridge University Press,

1988); and G. Cornelis Van Kooten and Henk Folmer, *Land and Forest Economics* (Cheltenham, UK, and Northampton, MA: Edward Elgar Publishing, 2004).

Additional references include John A. Dixon and Paul B. Sherman, *Economics of Protected Areas* (Washington, DC: Island Press, 1990); Richard Hartman, "The Harvesting Decision When a Standing Forest Has Value," *Economic Inquiry* 14, no. 1 (1976): 52–58; William Fischel, *The Economics of Zoning Laws* (Baltimore: Johns Hopkins University Press, 1985); Edwin S. Mills and Bruce W. Hamilton, *Urban Economics*, 4th ed. (Glenview, IL: Scott, Foresman, 1989); Robert A. Sedjo, Alberto Goetzl, and Stevenson O. Moffat, *Sustainability in Temperate Forests* (Washington, DC: Resources for the Future, 1998); and Roger A. Sedjo, R. Neil Sampson, and Joe Wisniewski, eds. *Economics of Carbon Sequestration in Forestry* (Boca Raton, FL: Lewis Publishers, 1997).

12

The Fishery Predicament

One of the most familiar and intractable natural resource problems worldwide is the overexploitation of ocean fisheries. Competition among commercial fishers has led to ever-expanding fishing fleets, a spiral of increasing fishing effort, and declining numbers of fish. The well-documented result has been financially shaky fishing industries and communities, despite the many unsuccessful efforts to correct the problems.

Ocean fisheries offer a classic example of how common pool resources can fall victim to the tragedy of the commons. The causes of fishery overexploitation are relatively easy to understand: the short-run incentives facing individual fishers conflict with the efficient long-term management of the resource. That puts us at point A, with too few fish and too many fishers. It is also relatively easy to describe what an efficient allocation for a particular fishery should look like, one with a larger fish population and sustained harvests that maximize net benefits. That gives us point B. Why is it so difficult to get from point A to point B? Understanding this predicament requires an appreciation of the constraints facing fishers on a year-to-year basis.

Of course, many fisheries are valued for more than their commercial harvests. In the same way that standing forests can have value beyond the value of the timber they contain, many fisheries have value beyond their value as food. Some fisheries, such as salmon, are increasingly valuable for recreational fishing. Other fisheries have important cultural and spiritual values; many efforts to protect fish, whales, turtles, and other marine species are motivated by their "existence value" rather than their direct "use value." These distinctions among different categories of value are discussed in chapter 14.

Although some of the decline in fish populations can be attributed to pollution or loss of habitat, excess harvest pressures continue to be a prime cause, and the remainder of this chapter focuses on the predicament that exists in commercially harvested fisheries.

The Fishery Problem as a Year-to-Year Problem

The classic economic model of a "steady-state" fishery developed by Scott Gordon in 1954 is a useful tool for understanding the dynamic equilibrium or steady-state relationships between stock, harvest rate, and harvest cost. But this model is less useful for understanding the year-to-year dynamics of a fishery, and it is these short-run incentives and constraints (e.g., uncertainty, fixed versus variable cost considerations, the effect of unexpected shocks) that make efficient fishery management so difficult. To understand how these forces work, we'll be using a new approach that helps identify these year-to-year pressures. The framework is a "discrete-time" or one-year model, where fishing takes place each year during the fishing season (e.g., in summer), and the growth in the fish population takes place in the off-season (e.g., in winter). This framework describes how the harvesting choices made in the current period affect harvesting opportunities in the next period. The relationships can be described as follows: The stock of fish at the beginning of the current period is denoted as S_I^1 (the initial stock in year one). Each fish caught in the current period will reduce the remaining stock by one fish, so that the relationship between stock and flow is one to one: harvest = $-\Delta$ stock.

Each fish harvested generates marginal net revenue (MNR) equal to the marginal revenue (fish price) minus the marginal cost of fishing effort. This marginal cost is assumed to equal the variable costs required to catch a fish (fuel, labor, etc.). If these variable costs are proportional to the time required to catch a fish, then the marginal cost can be expected to rise as the stock declines during the season, since it will take longer to catch each fish. Because of this, a point will be reached where the MNR goes to zero and then becomes negative (i.e., when the marginal revenue no longer exceeds marginal cost).

There are also fixed costs with fishing (e.g., boats, equipment, mooring fees, etc.), and these have an important effect on how fishers will respond to policy interventions. But first, let's return to the opportunity cost of harvesting fish in the current year. Anytime a fish is harvested this year, it affects the stock available at the start of the next season. This relationship is density dependent, meaning that it changes with the fish population. When the stock is high, the effect on next year's stock of taking one additional fish this year will be very small, since with large fish populations, the growth in the stock is limited by other factors such as competition for food among the fish. This means that at the beginning of the fishing season, when the fish population is high, the opportunity cost of harvesting is very low because the negative effect on next year's stock is small. Later on in the season, as the stock of fish declines due to harvesting, the effect on next year's stock of harvesting one additional fish this year will rise: with fewer fish, the growth rate of the stock between seasons is generally higher (fewer fish means higher survival and growth rates). This means that the opportunity cost of harvesting a fish this year varies inversely with the size of the stock.

When an opportunity cost involves two different time periods, economists often call it the **user cost**. **In this case, user cost is the cost of harvesting a fish today in terms of the present value of the marginal reduction in net revenues next season.** It is represented in the graph as MUC for marginal user cost. Figure 12.1

shows the relationship between marginal net revenue and the marginal user cost (associated with next period). Fishing involves moving from right to left along the horizontal (stock) axis, reducing the stock as fish are harvested. As fish are harvested, the MUC rises.

Individual fishers, however, cannot be expected to take MUC into account because they cannot count on being the one to benefit from leaving additional fish in the ocean this period: those additional fish are likely to be caught next year by somebody else! Each fisher has an incentive to fish until MNR = 0. In a sense, they can free-ride on others by catching more fish this year and letting the opportunity cost be shared by everybody next year. This is the open access or tragedy-of-the-commons situation. We denote this stock level as S_E^{OA}, where the E stands for the ending or "escapement" stock (think of this as the number of fish that escape being caught). The superscript OA denotes open access. If the initial stock at the beginning of the season was S_I, then the total net revenue for the entire fishery (ignoring fixed cost) in the current season can be represented as the shaded area under the MNR curve.

In contrast to the incentives facing individual fishers, the optimal management of the fishery collectively will involve taking into account MUC. This means harvesting only as long as MNR is greater than MUC. In figure 12.1 we can see that effi-

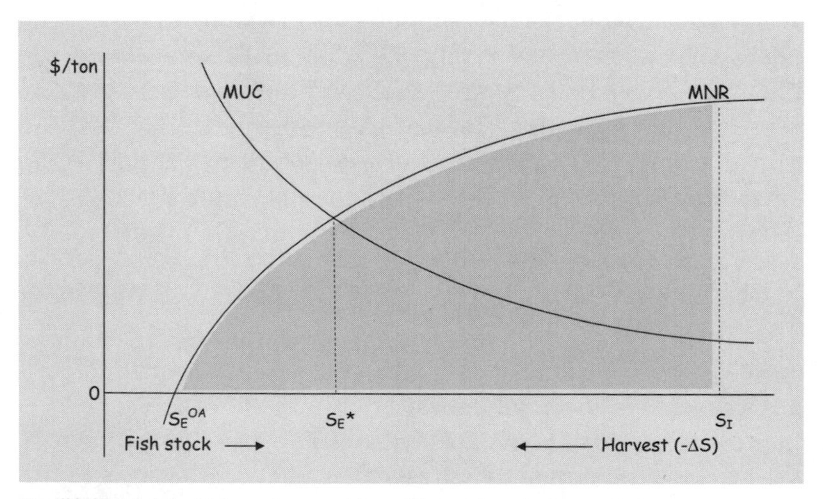

■ **FIGURE 12.1 Fishery harvest benefits and costs in current year**

ciency means fishing only until S_E*, where MNR = MUC. From a given S_I, the total net revenue for the efficient harvest will be lower (the part of the shaded area to the right of S_E*) than with open access (the entire shaded area), but the added benefits next season for the efficient harvest will be larger than what is given up this year. This is because next period's initial stock will be higher when this period's ending stock is higher.

The relationship between the escapement stock, S_E, in the current period and the initial stock, S_I, in the next period can be estimated based on the stock-growth relationship for the fishery between periods. This is a biological relationship that depends on the type of fish and the environment in which it lives. This relationship, $F(S_E)$, is represented in the portion of figure 12.2 below the horizontal stock axis. It shows how S_E in one period is related to S_I in the next period. For example, if fishing is halted at S_E* in the current period, the initial stock in the next period is found by finding the point on the $F(S_E)$ line directly below S_E*, and then moving horizontally to the lower portion of the vertical axis that corresponds to $f(S_E^*)$, which is $S_I \times (2)$. In the open access case, fishing continues until S_E^{OA}, which means an initial stock the following year of S_I^{OA} (2), which is much lower than if fishing were halted at S_E*.

What do we expect to be true if we manage the fishery efficiently? If we choose S_E* every year, then the shaded area (total net revenue) will be maximized for each period, and this would represent the optimal steady-state harvest rule. Any other S_E will produce a smaller shaded area over multiple seasons.

There are a couple of important factors to consider that don't appear directly in figure 12.2. First, these relationships are presented as though they are fixed or deterministic, with no surprises or shocks that affect the population of fish or net revenues from fishing. Obviously, this is unrealistic. The high degree of uncertainty and fluctuations for ocean fisheries is a major reason why these fisheries are so difficult to manage. But we can think of these figures as reflecting the average, or expected relationship.

Second, figure 12.1 appears to indicate that the total net revenue (the shaded area) is positive even for the open access situation. It's not. The fixed costs for things like boats, equipment, and mooring are not reflected in these figures, but they will affect

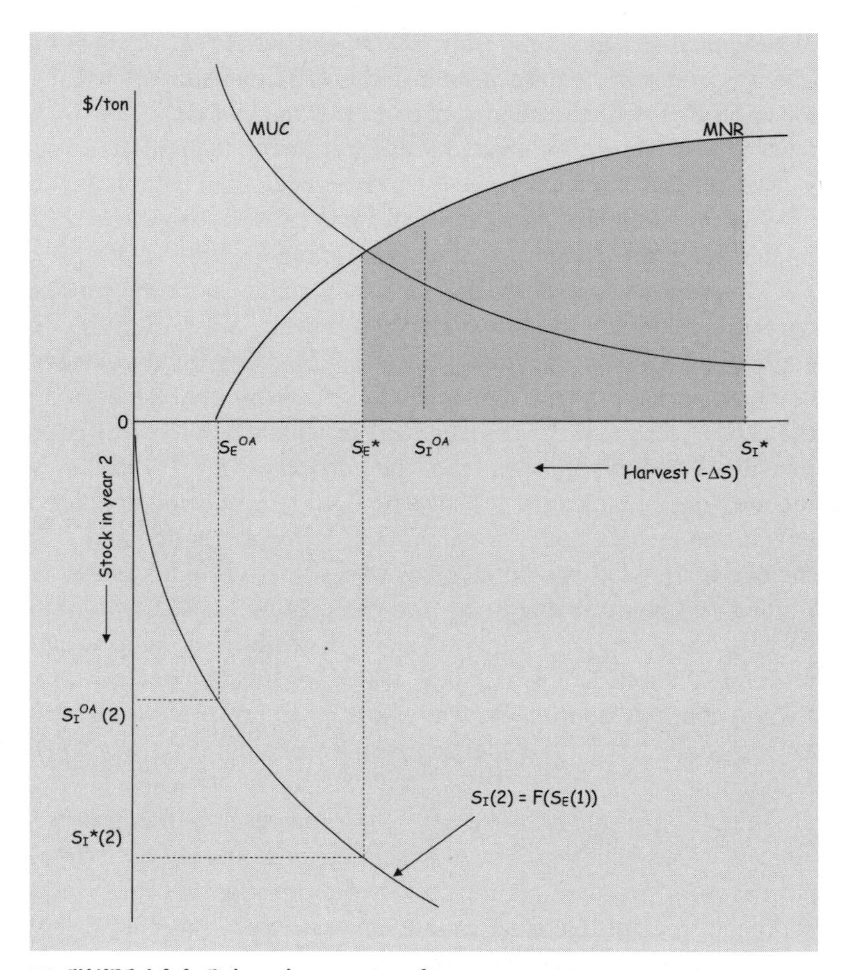

■ **FIGURE 12.2 Fishery harvest benefits, costs, and impact on subsequent year**

fishers' profitability. From the economics of firms (see chapter 3), we can say three things about how we expect them to operate:

1. If average revenue for an individual fisher is higher than average cost (including fixed costs), we expect additional fishers to enter the fishery in order to gain some of these profits. This entry will lower average revenues per fisher since each boat is likely to catch fewer fish as the number of fishers increases.

2. In the short run, if fishers are able to cover their average variable costs, but not their average total cost, they may continue to fish for a time since their fixed costs are "sunk costs" and cannot be recovered (their losses are less if they continue to fish).
3. In the long run, if fishers' average revenues are less than average (total) cost, they will shut down and leave the industry.

The upshot of these decisions is that the number of fishers and boats can be expected to adjust, so that the total net benefit will be just equal to fixed costs. For the open access case, this means that the total net benefit—the shaded areas in figure 12.1—will be just equal to fixed costs. What does that say about the net social benefit of the fishery overall? Zilch, zip. The fishery is exploited to the point where all potential resource rents or profits are dissipated because the value of the resource is offset by the cost of exploiting it. In effect, by attracting more than the optimal number of fishers, the resource ends up generating no net value to society—a tragedy indeed.

Solving the Fishery Predicament: Getting from Point A to Point B

This analysis helps us understand why so many of the world's fisheries are overexploited, and what that level of exploitation is likely to look like: S_I^{OA} and S_E^{OA} in figure 12.2, with open access meaning no net social benefits, and fishers barely able to cover their fixed costs. We can also identify what an efficiently managed fishery should look like: S_I^* and S_E^* in figure 12.2. The problem for economists and policymakers is figuring out how to get from the open access situation to the efficient situation. To do that, we need to understand why movement from one situation to the other is so difficult.

Figure 12.3 shows the open access situation, where the net social benefit or profit is zero because the number of individual fishers and the capital they have invested have risen to the point where the average revenue equals long-run average cost. In that case the size of the shaded area represents a break-even point:

any net revenues less than that will mean losses to the fishers; they will be unable to cover their fixed costs.

If this is our starting point, then what can be done to restore efficiency? The initial stock is lower than the optimal level, so it must be raised. The way to raise the initial stock in period t + 1 is to raise the ending stock in period t. But the way to raise the ending stock in period t involves reducing harvest, and this means reducing net revenues below the fishers' breakeven point. This is a large problem.

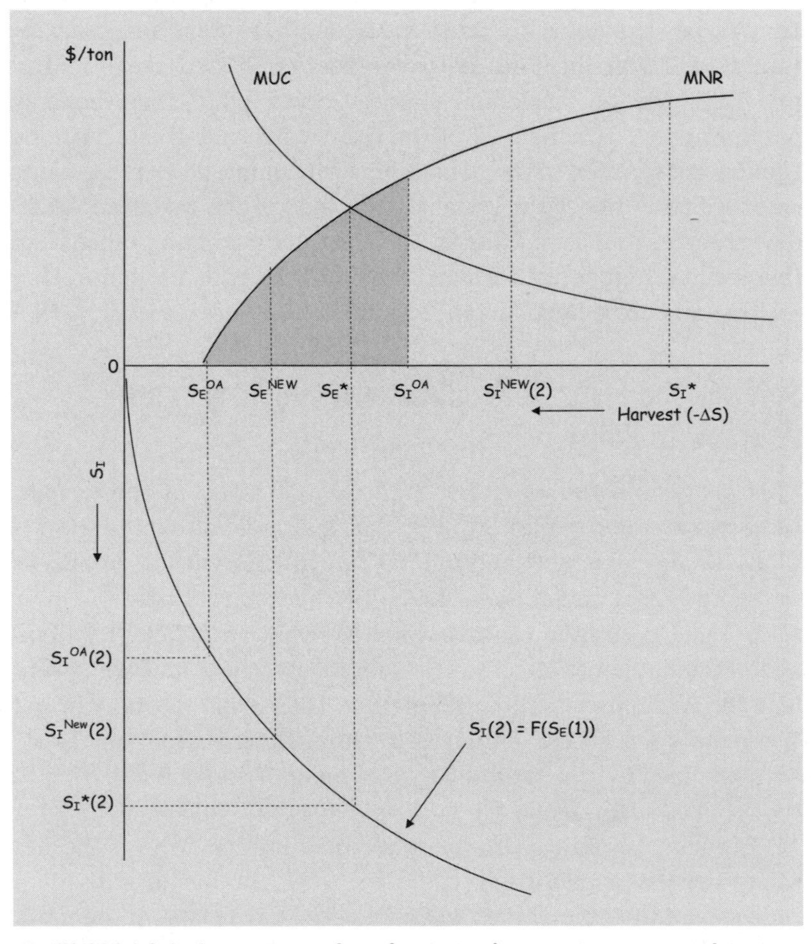

FIGURE 12.3 Economic benefits of reducing harvest in an overexploited fishery

Look at figure 12.3. If fishing is halted at S_E^{NEW}, this means that next year the initial stock would be higher, at $S_I^{NEW}(2)$. But to do this requires reducing the total net benefits—the shaded area—by the portion to the left of S_E^{NEW}. The loss of these revenues means that the fishers will not be able to cover their fixed costs, which could mean defaulting on a loan or being unable to cover personal expenses such as a home mortgage, a child's college tuition, and so on. Without access to emergency financing, fishing families would view this as a financial disaster—perhaps leading to bankruptcy. It may be possible to do this incrementally, imposing small costs on fishers in the near term, but this will also mean smaller gains in the immediate future. Keep in mind, too, that these graphical representations of fishery dynamics may be misleading if we think of them as changes that can occur from one year to the next. Many fish stocks grow slowly, and restoration to efficient levels could take many years or even many decades. Canada banned cod fishing off Newfoundland because of the devastation caused by overfishing, but the fish had yet to return after ten years. For some rockfish populations off the California and Oregon coasts, biologists estimate it will take more than one hundred years for them to recover.

The Pressures to Overexploit

Even in a well-managed fishery that is doing better than open access, there are constant pressures toward overharvesting. Consider figure 12.4, showing an efficiently managed fishery, and assume the shaded area is greater than fixed costs so that net social benefits are positive. In addition to pressures from other fishers who would like to enter this industry to earn profits, there are other shocks that create short-run pressures to overexploit. For example, a change in ocean conditions could reduce the initial stock from S_I to S_I' unexpectedly. In figure 12.4 this reduces total net revenue if fishing is halted at S_E^*. In a season like this, when fewer fish have been caught by the time S_E^* is reached, fishers can be expected to plead with fishery managers to raise the catch limit in order to meet their expected revenue levels and cover their fixed costs.

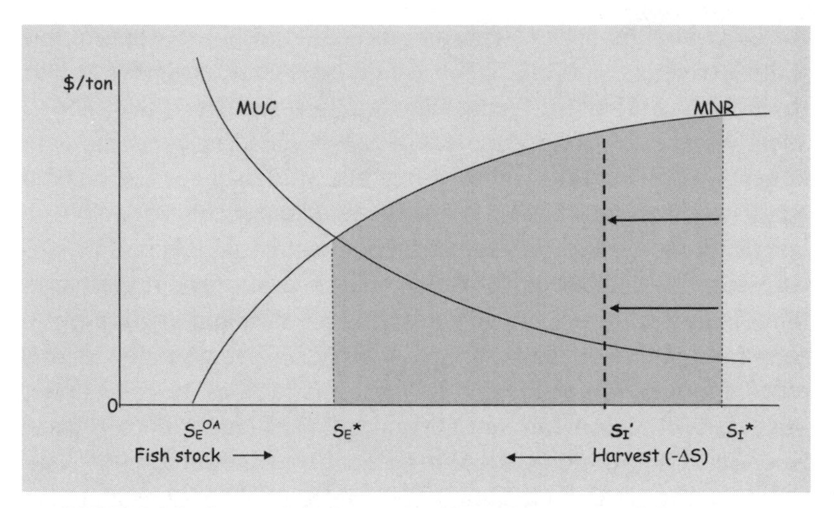

FIGURE 12.4 External shocks to an efficiently managed fishery

Similarly, if fish prices were to drop unexpectedly, this would shift the MNR curve down, and again the total net revenue earned by the time S_E* is reached would be insufficient to cover fixed costs. This situation would also lead to pressure on fishery managers to allow for increased harvests to compensate for the low fish prices.

Individual fishers often have strong incentives to impose costs on the fishery in the future. Given the uncertainty about things such as current and future fish stocks and current and future fish prices, there will be a tendency to give more weight to the certainty surrounding fishers' immediate needs for current income rather than to these long-term considerations.

Policy Alternatives

Given the dilemma facing fishery managers—that of making fishers worse off before they can be made better off—let's look at four alternative approaches that have been used or suggested for managing a fishery.

1. *Regulatory controls in equipment, timing, or location of fishing.* This is a widely used approach that can involve limits on the size of boats, the types of nets, the number of lines, or limits on the length of the season and/or the locations where fishing is

allowed. These constraints, however, raise costs by forcing inefficiencies on fishers. These kinds of management approaches may, indeed, be effective in reducing harvest levels and raising the escapement stock, but do they solve the open access problem? In general the answer is a resounding NO. This kind of fishery management has been referred to as irrational conservation because, in effect, it attempts to solve one inefficiency problem by creating another one. We can see this in figure 12.5. Beginning in open access, imposing inefficiencies on fishers will raise costs and thus lower MNR (it will also shift the MUC curve down). This is shown by the dotted line MNR′, and it means that instead of obtaining the shaded area in net revenues, only that portion of the shaded area below the dotted line will be available to cover fixed costs (and where fixed costs are equal to the entire shaded area given the initial open access situation). The effect of this intervention is to reduce net revenues so that they are below fixed costs. The policy will have the effect of raising S_E^{OA}, but what effect will it have on the net benefits of the fishery overall? Some fishers will leave because of negative profits, and the situation will return to one where net revenue (the new, smaller shaded area) once again is equal to fixed cost: the social value of the fishery is once again zero, just as it was before these controls were implemented. In terms of net social benefit, nothing has changed.

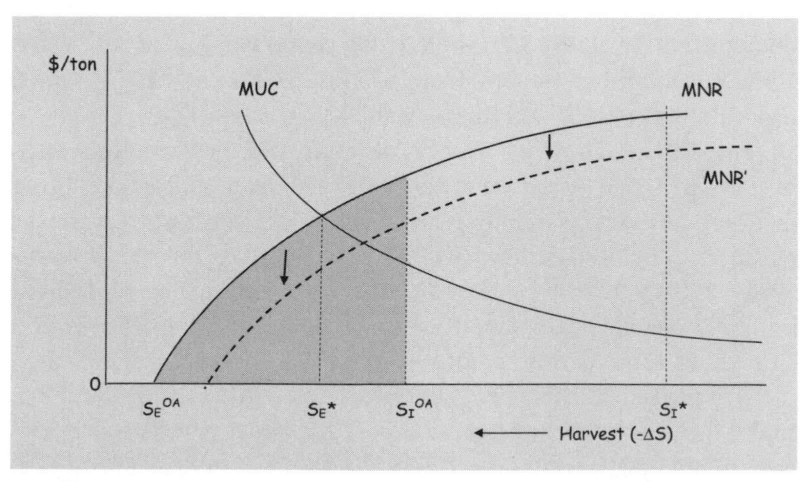

FIGURE 12.5 Fishery policies that amount to "irrational conservation"

It is important to note, however, that in some circumstances this approach may be useful as a component of a broader fishery management approach. For example, banning fishing when and where fish are known to reproduce, or where juvenile fish congregate, may actually increase the fishery's potential net benefits overall.

2. *Quantity restrictions on harvest*. This regulatory CAC approach involves a government agency imposing limits on the total harvest. Frequently, a harvest target is announced at the beginning of the season, although adjustments may be made as better information about the actual abundance of fish is acquired during the season. In principle, this approach could achieve efficiency, but experience suggests that the lobbying pressures on fishery managers to raise harvests above efficient levels will make it difficult to maintain an optimal policy. Free entry by fishers into this kind of fishery will exacerbate those political and lobbying pressures, for example, from recent entrants who have made capital investments in state-of-the-art boats and equipment. These tendencies may be even stronger if fishery commissions, charged with setting harvest targets, are dominated by representatives of the fishing industries themselves.

3. *Landing fees*. Charging fishers a fee per fish (or per pound of fish) is an approach similar to a pollution tax: it is intended to correct the misalignment between social and private net benefits. If a landing fee is set at the appropriate level, it will cause fishers to halt at the efficient ending stock, S_E^*, just like a Pigouvian tax on pollution. In figure 12.6 we can see that charging a landing fee t^* will discourage fishers from fishing below stock S_E^*, since their after-tax MNR will fall to zero at t^*.

In principle, landing fees could achieve efficiency in a fishery. In practice, there are major drawbacks that make them impractical. First, assuming our starting point is an open access or highly depleted fishery where net revenues narrowly cover fishers' fixed costs, the introduction of a landing fee on fishers will not be well received politically. In addition to causing fishers to reduce their catch (fishing will halt at a stock higher than S_E^{OA}), a portion of their net revenues will be lost as fee payments, making the fishers even worse off in the short run than if a harvest quota had been imposed. Even in the long run, or at the efficient level of fishing with an optimal, or Pigouvian, landing fee, the fishers are likely to be no better off than they were under open access: their net revenues are likely to end up being zero. Fishers will receive only the solid shaded area in figure 12.6, which, assuming some exit by fishers following the introduction of a landing fee, will end up equaling their fixed costs—just as it did in open access. Society will be better off because, in contrast to equipment restrictions, which raise the social costs and lower the social net revenues of fishing, the landing fee will transfer revenue from fishers to government—benefits that are not lost to society but are simply changing hands. In the current example, this transfer of net revenues from fishers to government in the form of landing fees will equal the diagonally striped shaded area in figure 12.6.

In addition to these disadvantages, the problem of uncertainty about prices, costs, and the underlying biological relationships in any given fishery makes it very difficult to ascertain what the "right" landing fee would be. In the face of such uncertainty, and the strong objections by fishers, the outcome of any attempt to introduce a landing fee is likely to be a fee that is far too low to achieve efficiency.

4. *Individual transferable quotas*. An individual transferable quota (ITQ) or individual fishing permit (IFP) is a property right created by government and allocated to fishers that entitles the

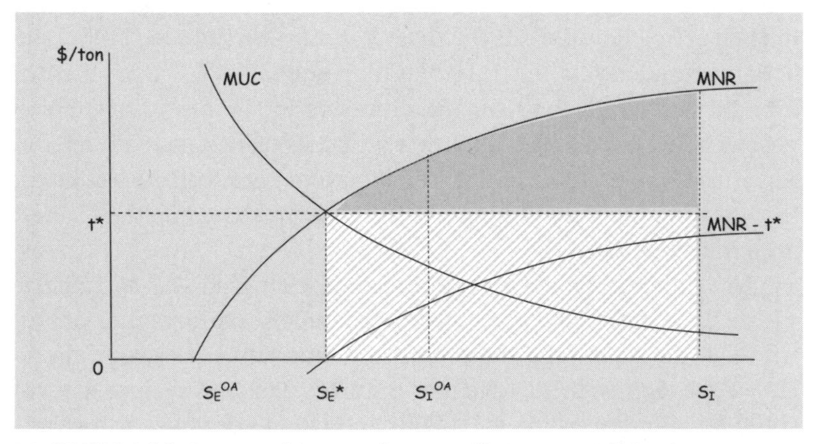

■ **FIGURE 12.6 Impact of landing fees on efficiency and fishers' incomes**

owner of each permit to a specified harvest level each year. Unlike tradable pollution permits, ITQs are generally permanent rights, ones that can be used for many years and then sold. In principle and in practice (based on limited, recent experience), this fishery management tool offers the most promise for reducing overfishing. What makes ITQs different and potentially more effective? First, with ITQs, no transfers of revenue to government are necessary—unlike a landing fee.

But if a depleted fishery is going to recover, there is no alternative but to reduce the catch in the short term so that stocks can be allowed to increase for the future, right? This is true of harvest quotas as well, so how are ITQs different? Let's consider a fishery that is currently in an open access situation, like the one depicted in figure 12.7. Assume that the situation is in equilibrium, meaning that net revenues are just equal to fixed cost. Let's start by doling out ITQs that give each fisher the right to catch exactly the number of fish each season that they have been catching. Now, what is the market value of each of these ITQs? Since we are initially operating in open access, the value should be zero. To see this, note that these fishers (now owners of ITQs) are still just covering their fixed costs and not making any profits. How much would you pay to buy a certificate that entitles you to make no money? Probably nothing!

Let's carry this situation a bit further. Let's assume there are twenty fishers, and we give each of them an ITQ that entitles them to one-twentieth of the allowed harvest. In order to move toward efficiency, the allowed harvest must be reduced below the open access harvest level, H^{OA}, which equals $S_I^{OA} - S_E^{OA}$. Beginning incrementally, let's consider a reduction in total allowed harvest to $H^0 = S_I^{OA} - S_E^1$ so that the ending stock is higher than S_E^{OA}. As a result, net revenues in the current year will be reduced, truncated to the shaded area in figure 12.7 rather than the shaded area in figure 12.3.

Next period, however, the initial stock will be higher, at S_I^1. This will permit fishery managers to keep the ending stock at S_E^1, while at the same time increasing the total harvest in year one to $H^1 = S_I^1 - S_E^1$, which is greater than H^0. This new harvest level could be maintained in every year following year one, as a result of the one-time sacrifice in year zero of the area labeled A in figure 12.7. *Now* what is an ITQ worth? That question can be answered in a fairly precise way if we make the following assumptions: First, assume that H^1 will be the (new) allowed harvest every year indefinitely and that this is understood by all fishers and potential fishers. Second, assume that fixed costs are unchanged from the initial open access situation. And third, assume the market interest rate is r. From figure 12.7 we can infer that net revenues are higher than fixed costs by an amount equal to (B + C) − A, the difference between these two areas (B + C) and A. Each fisher will receive one-twentieth of this as profits each year. Therefore, the price that potential fishers should be willing to pay, and that current fishers should be willing to accept, will be the present value of the permanent annuity, or perpetuity, for this annual amount. Using the simple formula for the present value of a perpetuity (see chapter 4), we can conclude that an individual ITQ should now sell for (1/20)((B + C) − A)/r, once the shift from H^0 to H^1 has occurred.

It's important to recognize that the reduction in harvest in period zero did not make the fishers worse off—as was the case with the other management approaches. In return for giving up net revenues A in period zero, the value of each ITQ rises from zero in period zero to (1/20)((B + C) − A)/r in period one. This must be true, otherwise the reduction in harvest in period zero

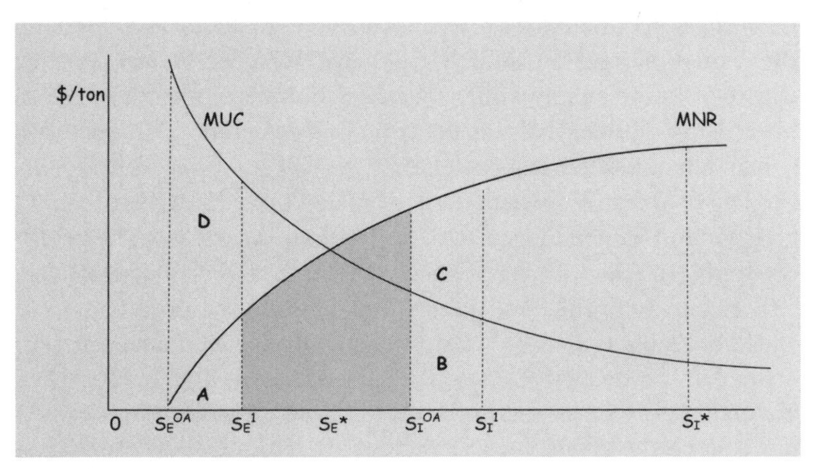

■ **FIGURE 12.7 Incremental gains when implementing an individual transferable quota**

and subsequent increase in harvests from period one forward would not be socially efficient. Another way to see this is by referring to the MUC curve. The present value of the future gains from sacrificing A in period zero is precisely the corresponding area under the MUC curve: area A + D. Any change that moves the fishery toward efficiency will increase the value of the ITQs by more than the short-term sacrifices, and this will be the case so long as MUC is above MNR for the change in S_E. In fact, it is useful to think of these sacrifices (giving up net revenues in any period in order to increase revenues in the future) as an investment (in capital—of the fishy kind), one whose return will manifest itself in the market value of the ITQ (which can now be seen as a share of stock, just like in a corporation).

An ITQ makes it easier for fishers to look to the future, because the value of their ITQ depends on the expected future profits from fishing. Overfishing in any particular year may earn them more income in that year, but it will likely reduce the value of their quota since it will reduce the expected future income from the fishery. Just like a stockholder of a corporation, fishers who own ITQs will have a strong incentive to protect the value of their stocks by focusing on the future prospects of the company (the fishery). So, ITQs cause fishers to be interested in their ability to meet their future needs, in addition to their current needs. If this sounds a little bit like one of the definitions of sustainability at the start of chapter 6, this is no accident. This policy tool, in the form of a private property right for ITQs, can be an effective way to promote sustainability because it alters private incentives toward the future, making them more consistent with society's goal of sustainable resource use.

The contrast between fisheries managed with effective institutions and those managed with ineffective controls can be pretty dramatic. In Rhode Island, where CAC policies are used, lobster fishers barely break even, often tending eight hundred traps and spending 240 days in the water chasing after two-pound lobsters instead of the twenty-pounders of three decades ago. By contrast, in Australia, where a system of tradable licenses has been in place since the 1960s, lobster fishers are limited to no more than 187 days on the water, and they have limited themselves to sixty traps each. The lobster trap licenses that sold for $2,000 apiece in

1984 were selling for $35,000 in 2000. Rather than fighting with government to increase harvests, these now-wealthy Australian fishers often impose stricter limits than those required by government or suggested by scientists.[1]

In the United States currently, there is a moratorium on ITQs. This is partly due to concern about market power, where ownership of Alaska's fishing quotas might end up being concentrated or in the hands of non-Alaskans. But the possibility of concentrated ownership or market power exists in many markets, including real estate and stocks, and there are ways to reduce the risks of such undesired outcomes. In the meantime, the situation in the United States still resembles open access, a tragedy of the commons.

Recommended Readings and References

The key references on common pool resources are Garrett Hardin, "The Tragedy of the Commons," *Science* 162 (1968): 1243–1248; which was preceeded by Scott Gordon, "The Economic Theory of a Common Property Resource: The Fishery," *Journal of Political Economy* 62, no. 2 (1954): 124–142.

On fisheries economics, see Lee Anderson, *The Economics of Fisheries Management* (Baltimore: Johns Hopkins University Press, 1986); and James A. Crutchfield and Giulio Pontecorvo, *The Pacific Salmon Fisheries: A Study in Irrational Conservation* (Baltimore: Johns Hopkins University Press, 1969). Two useful government reports are National Research Council, Committee to Review Individual Fishing Quotas, *Sharing the Fish: Toward a National Policy on Individual Fishing Quotas* (Washington, DC: National Academy Press, 1999); and Organization for Economic Cooperation and Development, *Toward Sustainable Fisheries: Economics Aspects of the Management of Living Marine Resources* (Paris: Organization for Economic Cooperation and Development, 1997). The seminal reference on the optimal fishery management is Colin W. Clark, *Mathematical Bioeconomics: The Optimal Management of Renewable Resources*, 2nd ed. (Hoboken, NJ: Wiley-Interscience, March 15, 1990).

[1]John Tierney, "A Tale of Two Fisheries," *New York Times*, August 27, 2000, 38–43.

13

Policy Failures

It would be a mistake to think that every market failure requires a policy solution. Some market failures surely have only small effects, and just as markets can fail, policies can fail, too. These can sometimes make the policy "cure" worse than the market failure "disease." This chapter summarizes some of the principal ways in which government policies can become more complicated, and less effective, than the discussions in recent chapters might suggest. The main point is not that government policies cannot correct market failure, but that they, too, have shortcomings. Good policymaking should try to weigh one kind of shortcoming against the other.

Of course, the observation that both markets and governments have failings is very similar to the recognition that both private property and common property involve transaction costs (see chapter 9) and that, in some circumstances, these transaction costs may be lower for private property than common property (or vice versa). The point we want to make here is no different. Sometimes government institutions may represent a more costly "solution" to a market failure problem than the problem itself. Indeed, government can be seen as just a more formal kind of common pool resource institution, and like all institutional arrangements, it involves costs and has various shortcomings. Let's turn now to some of the main types of policy or "nonmarket" failures.

The Visible Bludgeon

Rather than being like the "invisible hand" of efficient market allocation, government policies can often be a blunt instrument, more of a "visible bludgeon," especially when they impose a "one-size-fits-all" rule that does not take account of the differences in marginal benefits and marginal costs across firms, individuals, locations, and uses or over time. Whereas market forces and price signals can "target" efficient trade-offs for each individual or firm, government policies often cannot. For example, command-and-control emissions regulations assume all firms have the same marginal abatement cost curve and all individuals have the same air quality and identical willingness to pay for air quality improvements. Market-based policy tools bring important advantages by allowing firms to make decentralized decisions that reflect their own marginal abatement costs. But even these market-based instruments are blunt: pollution damages and highway congestion costs vary by location and time of day. A market-based policy like a statewide gas tax will be a crude way to control air pollution or reduce highway congestion because it imposes the same costs and incentives in rural areas where the air is clean and the roads are never congested. When the marginal benefits of abatement differ across sources of emissions, imposing either uniform controls or uniform costs on all air pollution sources will be inefficient and can lead to "hot spot" locations with high pollution or population concentrations where marginal damages are very high.

In contrast to the kinds of market-based instruments and other targeted policies outlined in other chapters, trade barriers constitute a very indirect and blunt instrument that will rarely be the most efficient choice. This is because trade restrictions affect the price and scarcity of the affected good in the same way everywhere in the economy. A tariff on gasoline imports aimed at reducing pollution will make it more costly to drive in LA, where pollution is a large problem, but it will also have the same effect in North Dakota, where air pollution from motorists is not a problem. As a result, imposing those unnecessary costs on motorists in North Dakota would be inefficient. In addition, trade restrictions affect the supply and demand for domestic currencies, and this will have an influence on the exchange rate, which alters the relative prices of all imports, exports, and nontraded goods (e.g., services). Any effect on the exchange rate caused by a trade barrier will permeate the entire economy rather than be narrowly focused on the actions that are causing environmental harm.

If other more direct mechanisms cannot be implemented effectively or with reasonable transaction costs, or if these alternatives are not socially acceptable for other reasons, then trade restrictions may be the only option. But it would be prudent to view trade as the "tool of last resort." This "last resort" justification would seem to be satisfied in the case of the ban on trade in endangered species. See box 8 in chapter 10 for more on the difficulties of controlling poaching of ivory and rhino horn.

It's also true that many developing countries lack effective formal institutions for protecting the environment. This leaves domestic environmental resources vulnerable to overexploitation by domestic users, and open trade can make matters worse by heightening the incentives to degrade the resources. Exports of timber from Cote d'Ivoire, Indonesia, and Brazil are examples fitting this scenario, as is the plundering of phosphates from the island nation of Nauru. These examples may not necessarily be lessons about the dangers of trade; they may simply reflect the dangers associated with dysfunctional institutions, corruption, and self-interested politicians.

The Private Goals of Public Agents

Probably the most common type of policy failure reflects what economists call **principal-agent problems.** Think of the "principal" as the owner of an apartment building, and the agent as someone hired to manage the rental units. The agent is unlikely to do things exactly the way the principal would like. If the building burns down, the agent loses his job but not his assets. If tenants leave without paying their rent, the agent is not responsible, and so will not make the same level of effort as the owner would in screening tenants or getting them to pay their rent on time. Anytime a principal assigns an agent with responsibilities, there are likely to be differences in motivation, incentives, and performance that lead to inefficiencies. This applies to any business with employees, or any contract for services.

Key Concept: *Principal-agent problems* 

The same thing holds for a society where public servants are charged with implementing the public's will. These civil servants are charged with running agencies, spending public funds, interpreting laws, and protecting communities and natural resources. One form of this principal-agent problem is what political scientists call an **internality or private goal.** Career government bureaucrats typically have their own careers to think about, and furthering their own career may motivate them in ways that diverge from the will of the people, for example, if job security or promotion depends on high spending levels or contract rates.

Key Concept: *Internality or private goal* 

In the case of elected officials, the time horizon for society (very long term) may be in conflict with the politician's time horizon (the next election). As a result, limiting logging to protect forests for future generations, spending public funds to clean up toxic waste sites, and taking timely action to slow climate change are examples of actions that may be in the public interest but are less likely to help with reelection.

This private goals problem can cause government entities to take on a life of their own because employees want to protect or enhance their jobs. When regional forest service budgets are tied to the level of logging contracts on public lands, it creates an incentive to promote high logging rates whether that is the stated policy goal or not. Economists call a similar phenomenon **regulatory capture,** which refers to a situation where government agents in charge of regulating an industry become so familiar and closely involved with the industry itself that they become advocates for the industry's interests rather than the public interest.

Key Concept: *Regulatory capture*

One other reason these principal-agent problems occur is that supervision of agents by principals is costly, and when there is "asymmetric information" (when the agents know things that the principal does not), conflicts of interest arise that create waste, inefficiencies, and opportunities for corruption.

It is important to distinguish between the economic rational for markets, trade, and comparative advantage on the one hand and the behavior of particular organizations such as the International Monetary Fund or the World Bank on the other. In recent debate about globalization, the distinctions between these two issues have sometimes been blurred. Recent critics of the International Monetary Fund and the World Bank include the Nobel Prize-winning economist Joseph Stiglitz.[1] He criticizes these international organizations for being heavy-handed and for offering bad advice to developing countries. But in doing so he is not abandoning economic reasoning about comparative advantage or the promise for increasing standards of living by promoting efficiently managed trade. Indeed, economics says little about whether a particular organization like the International Monetary Fund will always offer good advice or use its influence for the betterment of society.

Policy Distortions and Derived Externalities

A third type of policy failure is sometimes referred to as a **derived externality.** This occurs when a government policy aimed at addressing one kind of market failure creates some other kind of distortion. For example, in the interest of reducing urban hunger, many African countries tried to control food prices at affordable levels. This policy, however, lowered the

[1]See Joseph Stiglitz, "Globalism's Discontents," *American Prospect* (Winter 2002).

incentives for farmers to produce food (rather than export cash crops), and food production fell, actually making it more difficult to feed the poor. In another example, policies to encourage food production have sometimes included subsidies on fertilizer and chemicals, which in turn has led to overuse and worsened water pollution problems. Cheap coal in China and below-cost timber sales in the United States and many other countries are examples that show that one policy goal can be promoted at the expense of others. When these kinds of policies are recognized to be both inefficient and unjustified, abolishing them can create a "win-win" opportunity by eliminating two inefficiencies.

Key Concept: *Derived externality* 

A somewhat related problem is one that economists call **the theory of second best.**[2] This is a bit more subtle and not necessarily obvious. The basic idea is that in a world with two or more market failures (a "second-best" world), correcting one market failure could actually make society worse off. Free trade is an obvious example that was discussed in chapter 8. Opening an economy to trade should produce benefits owing to the gains from trade and market efficiency. But removing trade barriers may be welfare reducing if there are uncorrected externalities or insecure property rights in the domestic economy.

Key Concept: *Theory of second best* 

Rent Seeking

A fourth type of policy failure is **rent seeking.** Rent seeking refers to actions like lobbying to gain advantage through government action. A monopoly created or protected by government action is one example. Other examples include tariffs or import licenses that give certain individuals or groups benefits at the expense of others.

[2]Richard G. Lipsey and Kelvin Lancaster, "The General Theory of Second Best, " *Review of Economic Studies* 24 (1956): 11–32.

The theory of rent seeking has two parts. The first part involves the well-known idea that monopolies have the ability to influence prices in a way that increases profits for the monopolist at the expense of consumers. This monopolistic behavior can create large transfers from consumer surplus to producer (monopolist) surplus and will also create a deadweight loss. The second part of the theory focuses on what self-interested entrepreneurs will be willing to do to secure these large transfers. Given the possibility of extorting high profits from customers, potential monopolists can be expected to commit large amounts of resources to try to secure or maintain a monopoly position.[3] This is rent seeking.

Rent seeking does not, however, produce value for society. It just creates an opportunity for one firm or group to gain at the expense of others. How costly might rent seeking be to society? Rational entrepreneurs might be willing to invest resources in these efforts equal to the discounted value of the expected profits. These can be huge numbers. In one well-known study, the social losses from rent seeking were estimated to be 7% and 15% of national income in India and Pakistan, respectively.[4] Rent seeking in the United States can be seen in the lobbying for farm price supports on crops such as cotton, wheat, and rice; import restrictions on sugar; and promotion of ethanol fuel additives made from corn. Rent seeking is also widespread in the competition for government defense contracts and in other federal departments, as well as in state, local, and municipal governments.

Rent seeking will be more common and more successful when the benefits of rent seeking are concentrated on a small group of "winners" and the costs are spread across a large diffuse group of "losers." Trade restrictions, land use regulations, and farm support programs are just some of the areas where

---

[3]See G. Tullock, "The Welfare Costs of Tariffs, Monopolies and Theft," *Western Economic Journal* 5 (1967): 224–232).
[4]See A. O. Kreuger, "The Political Economy of the Rent-Seeking Society," *American Economic Review* 64 (1974): 291–303.

stakeholders with relatively narrow vested interests are able to promote policies that would not be supported on the basis of benefit-cost analysis or if voted on by the general public.

A counterargument can also be made here, however, that these are just the kinds of situations where comparisons of benefits and costs fail to adequately recognize the intensity of certain specific interests, or other considerations such as the protection of individual rights or fairness toward minority interests that are not adequately reflected in willingness-to-pay measures of value.

Recommended Readings and References

The idea of policy, or "nonmarket," failure was originated in Charles Wolfe, "A Theory of Nonmarket Failure: Framework for Implementation Analysis," *Journal of Law and Economics* 22 (1979): 107–139.

Other key references include Anne O. Krueger, "The Political Economy of the Rent-Seeking Society," *American Economic Review* 64 (1974): 291–303; Jean-Jacques Laffont and Jean Tirole, "The Politics of Government Decision-making: A Theory of Regulatory Capture," *Quarterly Journal of Economics* 106, no. 4 (1991): 1089–1127; Richard G. Lipsey and Kelvin Lancaster, "The General Theory of the Second-Best," *Review of Economic Studies* 24 (1956): 11–32; Richard A. Posner, "The Social Cost of Monopoly and Regulation," *Journal of Political Economy* 83 (1975): 807–827; George J. Stigler, "The Theory of Economic Regulation," *Bell Journal of Economics and Management Science* 2 (1971): 3–21; and Clifford Winston, "Economic Deregulation: Days of Reckoning for Microeconomists," *Journal of Economic Literature* 31 (1993): 1263–1289.

PART III
Measuring Values, Informing Choices

14

Valuing the Environment

Some people object to the idea of putting a value or price on the environment and would prefer that society make this kind of collective decision about the environment democratically, for example, by voting on proposals to establish a forest reserve, or to reduce air pollution, or to remove a hydropower dam from a river. For any one of these proposals, people would likely have differing views about the desirability of a particular environmental improvement, which would affect their willingness to vote in favor of it. There would of course also be costs to consider. For example, in the case of a forest reserve, the land might need to be purchased, and there would be infrastructure and maintenance costs. Voters would want to know what these costs would be and also who would pay them. If the costs were spread evenly across the community, for example, in the form of a uniform tax increase, then we would expect the percentage of voters voting yes to decline as the cost per person rose.

All voters will likely have a "reservation price," meaning a price above which they would switch their vote from yes to no. For the community as a whole, these reservation prices would vary depending on preferences and income, creating a distribution that might look something like the hypothetical example in figure 14.1. In this example, at a zero price everybody votes yes. At a cost of $25 per person, three or four voters would change their vote to no. And at a cost of $50 per person, a bare majority will vote yes, but above $50 there would not be a majority of supporters for the project.

This democratic approach will appeal to those who object to putting a price on the environment. But is it really different? People's votes reflect their willingness to pay. And people with higher income are likely to be willing to pay more, so people's willingness to vote yes is influenced by their "ability to pay," just like economic measures of value. Economic methods of estimating people's willingness to pay for a specific environmental improvement, and then comparing the mean or median of those estimates to the costs of the environmental improvement, amount to much the same thing as the voting approach just described. While there may be benefits to the voting process itself, voting is not a practical way to decide on thousands of potential actions related to the air, water, land use, and so on. The

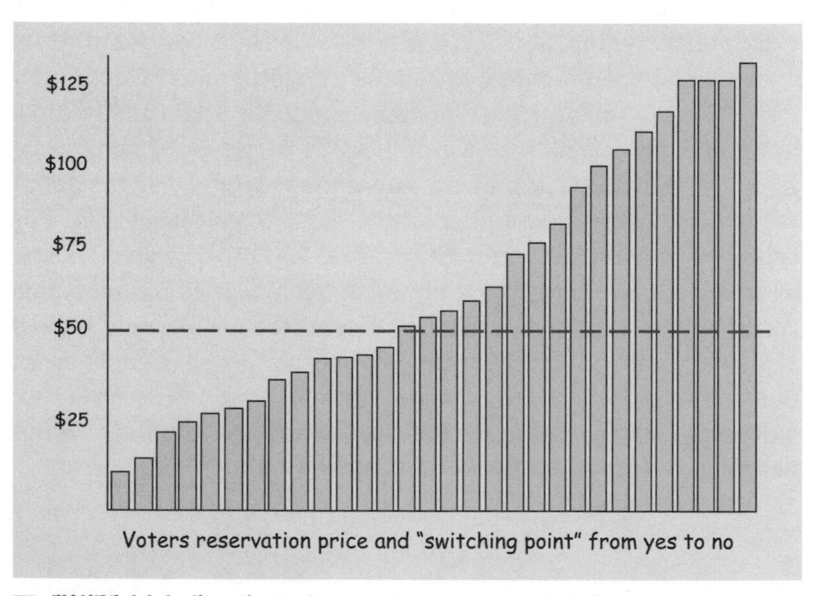

■ **FIGURE 14.1 Hypothetical voters "reservation price" for approving a forest reserve**

economic valuation methods described in this chapter attempt to ascertain the public's preferences without actually voting. So, while not identical to direct democracy, these valuation methods are intended to provide a close approximation.[1]

To make decisions about protecting the environment, policymakers need solid evidence about voters' reservation prices—their willingness to pay—especially when trying to justify actions that would impose tangible dollar costs on firms, consumers, or taxpayers. In cases where the environment affects the availability of market goods like wood, fish, and land, market data can provide useful information about people's willingness to pay. If we can estimate the demand curves for these goods and how that demand might change with policy, then we can evaluate the benefits or costs associated with a specified environmental change.

For *nonmarket* environmental goods and services, the task of valuation is more difficult but not impossible. In fact, one of the most important contributions by economists to the protection of the environment has been the development of a number of creative ways to measure the value people place on these kinds of nonmarket goods. In the days before these methods were developed, all too often the value of nonmarket environmental goods and services was effectively zero because there was no way to estimate their actual value.

Environmental economists make an important distinction between two main types of value related to the environment. The first is "use value" and the second is "passive-use" or "nonuse" value. The **use value** category includes market goods that come from nature, such as fish and game, wood and other forest products, and drinking water from a protected watershed. These goods can often be valued based on market-price information just like other commodities. Use value also includes many nonmarket goods and services, such as clean air, views of nature, enjoyment from visiting natural places, and recreational activities such as hiking, skiing, fishing, and hunting.

Key Concepts: *Use value, nonuse value* 

[1] I am grateful to Richard Carson for suggesting this comparison between voting and valuation.

In contrast, passive-use or **nonuse value** refers to the value people may place on environmental resources even if they do not consume them or benefit from them in any direct ways. Proximity is not required for passive-use value. These kinds of values often have to do with people's ethics or moral convictions about society's responsibility to act as steward for the earth. Passive-use values include people's desires to protect species from extinction (even if they do not expect to ever see the species) and to avoid another *Exxon Valdez* oil spill (even if they do not expect to ever visit Alaska). Passive-use values include the desire to keep parts of the Amazon rain forest pristine and to have clean air over the Grand Canyon.

Other terms are sometimes used to describe passive-use value, including existence value and bequest value. For the most part, these terms relate to a particular motivation or type of passive-use value. There is also a type of value called option value or option price, which is similar to the value of insurance, which mitigates risk associated with future events that might lead to regrets about current decisions or irreversible commitments.

The methods used to value nonmarket goods fall into one of two main categories. The first category looks at choices people actually make and identifies ways that those choices reveal something about the value they place on the environment. These techniques are called **revealed preference** techniques. If people travel long distances to visit a pristine beach, this reveals something about its value to them. And if people are willing to pay a higher price for a house in a part of town with clean air rather than in a part of town with dirty air, the price differences between houses in these two parts of town should reveal the strength of that preference.

Key Concepts: *Revealed preference, stated preference*

The second main category of techniques used to value nonmarket goods involves surveys, ones that ask people questions about how much they value the environment, or how much they would be willing to pay for a specified change in the environment. These approaches are called **stated preference** techniques.

Stated preference techniques are very important because in many situations there is simply no other way to come up with a measure of environmental values. There are good reasons to be cautious when interpreting what people *say* they are willing to pay when there is no commitment involved. But as we describe later, there are also good reasons to believe that, if done carefully and correctly, the stated preference techniques can provide very useful information about environmental values. In the rest of this chapter, we provide more detail on these main approaches to valuation.

Direct Use of Market Data

In some cases the value of the environment is directly reflected in the abundance of market goods (fish and game, wood and forest products, clean water). In other cases a change in environmental quality will impose additional market costs on individuals. These are cases where the value of the environment (or at least these components of the environment's value) can be evaluated on the basis of market information.

When water pollution in a river kills twenty thousand commercially valuable fish, we can estimate one component of the cost of the pollution based on the market value of those fish. (That does not mean that we simply multiply twenty thousand fish times the price that fish sell for in a supermarket. Since there are costs involved in catching, processing, and transporting the fish, we would need to subtract those costs first.) Alternatively, if there were fish hatcheries or fish farms where fish are reared and sold, we might take a "replacement cost" approach and estimate the cost of replacing the fish from a hatchery.

Agriculture is another area where market data can be used to evaluate environmental damage. Farm output can be adversely affected by contamination of soil, groundwater, or surface water or from loss of topsoil or air pollution. These environmental factors can lower yields or reduce the acreage that can be used in agriculture. If the costs of production are unaffected, then the loss would simply be the change in output multiplied by the price received by the farmer. In some cases environmental damage may not affect yields, but it may require additional actions by the farmer to avoid lower yields. A farmer may have to apply additional fertilizer to counteract the effects of a loss of topsoil. In this case these increased costs would represent the value (or loss of value) from the environmental change that has occurred.

Market and technical data can also be used to estimate the costs of reducing air pollution, as illustrated in box 9.

Some health effects of pollution can be valued using market data. If air pollution causes an increase in the frequency of morbidity such as chronic lung disease, the treatment (doctors' visits, medicine) and lost income from workers' absences will be components of the cost. Of course, people also prefer not to be sick for reasons extending beyond missing work and buying medicine, but there are no obvious market data to evaluate this aspect of health effects. In the case of death from exposure to pollution, there are several aspects to consider. There is a loss to society of the "human capital" and workforce productivity of a person who dies as a result of air pollution. But we would want some way of evaluating the very tricky question of what is called the value of a statistical life. One way to measure this value is found in the later discussion about hedonic pricing techniques.

Travel Cost Method

The travel cost method looks at how far people are willing to travel to enjoy an environmental nonmarket good such as a beach, lake, river, or wilderness area. Travel is costly in terms of time, fuel, and other expenses. We expect people who live closer to a pristine lake to visit it more often, on average, than people who live far away, just as we expect people to buy more pizza when the price is low than when the price is high. So, if we can estimate a demand curve for pizza using its price, then we can also estimate a demand curve for a pristine lake using the travel costs as a proxy for its price (where distance from the site means differences in travel cost). That is exactly what economists have been doing since the 1960s.

To explain how the travel cost method works, a simple illustration probably works best. In the upper portion of figure 14.2, we designate three rings or zones for people who live at different distances from the lake (five, ten, and fifteen miles). We conduct

BOX 9

Air Pollution in Mexico City: Assessing the Cost of Cleaner Air

In addition to estimating benefits from environmental improvements, economic analysis can often help policymakers estimate the costs. In the case of reducing air pollution, for example, policymakers face great uncertainty about the costs of air quality improvements and how those costs may differ for a wide range of possible actions under consideration. After they combine technical and economic data, it is possible for economists to estimate the marginal cost and changes in emissions for individual actions such as imposing emissions standards, retrofitting high-use vehicles such as busses and taxis, inspections for enforcement, fuel improvements, or fuel taxes.

In one study of this kind for Mexico City (Eskeland and Devarajan 1996), such estimates made it possible to construct a marginal cost or supply curve for emissions reductions. This was done by estimating the emissions reductions and marginal cost for a range of actions and then ordering them from lowest to highest cost. The results of that analysis produced a marginal cost or supply curve that looks something like the one below.

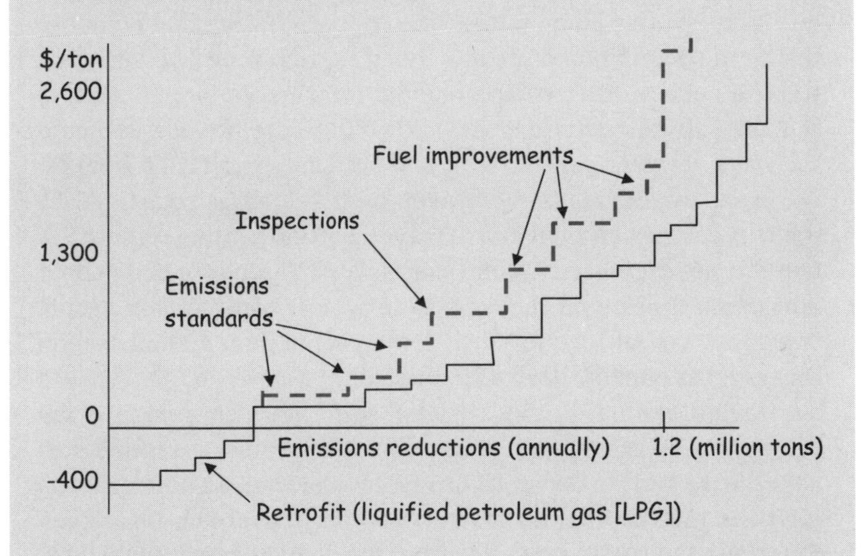

■ **FIGURE Marginal abatement cost for air pollution reduction in Mexico City**

Notably, the authors found that liquefied petroleum gas (LPG) and natural gas retrofitting had a negative cost because it was both cheaper and cleaner. Both emissions standards and inspections had lower marginal costs when applied first to high-use vehicles. And when a gas tax was omitted from the package of interventions, the MC curve was shifted higher as indicated by the dotted line above. The study demonstrates the usefulness of estimating costs of alternative environmental policies and also highlights how indirect policies, both CAC and economic incentives, can be complementary parts of an overall policy strategy.

Source: Gunnar Eskeland and Shantayanan Devarajan, *Taxing Bads by Taxing Goods: Pollution Control with Presumptive Charges* (Washington, DC: World Bank, 1996).

surveys of visitors to a lake to see where they come from and how often they visit. From a sample of visitors, we can estimate how many people come to the lake from each zone and compare that to the population of people living in each zone (we also may want to collect other socioeconomic information about visitors that may affect visitation rates). With this data, we can estimate the visits per year per one thousand residents from each zone.

Next, we estimate the travel cost, taking account of the method, cost, and time taken to travel. Putting a value on people's travel time is a bit tricky, and there are different opinions about how to put a price on the "opportunity cost of time" for people when they travel for pleasure. Some people may actually enjoy the travel as part of the experience.

Having estimated these travel costs, we can compare the three zones by graphing the visitation rates against the travel cost as in the bottom portion of figure 14.2. What we find—not surprisingly—is that demand is lower when the travel cost is higher. These points give us a sense of what the demand curve looks like.

Once we have estimated the demand curve, we can evaluate the net benefit, or consumer surplus, for the lake. We apply this demand curve to the population that lives at each distance from the lake: some people who live there will never visit the lake, while some may go only once because they are indifferent to the

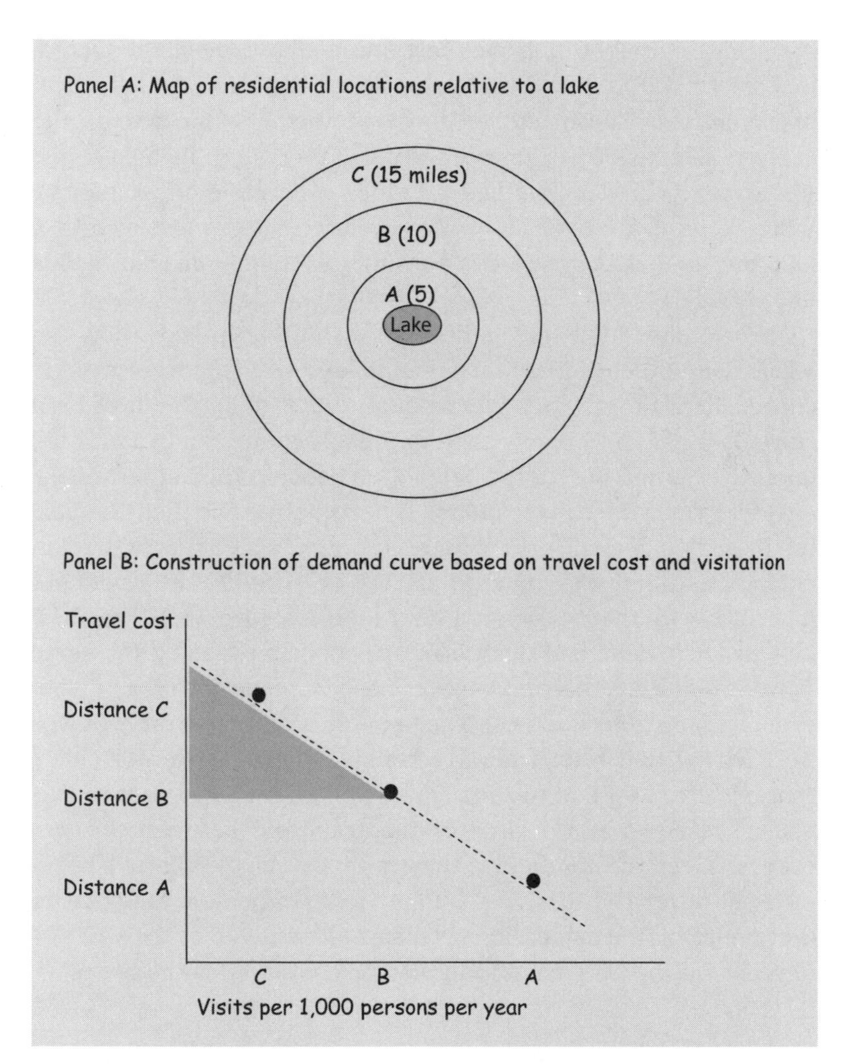

■ **FIGURE 14.2 Illustration of the travel cost method for lake recreation**

benefits from the visit and the costs (of travel). And some will visit frequently because the net benefits far exceed the costs. For distance B, for example, net benefit is the area of the shaded triangle representing the consumer surplus for people paying that "price." At greater distances, the consumer surplus will be small; for populations living near the lake, consumer surplus will be greater.

A large number of travel cost studies have been conducted, looking at things like beach use, sport fisheries, and hunting opportunities. These studies have produced estimates of the average net benefit or consumer surplus as high as $4,000 per visitor per year. This method provides concrete evidence of the value of natural resources and recreation sites, measured in a way that makes comparisons possible with other market goods and services.

What these kinds of studies can also do is to show how the whole demand curve for a particular kind of nonmarket good is shifted up or down depending on quality. The demand curve for a "dirty" lake is shifted down and to the left compared to a pristine lake (after adjusting for the population densities and other differences between the two locations). By estimating and then comparing these two demand or willingness-to-pay (WTP) curves, we can actually estimate the value to society of cleaning up a polluted lake. The way this is done is illustrated in figure 14.3. The WTP curves for a clean and dirty lake are superimposed on the same graph (adjusting the information based on the location, demographics, and other factors). The present condition is dirty (lower WTP curve), and a clean lake is estimated to produce a WTP curve that is shifted up and to the right. The benefit to society of this change is equal to the area of the trapezoid between the two curves. Given the numbers in the graph, we can calculate the benefits per person as $10 \times 10 + \frac{1}{2}(10 \times 5) = \$125$/person. Multiplying that figure by the population produces an estimate of the value of cleaning up the lake, which can then be compared with the cost.

Hedonic Pricing Analysis

The second major revealed preference technique is called hedonic analysis or the hedonic pricing method. The basic idea is that people are willing to pay different amounts for market goods with different characteristics. If some of these characteristics are related to the environment, we can gain an indirect measure of the value of the environment by looking at the differences in revealed preference for goods with/without a particular characteristic. For example, while residential housing prices will vary depending on the size of the house, number of bathrooms, and

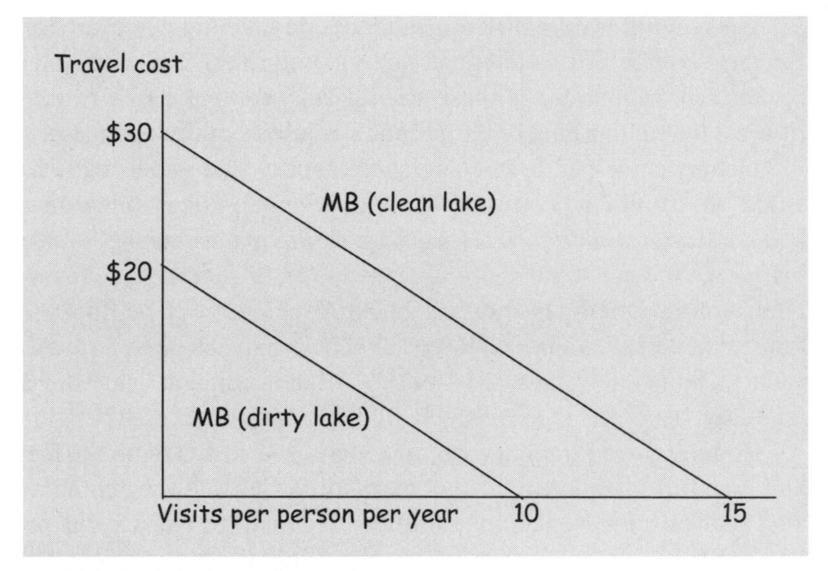

■ **FIGURE 14.3 Value of lake cleanup**

quality of construction, they also vary depending on the quality of the neighborhood schools, local crime rate, and distance from busy streets. The list of factors that may affect the market value of residential housing may also include the level of air pollution, distance from a toxic waste dump or superfund site, and the proximity to open space, such as a greenbelt.

Recall that the travel cost method relates the differences among people (distance from residence to lake) to differences in people's choices (visitation rates). By contrast, the hedonic method relates the differences among goods (attributes of a house/location) to differences in people's choices (willingness to pay a higher price for a house).

Among the most well-known types of hedonic analysis are hedonic housing price studies that take large data sets of home sales and housing characteristics, including things like air pollution levels and proximity to environmental goods (or bads). A statistical technique called multivariate regression analysis is used to sort out the value attributable to each characteristic, which can reveal the premium people are willing to pay, for example, for housing in areas with relatively higher air quality.

These studies reveal strong evidence in housing price data of the preference for reductions in air pollution. For example, results from a number of these studies suggest that a 10% reduction in a particular kind of air pollution would result in an increase in housing prices of 1–4%. The same method has been used to value environmental amenities such as open space and greenbelts. Estimates indicate residential housing prices can be 5–15% higher when near wooded areas, open space, or picturesque farmland. Similar methods indicate housing prices will be 10–20% lower when near major roadways. Traffic noise has been found to reduce housing prices by 10–15%. This kind of statistical approach is now used extensively in the real estate industry.

Hedonic pricing techniques are also used to value morbidity and mortality that might be associated with environmental degradation. In essence, this is where we need to put a value on life itself. In this context we refer to the value of a statistical life to distinguish the concept from putting a value on a particular individual's life. The approach looks at evidence of people's willingness to expose themselves to higher risks for higher pay, or their willingness to spend money to lower risks. One example compares the wages paid to workers in occupations that are similar in skill levels and other attributes but differ in terms of health risks (e.g., exposure to chemicals or accidents). In these comparisons, we observe a risk premium: workers in the more risky job are paid more, and the size of this "risk premium" is interpreted as evidence of what workers require as compensation for exposing themselves to risks. These and other studies tend to put the value of a statistical life in the range of $2–7 million.[2] Comparable results are found from other kinds of studies. For example, a hedonic housing price study involving housing in locations that exposed residents to cancer risk suggested a value of statistical life in the range of $4–8 million. A study of the market for automobiles with differing safety attributes indicates the value of a statistical life between $3 million and $4 million.

Even rough estimates of environmental costs based on these techniques can provide surprising and useful results, as illustrated in box 10.

[2]W. Kip Viscusi, "The Value of Risks to Life and Health," *Journal of Economic Literature* 31 (1993): 1912–1946.

BOX 10

Back-of-the Envelope Estimates

Developing countries cannot afford to conduct in-depth studies of every environmental issue, even though they may face dire environmental circumstances and have environment-conscious policymakers needing to rank needs and remedies. To move forward in a timely fashion, governments in countries like Mexico need rough, back-of-the-envelope estimates of the costs of various environmental problems to assist them in setting priorities.

Often it is possible to draw on existing data from the United States and other countries to produce order-of-magnitude estimates of the likely costs of things such as soil erosion, air pollution, and mining of underground waters, and the health effects of water and solid waste pollution, lack of sanitation, and ingestion of food contaminated by polluted irrigation. One such study did just that in the case of Mexico. The results are reported here:

Problem	Annual Cost ($ billions)
Soil erosion	$1.2
Health effects of air pollution in Mexico City:	
Particulates	$0.84
Ozone	$0.10
Lead	$0.13
Excess use of underground water	$1.0
Diarrheal diseases (from water and solid waste pollution, lack of sanitation, and foodstuff poisoning):	
Morbidity	$0.03
Mortality	$3.6
Mortality (with oral rehydration therepy available)	$0.0005

What these estimates show in dramatic fashion is that the estimated costs of diarrheal diseases is by far the largest cost of those estimated, followed by soil erosion. Moreover, when oral rehydration therepy is offered as treatment for diarrheal diseases, the mortality cost drops to about a half-million dollars per year. Given the rough nature of these estimates, none of them should be interpreted precisely, but even if we assume each one could be double or half the reported number, this still provides very useful information for policymakers.

Source: Sergio Margulis, "Back-of-the-Envelope Estimates of Environmental Damage in Mexico," in *Pricing the Planet: Economic Analysis for Sustainable Development*, ed. Peter May and Ronaldo Serôa da Motta (New York: Columbia University Press, 1996)

Contingent Valuation

The contingent valuation (CV) method is a survey-based approach to valuing nonmarket goods and services. In contrast to the "revealed-preference" techniques discussed, CV is the main "stated-preference technique," one of only a few feasible ways to measure passive-use or nonuse values. A typical CV survey will describe one or more alternative scenarios for possible actions by government. The most common format for a CV survey is to offer a choice between two alternative courses of action: one being the status quo and the other involving actions to improve environmental quality. The latter option also involves higher costs that may result in higher taxes, user fees, or higher prices. Given very specific information about the costs, actions, and anticipated outcome, the respondents are asked if they would be in favor of the alternative course of action.[3]

By varying the payment amount, and then surveying subsamples of individuals for different payment levels, the CV method provides information about the proportion of people willing to pay (at each level) to achieve the stated outcome. We expect this proportion to decrease with an increase in the cost, much like we expect visits to lake or beach to decrease with increased travel cost. After explaining the actions and expected outcomes, a questioner might ask, would you be willing to have your taxes increased by $100 per year in order to pay for this improvement in environmental quality? This format tries to emulate the voting approach described at the beginning of the chapter.

There are also two distinct ways to approach the question of valuation. The most commonly used approach asks people their **willingness to pay** (WTP) for something. This is quite similar to what we observe in markets; people buy things when their willingness to pay is greater than the price. But in using CV, we could also turn the question around and ask about people's minimum **willingness to accept** (WTA) compensation for some decrease in available goods or services. For example, would you be willing to

[3]Portions of this section draw on R. Carson, "Contingent Valuation: A User's Guide," *Environmental Science and Technology* (2000). Available at http://pubs.acs.org/journals/esthag/34/i108/pdf/es990728j.pdf.

accept $100 per month as compensation for living next to noisier neighbors or having somewhat dirtier air? For small changes in the amount of a good, economic theory tells us that these two values should be about the same (e.g., the marginal value for small increases or small decreases in the amount of a good consumed). However, there is overwhelming evidence that the responses to these two questions tend to be *very* different, with the WTA numbers being much larger than the WTP numbers. There is puzzlement and debate about why this is the case, and some of the debate has involved contributions by psychologists about what is sometimes called loss aversion. It is a fascinating issue, but we won't get into the details here.

Key Concepts: *Willingness to pay, willingness to accept* 

For our purposes, though, there is an important point about when to use WTP and when to use WTA. The correct measure to use will depend on the property right of the good in question. You wouldn't ask Bob if he would be willing to accept $100 to give up Suzy's bicycle. It's not his bike! WTP is the correct measure to use when a person does not have a right or entitlement to a good, and WTA is the correct measure to use when a person *does* have a legal right to the good. In the case of environmental goods, who owns the environment? What are the public's entitlements? Do individuals have an entitlement to enjoy environmental quality? Do landowners have a right to destroy wetlands? Do power plants have a right to emit particulates, SO_2 and CO_2, from their chimneys? The answer may be legally resolvable in some cases, but in many cases it is more a matter of opinion and cultural norms than legality, and it will influence how people respond to CV questions and how we should interpret the results.

CV has been in use for several decades now, and there have been several thousand studies conducted. The most famous study was an assessment of the damage from the *Exxon Valdez* oil spill in Alaska in 1989. The lost passive-use values from the spill were estimated at $2.8 billion using CV. The *Exxon Valdez* event and subsequent legal case that highlighted the estimates of damages led the National Oceanographic and Atmospheric Association

(NOAA) to commission a panel of preeminent experts—including two Nobel Prize–winning economists—to examine questions surrounding the use of CV. They concluded that CV studies can produce estimates reliable enough to be “the starting point for a judicial or administrative determination of natural resource damages—including lost passive-use values.”

CV continues to be used for a wide range of issues in research, in courts, and in government proceedings. CV has been used to estimate WTP to protect endangered species, such as the whooping crane, to reduce pollution that impairs visibility in places such as the Grand Canyon and to protect coral reefs and other unique ecosystems. Critics of CV argue that there may be biases in CV results if (a) respondents want to please the interviewer, (b) they may wish to make a “protest vote,” or (c) they feel unconstrained by the hypothetical nature of the payment. Some basis for concerns are evident in some survey results, for example, in cases where the average WTP seems not to vary even when the outcomes told to the respondents are increased by an order of magnitude (e.g., one thousand bird deaths avoided, ten thousand bird deaths avoided, or one hundred thousand bird deaths avoided). In recent years there has been a great deal of research on these problems and improvements in our understanding of how to avoid some of these potential biases. In cases where CV results can be compared with revealed preference results for the same environmental improvement, CV estimates tend to be slightly lower than other methods suggest. Nevertheless, one finds critics on both sides, some who think CV overestimates values and others who think the opposite.

Limits to Valuation

The valuation of benefits can be highly valuable to policymakers faced with difficult choices and limited budgets, as box 11 illustrates, but there are limits to how well these valuation techniques can capture people’s preferences. There are also limits to using any measure of individual’s willingness to pay as the sole basis for judging society’s priorities. There are many issues one could raise; several are described here:

BOX 11

Forest Preserves in Thailand

The number of protected areas worldwide has quadrupled in the past fifty years. Governments face difficult choices, however, because protected areas can be costly to manage and maintain, and they often displace people and shut off large areas to farming, logging, and other activities.

In Thailand, for example, the government has made efforts in recent years to establish and maintain a number of protected areas, including several national parks. One example is the 850-square-mile Khao Yai National Park in central Thailand, where economic analyses have evaluated some of the benefits and costs of the national park. Given the enormous difficulties involved, these analyses produce fairly rough estimates, but ones that nevertheless offer very useful insights. First, one aspect of the economics of environmental valuation has been to establish a checklist of the types of potential values for a complex resource like a national park. The checklist of values can include recreation and tourism, watershed values, ecological processes, biodiversity, education, research, aesthetic, spiritual, cultural/historical, option value, existence value, and global life support (Dixon and Sherman 1990). Even though some of these values may be impossible to quantify, identifying the categories can still be useful since a partial accounting of benefits and costs can sometimes be sufficient to give policymakers the information they need for a decision. In the case of Khao Yai, for example, the following estimates were made for some categories of benefits and costs:

	Millions of US$, annually
Benefits	
Watershed protection	$1.3
Soil erosion (cost of replacement)	$3.0
Recreation and tourism	$1.4
Trekking and camping	$0.1
Extractive values (local communities)	$2.2
Contribution to elephant survival	$4.9
Costs	
Enforcement expenditures	$−0.5
Opportunity cost (development)	$−1.6
Total Net Benefit	$10.8

Despite the roughness of the estimates and the omission of estimates for some categories of benefits, the numbers nevertheless support the value of protecting the park, suggesting a positive annual value of $10.8 million even with some benefits omitted.

Second, one way governments can minimize the costs imposed on nearby communities is by allowing certain kinds of activities (e.g., hunting, wood collection) in buffer zones rather than imposing uniform restrictions in all areas of the park. In the case of Khao Yai, economic analysis estimated that the net benefits from the park would rise by $5.3 million over fifteen years using this kind of multizone approach that allowed extractive activities in buffer zones, and that this would also provide incentives for local people to cooperate with preservation aims in other zones (Albers 2001).

And finally, differences in incentives for park protection from the national versus the global perspective were found not to be dramatically different since foreign tourists provided a strong preservation incentive to the Thai government (Albers 2001). Overall, analyses like these provide extremely useful information and insights for governments faced with managing complex resources where the benefits and costs can be very difficult to measure.

Sources: Heidi J. Albers, *A Spatial-Intertemporal Model for Tropical Forest Management Applied to Khao Yai National Park, Thailand*, Discussion Paper 01-35 (Washington, DC: Resources for the Future, 2001).

John Dixon and Paul Sherman, *Economics of Protected Areas* (Washington, DC: Island Press, 1990).

First, economic theory assumes that individuals know exactly what their preferences are so that they can state their willingness to pay for any given set of commodities. When it comes to buying the kinds of goods or services individuals are familiar with, such as clothing, restaurant meals, or cars, this may be a reasonable assumption. But when it comes to environmental or other public goods, is it reasonable to assume that people know what they want or would be willing to pay for? This problem doesn't apply only to environmental public goods, but to manufactured public goods as well. The contrast is revealing. For example, national security is an important public good that is provided in part by having a strong military. But we don't use CV methods to value, for example, the public's willingness to pay to make the nation's thirteenth aircraft carrier able to travel 35 miles per hour rather than 30 miles per hour. Most people are not well enough informed to make such a judgment, and the same is probably true for many environmental issues. Consider the following: what if careful surveys were conducted to estimate society's willingness to pay to take actions to keep the manatee, the Bengal tiger, or the panda from going extinct in the wild, but when we added up those amounts it turned out not to be enough to succeed? What would we conclude? Would we conclude that society is willing to let the species go extinct? Or might we wonder if some individuals may have thought success could be achieved at a lower cost per person and if they might revise their stated preference with more information?

Second, some observers worry about inconsistencies between people's behavior and economists' models of that behavior. Economic theory assumes people's preferences are continuous so that the marginal value of a small increase in consumption of good X will be about the same as for a small decrease in consumption of good X. But the "loss aversion" evidence on WTP versus WTA contradicts that assumption. Does that mean the theory is invalid and unusable? It's not clear what affect this has on these valuation methods.

Other behaviors don't exactly fit with the "rational optimizer" model of behavior. There is evidence that people often behave by following "rules of thumb" in a complex and uncertain world rather than evaluating the marginal trade-offs for every effect of every decision. And there is strong evidence from laboratory "games" in psychology and experimental economics showing that people don't always act in a self-interested way, but sometimes cooperate or act in ways that may appear to be altruistic. These kinds of inconsistencies between certain kinds of economic predictions and actual behavior raise questions about the degree to which economic valuation measures may be misleading when used to measure changes in social welfare. But again, it's just not clear how serious these problems may be.

Finally, an argument can be made that in some cases society should not base policy choices simply on an adding up of individuals' willingness to pay.[4] It may be that what people want to achieve for society, the kind of world they want to live in, is not adequately reflected in their own, day-to-day choices or stated preferences. At times we observe people benefiting from free riding; at other times we see people willing to pay taxes and to contribute to the common good (including approving of speed limits lower than their own habits would suggest). These differences probably reflect a more complex relationship between what people think is good for society and what choices they make for themselves.

Recommended Readings and References

A standard reference on valuation is A. Myrick Freeman, III, *The Measurement of Environmental and Resource Values: Theory and Methods*, 2nd ed. (Washington, DC: Resources for the Future, 2003). An excellent survey is found in Charles Perrings et al., "The Economic Value of Biodiversity," in *Global Biodiversity Assessment* (Cambridge: Cambridge University Press, 1995), 824–914. See W. Kip Viscusi, "Mortality Effects of Regulatory Costs and Policy Evaluation Criteria," *Rand Journal of Economics* 25 (Spring 1994): 94–109) for discussion and estimates of the value of a statistical life. For a useful case study, see R. David Simpson, Roger A. Sedjo, and John W. Reid, "Valuing Biodiversity for Use in Pharmaceutical Research," *Journal of Political Economy* 104, no. 1 (1996): 163–185.

On contingent valuation, see Robert C. Mitchell and Richard T. Carson, *Using Surveys to Value Public Goods: The Contingent Valuation Method* (Washington, DC: Resources for the Future, 1989). See also Kenneth J. Arrow et al., *Report of the NOAA Panel on Contingent Valuation* (Washington, DC: Government Printing Office, 1993); and Arild Vatn and Daniel W. Bromley, "Choices without Prices without Apology," *Journal of Environmental Economics and Management* 26 (1994): 129–148.

[4]See Arild Vatn and Daniel W. Bromley, "Choices without Prices without Apology," *Journal of Environmental Economics and Management* 26 (1994):129–148.

15

Project and Policy Evaluation

When making an important decision like buying a car or attending college, you are likely to spend some time thinking through the implications of different options. There will be financial implications now and in the future, side effects on your lifestyle, direct and indirect effects on friends and family, and risks. Should you buy a new or used car? Pay extra for side airbags? Should you take out a loan to go to a more expensive college? Will the extra cost be worth it if you don't end up getting a better job after spending four years far from friends and family? With many different options and their many different implications, you might want a systematic way to evaluate and weigh all the positive and negative implications for each option.

Similarly, when society considers building a dam, a highway, or a waste treatment plant, or changing a policy to control air pollution or regulate effluent, it would be very helpful to have a systematic way to evaluate and weigh all of the positive and negative implications.

Several analytical techniques have been developed to estimate the benefits and costs of a particular project or policy change. Benefit-cost analysis (BCA) is the most general and the most widely used of these methods. Most of this chapter is devoted to introducing the reader to BCA. In the same way that we expect consumers to buy commodities so long as the net benefit is positive, BCA is a framework for judging whether a project or policy has positive net benefits.

Two other methods are also discussed in this chapter. The first is cost-effectiveness analysis, which is a variant of BCA. The second is regional impact or input-output analysis, which is quite different from either BCA or cost-effectiveness analysis.

Before we dive into specifics, it's important to recognize that applying these methods to specific projects or government actions can be a complex and technical procedure. This chapter is only intended to introduce the reader to the methods and to highlight some of their strengths and weaknesses. In order to actually perform a benefit-cost analysis, or even to evaluate and critique an existing BCA, you will need to study these methods in more depth, for example, by studying some of the recommended readings noted at the end of this chapter.

Benefit-Cost Analysis

Doing BCA can be divided into four steps: identify the impacts of the project, estimate the dollar value of those impacts as benefits and costs, discount across different time periods, and evaluate.

1. Identifying impacts. In order to identify the impacts of a project, you first need to answer the question, who has **standing,** or what is the **accounting stance** of the analysis? By this we mean, whose benefits or whose costs count in the analysis? This question is sometimes answered in terms of the "accounting stance," which implies a geographic boundary around a nation or region. Benefits and costs to individuals within the region count; those affecting people outside the region do not count. There is a strong case to be made for taking a very broad accounting stance in order to avoid omitting some of the benefits or costs that could be significant. However, when building prisons, do we include the values of the criminals? What about future generations, undocumented aliens, future immigrants, or future emigrants?

Key Concepts: *Standing, accounting stance* 

2. *Estimating values*. The costs of a project need to be measured in terms of the opportunity cost of the inputs required. If markets are competitive and the project is small relative to the size of the market for a particular input, then this opportunity cost will be reflected in the price of the inputs in the market. This indicates the willingness to pay for putting those inputs to their "next best use." Benefits should be measured based on the incremental increases in goods and services, net of their incremental costs.

As an example, let's look at a project to construct and operate a waste treatment plant (see figure 15.1). The plant will require energy to operate. We can characterize this as a shift in the demand for energy in a regional power grid, shifting demand from D_1 to D_2. Given a constant price of energy, this cost will equal the shaded area, equal to $P \times (Q_2 - Q_1)$.

A similar approach can be taken in some cases for changes in outputs due to government action. When the change occurs in a

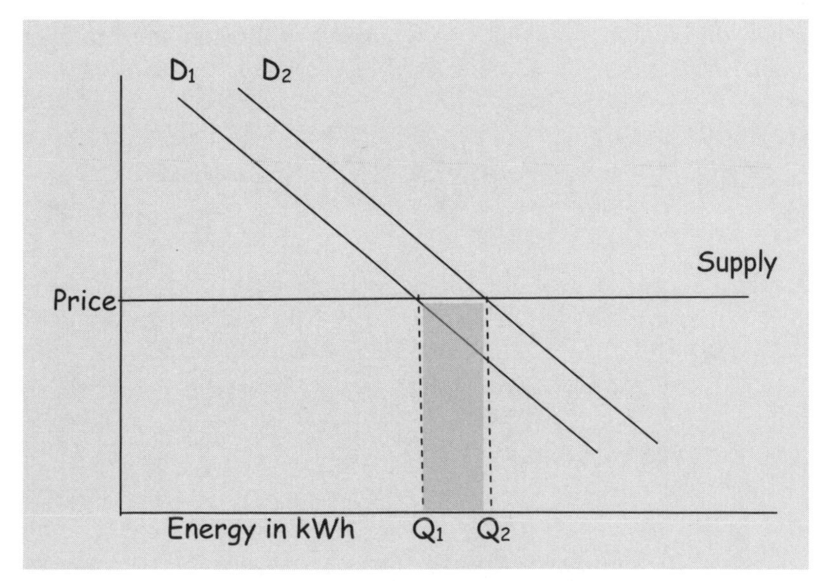

■ **FIGURE 15.1 The opportunity cost of project inputs**

large competitive market, so that the change in supply does not affect the price appreciably, the marginal value of the change in supply can be approximated by the market price, which reflects individuals' (or firms') willingness to pay. For example, removing a hydropower dam to restore free-flowing rivers and fish habitat will reduce the supply of energy in the marketplace. In figure 15.2 we illustrate this as a shift in supply from S_1 to S_2. The reduction in benefits is reflected in the willingness to pay in the market, or the shaded area equal to $P \times (Q_1 - Q_2)$.

3. Evaluation. Although BCA is sometimes described as providing a self-contained decision rule, this is not a wise interpretation given its limitations. BCA looks only at whether the discounted present value of net benefits is positive, which implies that this approach does not satisfy the Pareto criterion since it does not require a positive net benefit for everybody. What it does satisfy is the "potential Pareto criterion," which means that although there are winners and losers, the winners under the policy *could* compensate the losers for their losses and still be better off than they were without the policy. BCA does not, therefore, take account of the way in which those benefits or costs are distributed across individuals or groups, nor does it take account of other kinds of factors that policymakers will often want to take

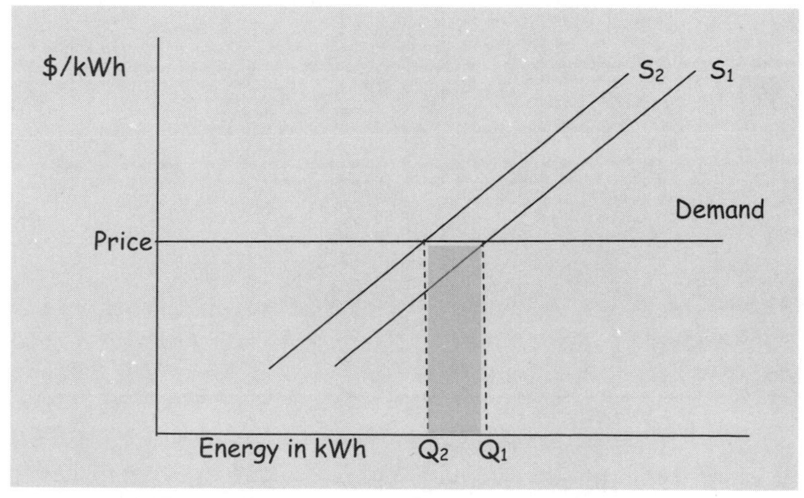

■ **FIGURE 15.2 The willingness to pay for change in outputs**

into account, such as rights or fairness. For some government actions or projects, this BCA criterion alone may be adequate, but in many settings where policymakers are mindful of multiple objectives, including the distributional or equity consequences of a policy, BCA should be considered alongside these other criteria.

Key Concept: *Net present value* 

When benefits and costs occur in different time periods, BCA will require discounting to estimate the project's **net present value** (NPV). NPV can be described mathematically for periods 0 through t, and for the discount rate r, as:

$$NPV = (B_0 - C_0) + \frac{(B_1 - C_1)}{(1 + r)^1} + \frac{(B_2 - C_2)}{(1 + r)^2} + \frac{(B_3 - C_3)}{(1 + r)^3} \ldots\ldots + \frac{(B_t - C_t)}{(1 + r)^t}$$

This gives us the present value of the net benefits of the project. When choosing among policies or projects, we may want to look for the one with the highest net benefit. However, when a government agency has a fixed budget, it may want to get the most for its money, in which case it may want to look at the ratio of benefits to costs: if a project with a high net benefit is also very costly, then it may be that a project with smaller benefits but much smaller costs may be preferable. By choosing the set of projects with the highest benefit-cost ratio, the agency can get the most out of its budget.

4. *Risk and expected value*. Since the future costs and benefits of a project can never be known with certainty, we always face uncertainty about what future net benefits will be. Often we have in mind a number of different contingencies, or future conditions, that will affect the costs and benefits. If we can evaluate the probability of each contingency or set of future conditions and estimate the benefits and costs for each, then we can also calculate the "expected value" of the net benefits as a weighted average of the net benefits for each contingency, weighted by its probability.

For cxample, consider a project to build improved flood controls in a flood-prone area that would cost $1 million in the first year but is expected to generate benefits by limiting flood damages—but only in years when there are floods. If there are no floods for twenty years, then the present value of the benefits may be quite small compared with the $1 million cost. We can estimate the expected net benefit in each year, however, by multiplying the probability of a specific type of flood event by the benefit that would occur as a result of the flood control investment. The probability of a "hundred-year" flood in any given year will be 0.01. So for every year into the future, we multiply 0.01 by the benefits of the added protections the project would provide, and then discount these to obtain the "present value of expected future benefits." If the benefit (reduction in flood damage) for the project in the event of a hundred-year flood is $6 million, then the present value of expected future benefits in millions of dollars can be estimated as:

$$\text{NPV} = \frac{(0.01) \times 6}{(1 + r)^1} + \frac{(0.01) \times 6}{(1 + r)^2} + \frac{(0.01) \times 6}{(1 + r)^3} + \ldots + \frac{(0.01) \times 6}{(1 + r)^t}$$

When this kind of discounting problem is estimated for a long time period, the NPV will approximate the value of a perpetuity that has a simpler formula of NPV = 0.01 × $6million/r, which would be $300,000 when the discount rate r = 5%.

Cost-effectiveness Analysis

If policymakers are aiming to prevent the extinction of a species, eliminate poverty, or promote equality, the notion of efficiency may seem irrelevant. But any effort to achieve these goals will likely involve public funds, or costly actions that affect previously existing market and policy failures, and thus will cause deadweight losses that merit consideration. If government has a fixed budget for this aim, then considering how best to use scarce funds will involve comparing the costs of alternative options along with the differences in their outcomes.

If the policy goal has been predetermined or when the objective is impossible to quantify in monetary terms, cost-effectiveness analysis may be preferable to BCA. When the goal can be quantified in noneconomic terms (number of families escaping poverty, number of species protected from extinction, etc.), then cost-effectiveness analysis can also be applied without putting a monetary value on the benefits. Cost-effectiveness analysis can be approached in two ways. The first approach is applicable when there is a fixed level of available funds to use, and policy alternatives can be compared on the basis of their expected level of benefits (measured in whatever quantitative terms are available). The second approach identifies a target goal or level of benefits and then compares the costs of alternative approaches to meeting that target.

For example, city officials may have a goal of reducing urban air pollution by a given amount, and they are considering a range of options, such as levying a gas tax, raising emissions standards on private vehicles, requiring high-use vehicles like taxis and delivery trucks to be retrofitted for liquefied petroleum gas, requiring gas stations to recover vapors, using only electric busses, and so on. Without quantifying the value of benefits, these alternatives can be compared in terms of their cost-per-unit reduction in air pollution. If no single action achieves the goal, a combination of these actions may be taken, starting with the lowest cost alternative (for an example, see box 9 on air pollution in Mexico City).

Regional Impact Analysis with Input-Output Models

Local public officials often want to know how a project or change in policy will affect income and employment in their jurisdiction. One approach to estimating these effects is a regional input-output (I-O) model. In the past two decades, these models have become widely used to evaluate the impact of a range of policies and projects on local economies, such as the evaluation of federal land use policy changes or actions requiring environmental impact statements.

I-O models contain a mathematical representation of the level of output for each activity or industry in a region, and the linkages between the industry's production and its inputs (backward linkages), as well as linkages between the industry's production and processors or users of that output (forward linkages). If those linkages occur within the region, then a change in production will cause a ripple effect that affects other parts of the regional economy. These feedbacks are known as the **multiplier effects** of an initial change or shock in the regional economy. The size of the multiplier effect will depend on the strength of these linkages for the industries affected.

Key Concept: *Multiplier effects*

The regional effects of a project are divided into direct, indirect, and induced effects. The direct effect is the project itself and the changes in income and employment resulting directly from it. The indirect effects are the changes in income and employment in the industries affected by the project through backward and forward linkages. For example, a construction project will give a boost to local mechanics doing equipment repair.

Induced effects refer to how the income generated by a project is spent. The project will generate additional payments to laborers and owners of land and capital in the region. These individuals can be expected to spend this additional income. If they spend it on a trip to France, there will be no "induced effect." If they spend it locally at restaurants, stores, hair salons, or to remodel their house, there will be an induced effect that adds to the income and employment multipliers.

Caution: *Misuse of impact analysis*

These kinds of estimates can be useful, but I-O models are easy to misuse and misinterpret. One way they are often misused is by referring to the changes in output or "final demand" (along with the output multiplier effects) as if it were a change in income. For example, building a $500,000 interpretive center at a wildlife preserve may involve employing a local contractor to build the structure. The direct change in output for this project will be $500,000. However, the contractor will purchase some materials from outside the region (windows, plumbing, electrical parts, timber, stone, etc.) and these costs come out of the $500,000 increase in final demand. The value-added or income paid to the contractor and his workers may only be $75,000. If we are interested in who benefits locally from the project and by how much, this is the proper measure: the value-added or income measure. Of course, there are likely to be indirect and induced multiplier effects from the building project, but again we would want to look at the income (value-added) multiplier, not the output multiplier, to assess these benefits for members of the local community. The change in output will often be several times larger than the changes in income depending on the activities involved.

Two other characteristics of input-output analysis can also limit its usefulness for economic analysis. First, unlike most BCA, regional I-O models adopt a limited geographical accounting stance that overlooks any benefits or costs that occur outside the defined region. Local public officials are understandably interested in the local effects of a project, but gains to one region may often be offset by losses in other regions. For example, projects that generate employment nearly always represent a redistribution, or transfer, of jobs and income from one region to another. If these changes were viewed from a national accounting stance, they might indicate zero or negligible changes in employment and income. Remember also that regional economic activity—whether measured as income or output—will increase following an earthquake, flood, fire, or war. So, just looking at ways to increase local economic activity rather than examining benefits and costs more comprehensively can be highly misleading.

Second, these models assume a fixed relationship between inputs and outputs in each industry and do not allow for the kinds of substitutions or changes in prices that would occur in a real economy, especially over a period of time. If a policy reduces the number of jobs in a particular industry, these models essentially assume that the unemployed workers are remaining permanently idle, rather than looking for work in other industries or in other regions. The model also does not allow for downward pressures on wages in response to this excess supply of labor. Similarly, if land were set aside for open space, these models do not allow for any changes in land values or tax revenues in response to an increased scarcity of residential or commercial land. As we saw in chapter 2, the real-world effects of such a change on land prices and tax revenues can be quite important.

For many short-run projects or impacts that begin and end in one or two years, these limitations may not bias the model's results greatly. But when evaluating permanent changes in a region's economy, the assumption that losses or gains in income and jobs are permanent represents a seriously misleading picture of how most economies adjust to economic changes, especially in regions with high workforce mobility.

Taking a local accounting stance that focuses only on the local community may be justified with an isolated community or small island nation with little immigration. The impacts of a project in this case may be more long lasting, and the value of focusing on the local income and employment impacts over long periods of time may be justified. For example, in Caribbean island nations, investment in tourism can have valuable long-run implications for jobs and income. Island governments will be very interested to learn that the income multipliers for a large foreign-owned hotel are very small because so much of the materials, including food, linens, and management personnel come from outside the country. Regional I-O models could help the governments identify alternative investment opportunities with larger income multiplier effects, but they should also look at the benefits, costs, and profitability of those alternatives before promoting one activity over another.

Recommended Readings and References

Excellent references for more detail on applied policy analysis include David L. Weimer and Aidan R. Vining, *Policy Analysis, Concepts and Practice*, 4th ed. (Upper Saddle River, NJ: Prentice Hall, 2005); Edith Stokey and Richard Zeckhauser, *A Primer for Policy Analysis* (New York: W. W. Norton, 1978); Richard O. Zerbe, Jr., and David D. Dively, *Benefit-Cost Analysis in Theory and Practice* (New York: HarperCollins, 1994); and Robert H. Haveman and Julius Margolis, *Public Expenditure and Policy Analysis*, 2nd ed. (Chicago: Rand McNally, 1977).

The first book on benefit-cost analysis was Edward J. Mishan, *Cost-Benefit Analysis* (New York: Praeger, 1971). See also Edward J. Mishan, *Economics for Social Decisions: Elements of Cost-Benefit Analysis* (New York: Praeger, 1973). A classic example of intertemporal benefit-cost analysis that had important policy implications was the study conducted for the Hells Canyon dam on the Snake River in John V. Krutilla and Anthony Fisher, *The Economics of Natural Environments*, 2nd ed. (Baltimore: Johns Hopkins University Press).

16

Economics and Morality

Economic analysis is not "value free." That is, it is not neutral or independent with respect to moral or ethical considerations. Economics, in fact, has a very specific moral basis—the one that leads economists to say that resources "ought" to be allocated efficiently or that policies with high net benefits "ought" to be preferred over ones with low net benefits. In economics, the basis for these value judgments is people's preferences and the central idea underlying economic value judgments is that the more we can satisfy people's preferences, the better.

It's hard to argue with "preference satisfaction" as a worthy goal when, for example, we think about alleviating hunger, reducing poverty, curing disease, or making possible the enjoyment of the arts or nature. After all, preferences are just what individuals want, and economists simply try to measure and add up people's preferences. The underlying idea is to promote greater social well-being or welfare, and promoting greater well-being should not really be very controversial. All moral approaches to judging the state of things in society embrace *some* notion of individual "utility," "good," "welfare," or "well-being." But there are many differing moral concepts and a range of moral viewpoints, and advocates of some of these moral views are highly critical of welfare economics and argue against using it for judging society's choices.

These are complex issues to address in a brief chapter. Let's start by distinguishing between two main types of moral theories. First, there is the approach that focuses on individual behavior: personal virtue, judgments about right and wrong, rules like the Ten Commandments, and moral views on pornography, drugs, or homosexuality. This approach to morals is referred to as **deontological,** and centers on the morality of individual actions, not the outcomes of those actions. The second type of moral theory is referred to as **consequentialist,** a doctrine that judges the morality of things by their consequences. Welfare economics is definitely consequentialist. It focuses on questions about the welfare or well-being of society.

Key Concepts: *Deontological, consequentialist*

The moral approach of welfare economics is also closely related to another consequentialist theory, utilitarianism, which seeks to maximize the good of the whole of society. Although economics is sometimes described as utilitarian, there are some important distinctions between the two. Economists sometimes define social welfare in theoretical models in a utilitarian way, as the sum of individuals' utilities. But as a practical matter, we cannot measure utility directly or compare the utility of different individuals. As a result, economists instead rely on the behavior of each individual and take her choices as a reflection of her own preference ordering (e.g., a preference for A over B is based on evidence of choosing A over B, etc.).

To make this connection between choices and preferences, economists assume that individuals are rational, so that actual choices reflect the maximization of utility at the individual level. Then, based on this ordering of preferences at the individual level, the economics approach adds up these preferences across individuals (using dollars as the common unit of exchange), to obtain a measure of the aggregate willingness to pay for a given change in resources or goods. An action or policy that is efficient will be one that allows more individuals to satisfy more of their preferences, and this is interpreted as achieving a higher level of social welfare. Each individual's willingness to pay carries the same weight, even though these dollar values may reflect very different utilities.

How then should economic analysis be interpreted in the context of other moral viewpoints that may conflict with economics? The view offered here, and elaborated on later, suggests that economics should not be viewed as an "all-purpose decision rule" for making all policy decisions because there will often be other issues to consider. These other issues include moral notions of equality, rights, and fairness, which in some cases may be very important. This is not to suggest that economic analysis should be abandoned in these cases. What is needed is a balanced consideration of the strengths and limitations of both economics and other approaches.

Other Moral Viewpoints

Let's consider several alternative moral considerations. Equality is an important idea in many Western traditions, and it is a very influential practical concern in debates about economic policy. It's easy to be in favor of equality, but unanimous support for equality quickly dissolves when one asks, equality of what? What are we trying to equalize? Libertarians want equality of rights; utilitarians want everyone's welfare to count equally; some observers favor equality of respect and others promote equality of opportunity.

Most people would agree that notions of rights, freedom, and liberty are relevant to judging what is good for society. But, once again, there exists below the surface a mind-boggling array of disparate and conflicting questions about their definition, justification, and weighting for judging what is morally good. Autonomy and self-determination are important aspects of freedom, but freedoms for one individual often conflict with the freedoms of others; often constraints imposed on one kind of freedom will serve to remove obstacles of another kind (e.g., a stay-to-the-right rule constrains individual actions but enlarges the freedom of movement for all). To evaluate morally significant freedoms requires judging which objectives are most important to people and what kinds of obstacles are of moral concern.

Questions of justice may come up whenever there are conflicts among individuals in society. Justice has to do with agreements, cooperation, negotiations, or contracts and moral judgments about those arrangements. The idea of justice can be seen as a way to referee individual interactions and conflicts of interest so as to secure the benefits of cooperation. But the main hitch here is that notions of justice are compatible with the ideas of both libertarians and utilitarians. For libertarians, justice comes down to respecting the rights that libertarians recognize. For utilitarians, justice involves rules that maximize utility by facilitating cooperation and diffusing conflicts of interest. If income inequality is unjust to one group on equality grounds, redistributing that income will be unjust to another group on the grounds of violating rights and freedoms.

Means, Ends, and Instruments

Philosophers recognize that a crucial question for moral views is their justification. As mentioned at the start of this chapter, deontological theories view moral rules as justified in absolute terms: they are simply "right" or "good" in and of themselves (e.g., telling the truth). The alternative view sees moral rules as justified in terms of their ends or consequences, and consequentialist moral views include welfare economics, utilitarianism, egalitarianism, notions of fairness, justice, and social contract approaches.

Consequentialist theories are highly compatible with an **instrumentalist** interpretation that sees moral rules as instruments or tools for achieving a desired outcome. In economics, this is similar to our understanding of institutions generally: as mechanisms that constrain, alter, or limit individuals' choices and actions—with the consequences benefiting society. Moral views along these lines include the golden rule and Kant's categorical imperative. We are all better off in a society where people tell the truth, don't steal or litter, and stay to the right when walking on the sidewalk. The idea here is that institutions including laws, policies, and moral rules come to exist because they serve as instruments, ones that benefit society overall. A society where it is immoral to murder, lie, walk on the grass, shirk work, or steal from others is more likely to achieve higher general levels of well-being than societies where these moral codes do not exist. Moral codes are not always sufficient to achieve the desired outcome (like teaching your children to always tell the truth). Often we need to reinforce or complement moral rules with laws, penalties, and regulations. In the same way that consequentialist moral views emphasize ends rather than means, this same underlying approach is the way economists tend to look at policy issues.

Economics and Morality in Practice

Trade policy and globalization are controversial topics, in part because they magnify the relationship between moral and economic issues. To highlight some of these issues, let's take a look at an infamous 1991 memo by Larry Summers, who was then chief economist of the World Bank and is now president of Harvard University (see box 12). We want to consider the arguments in the memo and the objections to them. We also want to distinguish moral issues from other kinds of issues.

The basic idea in the memo is that the relocation of some highly polluting industries from rich countries to poor countries could be mutually beneficial to the people in both rich and poor countries (it would increase allocative efficiency). Summers is suggesting that industries that generate pollution be encouraged to relocate to less-developed countries (LDCs), and that this be done in ways that involve market transactions and voluntary exchanges undertaken with the approval of each government (and perhaps with some initial encouragement or support from the World Bank). As compensation for more pollution, LDCs would have more jobs and income from the polluting industries. In high-income countries, the loss of some jobs and income would be compensated for by improved environmental quality. Summers suggests that the net benefits of such a shift would be positive for both countries, and he gives several reasons why.

BOX 12
The Infamous Memo

In 1991 Larry Summers, chief economist of the World Bank, sent an internal memo to colleagues at the World Bank. The memo attracted a lot of attention, and the following portions were published in the *Economist*:

Just between you and me, shouldn't the World Bank be encouraging *more* migration of the dirty industries to the LDCs [less developed countries]? I can think of three reasons:

(1) The measurement of the costs of health-impairing pollution depends on the foregone earnings from increased morbidity and mortality. From this point of view a given amount of health-impairing pollution should be done in the country with the lowest cost, which will be the country with the lowest wage. I think the economic logic behind dumping a load of toxic waste in the lowest-wage country is impeccable and we should face up to that.

(2) The costs of pollution are likely to be nonlinear as the initial increments of pollution probably have very low cost. I've always thought that under-populated countries in Africa are vastly *under* polluted; their air quality is probably vastly inefficiently low compared to Los Angeles or Mexico City. Only the lamentable facts that so much pollution is generated by non-tradable industries (transport, electrical generation) and that the unit transport costs of solid waste are so high prevent world-welfare-enhancing trade in air pollution and waste.

(3) The demand for a clean environment for aesthetic and health reasons is likely to have a very high income-elasticity. The concern over an agent that causes a one-in-a-million change in the odds of prostate cancer is obviously going to be much higher in a country where people survive to get prostate cancer than in a country where under-5 mortality is 200 per thousand. Also, much of the concern over industrial atmospheric discharge is about visibility-impairing particulates. These discharges may have very little direct health impact. Clearly trade in goods that embody aesthetic pollution concerns could be welfare-enhancing. While production is mobile the consumption of pretty air is a non-tradable good.

The problem with the arguments against all of these proposals for more pollution in LDCs (intrinsic rights to certain goods, moral reasons, social concerns, lack of adequate markets, etc.) could be turned around and used more or less effectively against every Bank proposal for liberalization.

Source: Economist, February 8, 1992.

First, Summers believes the cost of a given amount of pollution may be lower in LDCs because they often have lower population densities, so a given amount of pollution will have fewer human impacts in a sparsely populated area than in a densely populated area. His comment about "nonlinearity" means that spreading pollution thinly over a wide area may be far less costly than having the same amount of pollution concentrated at higher densities in only a few locations. He also points out that some health risks from pollution occur late in life (e.g., prostate cancer), so that those impacts would be smaller in a population where fewer individuals typically reach the relevant age. He also believes that people with high incomes place a higher value on clean air (are willing to pay more for cleaner air than poor people), so that the improved air quality in high-income countries would be valued more by those people, and that this gain would be larger than the losses from a decline in air quality for the people living in poor countries.

So far the arguments are fully consistent with the basics of welfare economics. Summers doesn't always explain himself well or delicately, but then this was an internal memo aimed at other economists, not for public distribution. Fundamentally, though, he is suggesting that the relative price of clean air (the value of clean air relative to the value of income or jobs) is lower in poor countries than in rich countries and that, as a result, there are potential gains from trade.

One thing that gets Summers into trouble is the way he begins his memo, when he suggests that the cost of health-impairing pollution depends on the forgone earnings from increased morbidity and mortality, and thus this activity should be done in the country with the lowest wages. This statement cannot be supported by economics. The impression this statement gives is that people are only as valuable as the income they earn during their lifetime, so that the lives of low-wage earners are less important than are the lives of high-wage earners. Remember, welfare economics provides no basis for making interpersonal comparisons of utility, so we cannot say anything directly about what one person's life is worth relative to another person's life. This point is especially germane to making moral value judgments because morality is concerned with the basis for judging the moral worth of individuals and their characteristics. Here, Summers gets it wrong.

What economics does allow, however, is recognition of the differences in people's willingness to expose themselves to health risks. Economic analysis might conclude that people in poor countries are, on average, more willing to give up air quality in exchange for income than are people in high-income countries. If so, then this is just like any difference in the relative willingness to pay between poor and rich countries, and it represents an opportunity for gains from voluntary, mutually beneficial trade.

But there are a number of potential problems with that conclusion, too. First, we can't be sure that people in poor countries would be well-enough informed about the health risks from pollution to make informed decisions or to act to avoid unnecessary exposure. Since economic analysis is based on "full information" as the basis of choice, the absence of adequate information or false information could, indeed, invalidate the economic conclusion about gains from trade. Second, we can't be sure that the benefits of these kinds of investments in LDCs will trickle down and actually benefit the poor. If a program of industry relocation were negotiated government to government, without the consent of the people who would be most adversely affected, then it is possible that some previously disadvantaged individuals might see none of the anticipated benefits, while bearing much of the burden of increased pollution. Government corruption may siphon off some or all of the benefits rather than distribute them to the population. This is certainly a common concern for any kind of dealings between countries, whether the transfer is cash, food, or dirty factories. Corruption and cronyism are examples of the kinds of policy failures discussed in chapter 13.

Third, LDCs typically have lower pollution standards and weaker enforcement than high-income countries, so moving a polluting industry to an LDC may result in higher levels of pollution after the move. This result, however, may be entirely consistent with people's preferences: air quality may have a lower value relative to income in LDCs—as suggested in the discussion of the environmental Kuznets curve in chapter 7. If people in the LDC value additional income much more highly than additional clean air, then we would expect their air quality standards to be lower, and their enforcement agencies to be weaker, than in a high-income country where air quality has become a much higher priority. Indeed, in the same way governments in LDCs are likely to spend less on museums and performing arts, environmental quality also has a lower relative priority given the prevalence of poverty, the scarcity of jobs, and the dearth of public funds.

The moral dimensions to these issues are complex and ultimately ambiguous. Egalitarians will want to know whether the relocation of pollution to poor countries would promote equality, but equality of what? Pollution? Jobs? Income? Opportunity? How would rights and freedoms be affected by the relocation of pollution? The proposal conflicts with the idea that people in developing countries have a right to breathe clean air, but what about a right to jobs and income opportunities that might come with it?

What is evident in the debate on this topic is that some observers who object to the relocation of pollution to LDCs view pollution quite differently from the way they view other inputs into production, such as labor, land, or capital. There is a sense that pollution itself is immoral and that allowing pollution to be traded is similar to hiring an assassin, creating a market for cocaine, or endorsing child labor. Economics tends not to attribute moral connotations directly to polluting or the cocaine trade, but instead focuses on the consequences and especially the externalities that may arise. If there is a case to be made for reducing pollution or banning cocaine because of their externalities, then economic analysis will come to that conclusion, and economists will seek the most cost-effective means. If attaching a moral stigma to polluting will get the job done, that's great!

There are many potential considerations for judging whether polluting industries ought to be encouraged to relocate to LDCs, but there is no clear conclusion. For every moral argument against the idea, there seems to also be a moral counterargument. To come to a conclusion, one needs to weigh and balance the different issues and considerations. But there is still one more issue, and that is *who* is to do the weighing? If Americans generally judged the Summers's plan to be morally questionable, should their view be decisive? Should the question be left up to the citizens of poor countries? Their governments?

This raises ethical questions about sovereignty and self-determination. Evidence suggests that the citizens of one country are willing to respect sovereignty and defer to the people or government of other countries, depending on the type of moral issues. However, many people would also agree that it is acceptable, or at times morally necessary, to interfere (e.g., with trade sanctions), as in the case of apartheid, child labor, or slavery. But this moral argument may be outweighed by the rights of sovereignty at some point along the continuum of issues, such as those involving the traditional roles of women, capital punishment, animal rights, sacred cows (as in India), forest protections, and so on. Clearly, this is a complex issue with multiple dimensions and conflicting moral aspects that will be interpreted differently by different individuals. Summers, by contrast, does not appear to have appreciated these complexities and instead saw a path to an unambiguous and firm conclusion based on a narrow application of welfare economics.

What Should We Make of All This?

Economics provides an approach to making value judgments that is neither perfect nor comprehensive. Still, any of the alternatives that might have widespread support in society appear also to be imperfect, ambiguous, and incomplete. Some might argue that the economics approach has fewer flaws and commands more widespread agreement than any of the other options, but the more important point to emphasize here is that judgments about what society ought to do should consider multiple views and criteria. In many settings, estimating net benefits may be the dominant consideration, for example, if the effects on equality, rights, or fairness are neutral, offsetting, or ambiguous. In many other settings, however, concerns about rights, equality, or fairness will trump efficiency, and it would be a misuse of economics to ignore that reality.

It is worth emphasizing that economics does not, by itself, provide a direct way to identify the difference between "moral" goods and "immoral goods." People's willingness to pay suggests potential net benefits from market exchange, but what about markets for babies, kidneys, heroine, or slaves? The issue is not just where to draw the line, and how to draw such lines. To some, this is a moral question; some kinds of goods and services are simply immoral. But isn't it also a question that could be informed by the effect on welfare? Would a market for kidneys increase welfare through mutually beneficial exchange?

Overall, there seems to be a strong case for humility in proposing the use of any particular moral viewpoint as a basis for policy decisions. A composite or combination of approaches is easy to endorse, recognizing that each approach has shortcomings. In the real world, this is what we often (but not always) observe: the promotion of efficiency being tempered by consideration like rights, fairness, and equality. Some will object to the idea that morals should be tempered by humility if these morals are understood to be absolute, watertight judgments about right and wrong. Herein lies what some will see as a major weakness of economics: its methods attempt to find common ground or a compromise position by averaging the values of all individuals, as revealed in their preferences. In a society with many different moral viewpoints, from libertarianism to communitarianism, and many different views of nature from biocentrism to ecofeminism, to deep ecology, an averaging of these positions will be unsatisfactory to some individuals. Economics doesn't invalidate any of these points of view. Rather, it attempts to take an approach that offers equal treatment to all of these viewpoints to the extent that they are reflected in people's preferences.

Recommended Readings and References

An excellent discussion of these issues is found in Daniel Hausman and Michael McPherson, *Economics Analysis and Moral Philosophy* (New York: Cambridge University Press, 1996). Other recent discussions are found in Daniel W. Bromley and Jouni Paavola, *Economics, Ethics and Environmental Policy: Contested Choices* (Oxford: Blackwell Publications, 2002). Some well-known contributions include Amartya Sen, "Rational Fools: A Critique of the Behavioral Foundations of Economic Theory," *Philosophy and Public Affairs* 6, no. 4 (Summer 1977): 317–344; and Amartya Sen, *Development as Freedom* (New York: Anchor Books, 1999). See also Vatn Arild and Daniel W. Bromley, "Choices without

Prices without Apologies," *Journal of Environmental Economics and Management* 26, no. 2 (1994): 129–148; and William K. Jaeger, "Is Sustainability Optimal?: Examining the Differences between Economists and Environmentalists," *Ecological Economics* 15 (October 1995). For a historical view on economics and ethics, see the wonderful essays in Frank Knight, *The Ethics of Competition and Other Essays* (New York: Harper and Brothers, 1935).

PART IV
Wrapping Up

17

Closing Arguments

Limits of Economics

This book has made the case that economic analysis offers a valuable set of tools for identifying and solving problems and influencing policy debates in positive ways, yet it has also pointed out that economics has some important limitations, such as the lack of a direct and comprehensive way to take account of equity, rights, and fairness, and the problems associated with discounting. Several additional limitations of economics deserve mention.

One problem relates to measuring values based on people's current preferences, even though it's generally recognized that our preferences change as a result of learning, habit formation, and the influences of our experiences, culture, and society. Why is this a potential problem? In the short run, it may not matter much. But over long periods of time, if preferences evolve and change, then so do our values. But if values are measured and policies are evaluated based on current preferences, these may not reflect future values. In particular, there is the possibility that a given policy change will alter the path of changes in people's values.

Since each different policy is likely to alter preferences in its own particular way, our ability to say anything about which policy does the best job of satisfying (future) preferences becomes like quicksand under our feet.

This may seem like a fatal flaw of economics, but as we observed in chapter 1, difficult choices are difficult choices, and this dilemma is a fundamental one facing society, not primarily a defect of economics. Society's choices, and the preferences that inform them, are **path dependent,** meaning that choices we have made in the past affect current preferences and options, and the choices we will make now and in the future. As a result, we may become "locked in" in the sense that certain options that might have been possible or even likely, if we had made different choices in the past, may no longer be feasible or desirable. This idea of path dependence or "lock-in" has been applied most frequently to technology (steam engine versus internal combustion gas engine, etc.), but these same ideas apply to preferences and choices when changes are interdependent and self-reinforcing.

Key Concept: *Path dependent*

What this observation suggests is that we should be somewhat tentative when placing weight on economic estimates of benefits and costs if we have reason to believe that the preferences underlying those particular measures may change over a long period of time. If we try to imagine what kinds of paths we might become "locked into" (e.g., further dependence on the automobile and fossil fuels), then it might be prudent in our policy discussions to give less weight to economic measures reflecting that dependence (e.g., climate change policy). Indeed, these concerns open up a philosophical debate about "preferred preferences," and the kinds of questions asked by the economist Frank Knight, who in the early 1920s concluded that many issues in welfare economics ultimately dissolve into questions about aesthetics and morals.[1]

[1]Frank Knight, *The Ethics of Competition and Other Essays* (New York: Harper and Brothers, 1935).

Potential Biases in Economics

Two specific sources of potential bias in economic analysis deserve mention here. The first is **status quo bias.** Economists recognize that welfare measures that are based on people's willingness to pay reflect the existing set of institutions, especially property rights and government regulations. When evaluating a change in existing institutions (e.g., a transfer of rights), the comparison of benefits and costs is likely to favor retaining the existing institutional structures, the status quo. This is a subtle concept, and one that is probably best explained by example.

Key Concept: *Status quo bias* 

Consider the group of upstream farmers and downstream fishers used in the discussion of the Coase Theorem in chapter 9, where the farmers have the right to withdraw water and pollute the river. As a result of this favorable assignment of rights, the farmers are relatively rich and the fishers are relatively poor. A policy to limit water diversions to level X and instream pollution to level Z is being evaluated on the basis of benefits and costs. Because the farmers are rich, their preferences carry more weight in those value measures than the poor fishers. The analysis may find that the costs of the policy to limit water diversions would exceed its benefits.

Now consider a different starting point. Suppose that the fishers had a right to ample clean water to protect their fish, whereas the farmers could not divert water or pollute the stream. In this situation the fishers would be richer and the farmers poorer, and as a result of this our measures of benefits and costs will be different. From this alternative starting point, there is a good chance that the net benefits of a policy to raise water diversions to level X and to raise pollution to level Z would also find that the costs exceeded the benefits. In both cases economic analysis would tend to protect the interests of the groups who benefited most from the "status quo" set of institutions.

The second kind of bias involves **status goods.** When people buy big houses or expensive cars or have cosmetic surgery, they may be trying to enhance their status, or relative standing, in society. This "keeping up with the Joneses" is part of human nature, and while it may be wasteful in some settings (conspicuous consumption), it likely also contributes to civic society in other ways (e.g., respect for honesty, charity, or compassion). Nevertheless, efforts to raise one's status are to some extent zero-sum: if we all build bigger houses or drive more expensive cars, our status, on average, will not be higher. But if economic analysis simply adds up people's willingness to pay when estimating the net benefits of a policy, it will not recognize the self-canceling nature of these status-seeking values.

This wouldn't be a problem if the desire for high status affected all goods and services in the same way, but these kinds of desires do not. We may pay more for things like fashionable clothing because they bring us status. But this isn't true for the ozone layer, biodiversity, or the global climate. The estimated value of these public goods will not be inflated by status seeking, but the opportunity cost of protecting these public goods may be inflated by the zero-sum status seeking of individuals.[2]

Systems Approaches

A key question when doing economic analysis is whether the natural world is adequately and appropriately represented in the analysis. It is now widely recognized that a "systems approach" is often needed when addressing these kinds of issues, one that understands the workings of the natural system, the socioeconomic system, and how the two interact. Historically, academic researchers in most fields have faced strong incentives not to

[2]See Kiell Arne Brekke and Richard B. Howarth, *Status, Growth and the Environment: Goods As Symbols in Applied Welfare Economics* (Cheltenham, UK, and Northampton, MA: Edward Elgar Publishing, 2003); and William K. Jaeger, "Is Sustainability Optimal?: Examining the Differences between Economists and Environmentalists," *Ecological Economics* 15 (October 1995).

venture too far outside their own discipline. As a result, it is not surprising to see economists, biologists, and others working independently on topics where collaboration would be beneficial. In recent years, however, there is much more interdisciplinary research and analysis involving both economists and natural scientists working together on policy-relevant topics. This has been due to a growing recognition of the importance of this kind of work, growth in interdisciplinary programs on university campuses generally, and growth in funding sources that encourage this kind of work.

Professional associations have also emerged to promote and encourage interdisciplinary research of this kind. One notable example is the interdisciplinary "ecological economics" movement founded in the late 1980s by the International Society of Ecological Economists "to promote understanding between economists and ecologists in the development of a sustainable world." This idea resonated with a large number of people, including many economists and ecologists. As a result, the organization grew rapidly in the 1990s and established an interdisciplinary journal, *Ecological Economics*. Factors that contributed to the appeal of ecological economics included widespread interest in sustainability and a growing interest in breaking down some of the barriers separating disciplines at universities.

The example of ecological economics also demonstrates, however, the difficulties inherent in promoting high-quality interdisciplinary research and analysis. Despite its promising start in the late 1980s and early 1990s, ecological economics has come to mean different things to different people, with many self-identified ecological economists being neither economists nor ecologists. As a result, some of what currently passes for ecological economics in the United .States is either noneconomic or antieconomic. By contrast, the European Society for Ecological Economics has a notable record of innovative, high-quality research and analysis, bringing together economic, social, and natural sciences.

Critics and Critiques

Although there are many valid limitations of economics, there are also some misguided critics and misleading critiques. The aim here is not to defend economics per se but rather to point to examples where some critics seem to have missed the mark. So here is some guidance.

First, don't shoot the messenger. Economists do not create economic data; they only collect information and report on what people want and how they behave. If people want huge houses, SUVs, disposable commodities, cheap gasoline, and lower taxes, this information is a reflection of our society, not something created by economists. Some environmental advocates seem to want to hold economists responsible for the greed, materialism, and consumerism in America and elsewhere. Describing economists and the field of economics in these terms can be found in many places, such as the writings of populist advocates like Vandana Shiva, Hazel Henderson, David Suzuki, Ralph Nader, and Donella Meadows, to name a few. Meadows, for example, coauthor of *Limits to Growth*, claimed that environmentalists "don't share the religious beliefs of economists, who love trade as indiscriminately as they love growth."[3] She also claimed that unlike economists, environmentalists "are inclined to ask questions." Her questions, however, do not appear to include asking whether poor people in poor countries would prefer a low-paying job to no job at all, or whether they are willing to give up their chance to escape chronic poverty in order to protect tropical forests.

Second, some critics seem bent on perpetuating and even exaggerating an outdated caricature of economists as people who completely ignore the effects of the economy on nature, and who believe that the gross domestic product is a measure of social welfare or quality of life. Economists, of course, have long recognized that GDP is not a measure of welfare but only a measure of the quantity of goods and services produced in an economy in a year. But despite a large literature on this point, these critics seem to believe that they have discovered something new that the entire economics profession has overlooked: "The nation's central measure of well-being works like a calculating machine that adds but cannot subtract. It treats everything that happens in the market as a gain for humanity, while ignoring everything that

[3]Donella Meadows, "Why Greens Don't Love the WTO," *The Global Citizen*, November 25, 1999.

happens outside the realm of monetized exchange, regardless of the importance to well-being."[4] No doubt many politicians are too focused on growth in GDP, but economists have been writing about the shortcomings of GDP for decades. In fact, improving the systems of national income accounting has been the subject of study by economists for many years, especially efforts to develop "green national accounting" beginning in the 1990s.

Both of these types of criticism (shooting the messenger, and creating and then attacking a caricature of economics) can be found in the writings of some self-described ecological economists.[5] In addition to their misleading characterizations of economics, these critics claim that ecological economics is a fundamentally distinct discipline from conventional economics because it encompasses theoretical features that economics does not. A careful examination of their writings, however, reveals no such distinctive theoretical features.[6] There are differences in emphasis, but the fundamental difference here is their strong advocacy: these economists wish to imbue their brand of economics with an overriding commitment to the urgency of protecting the ecological system and to their personal vision for fostering environmental sustainability. As an agenda for an advocacy group trying to change public opinion, these goals are easy to appreciate. But these goals also make their agenda fundamentally different from

---

[4]Clifford Cobb, Ted Halstead, and Jonathan Rowe, "If the GDP Is Up, Why Is America Down?" *Atlantic Monthly*, October 1995, 59–78.

[5]See Herman E. Daly and Joshua Farley, *Ecological Economics: Principles and Applications* (Washington, DC: Island Press, 2003); and J. M. Gowdy, "The Revolution in Welfare Economics and Its Implications for Environmental Valuation and Policy," *Land Economics* 80, no. 2 (204): 239–257.

[6]Daly and Farley (*Ecological Economics*, 314–317) take exception to one key theoretical point in economics, the theory of comparative advantage. They claim that capital mobility makes the theory of comparative advantage invalid in the sense that trade can no longer be expected to benefit both countries. Several assumptions underlying their claims are flawed, however, including the assumption of "perfectly mobile" capital, since many forms of capital are not mobile (natural capital, institutional capital, human capital, capital embodied in location-specific technology, and social and cultural capital). Nevertheless, they claim that because of capital mobility, trade flows will follow "absolute advantage" between countries, and because of this the disadvantaged countries will lose jobs and income as capital moves abroad. Daly and Farley offer no rigorous theory, however, and no empirical evidence to support their claim. Nor do they mention the many empirical studies that have been conducted, described in chapter 8, that show strong evidence of a positive effect of both trade and capital flows on per capita income.

economics. Economics tries to measure people's preferences and values, not to influence them.

Nevertheless, these criticisms raise an important distinction between the practice of economics and the practitioners of economics. There are, no doubt, many biased economists and bad economic analyses. There are also many nonacademic forms of economics analysis that have been distorted in the promotion of political and ideological agendas, some of which have been well documented by Paul Krugman.[7] Another example relates to global climate change. In the past fifteen years, some of the economists who have evaluated benefits and costs for slowing climate change have drawn strong policy conclusions that are, to this author, simply irresponsible given the degree of uncertainty, the large omissions in their analysis, and our limited ability to measure, value, and predict what may or may not occur over the next one hundreds years or more.[8] However, the large majority of academic economists are committed to doing careful and balanced studies.

The Last Word

The perspective offered in these pages suggests that when used as directed, economic analysis can provide powerful insights into the causes of environmental problems. These insights are made possible by a conceptual framework that sees public goods, externalities, market failures, and policy failures as contributing to the situations we observe around us, situations where the existing set of institutions, including markets, government, and social norms, are sometimes unable to effectively resolve the incompatibility between individual incentives and collective goals.

Economic analysis also provides a toolbox of methods for measuring the costs of environmental problems and comparing the costs of correcting them. Here economics can be used to offer

---

[7]See, for example, Paul Krugman, *The Accidental Theorist: And Other Dispatches from the Dismal Science* (New York: W. W, Norton, 1998); and Paul Krugman, *Peddling Prosperity: Economic Sense and Nonsense in the Age of Diminished Expectations* (New York: W. W. Norton, 1994).

[8]See, for example, William D. Nordhaus, "An Optimal Transition Path for Controlling Greenhouse Gases," *Science* 258, no. 20 (1992): 1315–1319.

quantifiable evidence of just how important—or unimportant—a particular kind of environmental damage is, and thus provide some evidence about how valuable it might be to society to correct one problem as compared with addressing other problems. The common use of these approaches is in stark contrast to the situation fifty years ago, when economic methods had not yet been developed to measure environmental values, often leaving proponents of environmental protection waving their hands and making qualitative arguments. Such qualitative arguments were frequently less effective than the counterarguments about the costs of environmental policies because those costs could be easily measured in cold hard cash.

In cases where a policy goal has been identified, such as reducing pollution to an agreed-upon level, economic analysis can be used to evaluate and rank alternative ways of achieving that goal in terms of their cost-effectiveness. In this case, "use as directed" implies recognizing that cost-effectiveness and efficiency are not the only criteria to consider when ranking alternative policy approaches. Ultimately, policymakers, politicians, and the general public need to have economic information to weigh alongside other considerations—like fairness, rights, or equity—that may be less amenable to quantification.

How do we coordinate a world where individual actions and incentives often conflict with society's collective goals and well-being? Economics sees an abundance of mechanisms that society has devised to resolve these kinds of conflicts. Economists call them institutions, and they are the rules of the game. They include not only simple and effective rules, such as stay to the right when walking down the sidewalk, but also property rights, traffic signals, social norms, international treaties, legal statutes, common law, moral rules, and first-come, first-served. This multilayered, complex, and overlapping set of institutions that constrains and guides individual actions in our society is the hallmark of civilization; it enables us to avoid a Hobbesian world where life is poor, nasty, brutish, and short.

How does economics contribute to this accumulation of "institutional capital"? It offers a perspective that recognizes how the relative effectiveness and cost of alternative institutional approaches to resource allocation (e.g., private property, common property, or government policy) can vary depending on the social and economic circumstances, and on the characteristics of the resources themselves. One important lesson learned is that we rarely face a binary choice between markets and government to achieve successful resource allocation. What tends to produce the most effective and successful coordination in societies around the world is a combination of complementary and mutually reinforcing institutions introduced at various geographic and jurisdictional levels. The success of markets, private property, the local commons, government policy, and international agreements all tend to be interdependent.

In the same way that advances in physical technology have taken us from the plow to the combine, and from the telegraph to cell phones, advances in "institutional technology" by innovators in economics, political science, law, and nongovernmental organizations have given us creative policy tools that lower the cost, raise the effectiveness, increase the flexibility, or overcome other obstacles to resolving environmental issues. Some of the most notable advances are emissions trading, individual fishing permits, green tax reform, deposit-refund systems, transferable development rights, green labeling, and conservation easements. Innovative approaches like manipulation of the market for rhino horn (see box 8 in chapter 10), or a safety value carbon trading policy, have yet to be tried.

One of the important strengths of economics may also be one of its weaknesses. The economic approach to weighing people's preferences, or values, takes those varied preferences at face value and tries to find a middle ground. When used as directed, economics attempts to add up people's preferences as reflected in their actions or stated desires and evaluate the social benefits and costs based on those measures of aggregate value. Yes, this approach gives more weight to the preferences of high-income earners since their greater willingness to pay will carry more weight in markets and surveys (and this group may be more inclined to support some environmental goals than the poor). Yet aside from this weighting of willingness to pay based on ability to pay, economics does not include a mechanism for discriminating among preferences, or for judging certain values or ultimate goals to be more legitimate or worthy than others. It contains no basis for distinguishing the vain or frivolous wants reflected in the preferences of one person, from the life and death choices faced by others. This can be a dangerous weakness if we fail to use economic analysis fastidiously, by looking beyond the numbers in situations where common sense tells us that other considerations should carry weight in the social calculus.

This weakness is also closely tied to a vital strength of economics. The fact that economics does not take sides (at least to the extent that it tries only to add up all people's revealed and stated preferences without explicitly discriminating among them) is one of the reasons that economic analysis has achieved a high level of credibility and legitimacy in policy discussions and political debates that it would not have if it advocated a particular set of values or ethical position (e.g., ecological, Gaia, libertarian, or ecofeminism). For that reason, economics does not lend itself to advocacy as easily as some activists might like, except to the extent that economists advocate paying attention to what people prefer, how people make choices, and how the economy works (or doesn't work). While this kind of neutrality may frustrate some advocates at either end of the political or environmental spectrum, it's a primary source of the influence economics has on public policy.

Acknowledgments

This book's gestation began at Williams College in the early 1990s when I began to teach courses in environmental and natural resource economics, sustainable development, and institutional economics, and where I participating in a series of faculty research seminars aimed at fostering faculty collaboration across disciplines. The thorny questions raised by students in and out of class, along with my attempts to explain economics to skeptical faculty in biology and elsewhere, made me realize that the straightforward way economics could be explained and applied to some issues was not adequate for addressing the environment, and certainly not up to the task of getting skeptics to appreciate the powerful tools economics has to offer. The challenges I faced included teaching environmental studies undergraduates with strong doubts about the relevance of economics to the environment, and at the same time teaching economics graduate students from developing countries with strong doubts about the relevance of the environment to economics. During two sabbatical stints first at the University of Washington in 1994 and later at the University of Oregon in 1998, I continued to learn from the many stimulating encounters I had with faculty and students in the natural sciences, social sciences, law, planning, and public affairs. These encounters helped me hone my messages, often by trial and error, as I observed which explanations, examples, and analogies resonated, and which ones fell flat.

It is in that context that I owe a debt of gratitude to all those students and faculty who engaged and challenged me. I learned an enormous amount by listening to what they had to say. I am also especially grateful for the encouragement from, and stimulating conversations with, my economics colleagues at Williams College including Roger Bolton, Henry Bruton, Michael McPherson, and

David Zimmerman. Also, I owe a special thanks to former graduate school peers and friends, Don Bovee and Jerry Hembd, who read early drafts and offered vital comments, feedback, and criticisms that improved the book greatly. In fact, their contributions to these pages, like those of David Zimmerman at Williams, also stem from many conversations over the years about economics--and much more.

With regard to actually publishing this book, I owe a special thanks to John Dixon, then at the World Bank, for encouraging me to go forward. At Island Press I was greeted warmly and professionally by Todd Baldwin who guided the process. I am grateful to him and to the production editor, Jessica Heise, and the copy editor, David Sweet, for their hard work and attention to detail.

Closer to home, I want to thank my daughters, Aleah and Marika, for reminding me regularly why this book was worth doing. And finally, I am grateful to my wife, Suzy, not only for her copious editing and advising at every stage, but also for her dependable support, caring and encouragement. A book project shifts responsibilities and adds pressures within a family, and in that sense it has definitely been a joint effort with shared sacrifices.

Index

Island Press Board of Directors